Praise For Card Games For Dummies

"*Card Games For Dummies* is an excellent introduction to the most popular card games in the world. The writing is clear and accurate. I highly recommend this book to all card players."
> — Fred Gitelman, Leading Developer of Bridge Software and Member of Canada's National Bridge Team

"Dummies rarely play card games. However, it's time they did; and this book is an excellent starting point. Barry Rigal lucidly explains the rules and tactics of the games, so that they will have no trouble defeating other dummies and declarers (that's a Bridge joke — see Chapter 7)."
> — Phillip Alder, Syndicated Bridge Columnist

"From Poker to Pinochle, from Blackjack to Slapjack, or from Barbu to Oh Hell!, Barry Rigal is your tour guide into the many worlds and traditions of card games. Deal by deal, Barry shows you how to play your cards right and score big with your friends. And what's neat is that you can open up this book anywhere and join right in!"
> — David Galt, Game Designer and Playing Card Authority

"Barry Rigal presents us with a genuinely new collection of the best known modern card games and variations. Popular games rarely found in books, such as President, Spades, Barbu, and Palace, are fully described here. There are useful hints on play as well, and Barry even mentions card-playing resources on the Internet. A truly fresh approach to the subject and a fine introduction to card playing."
> — John McLeod, Editor of the Card Games Web site (www.pagat.com)

"This is the best introduction to card games I've read, bar none. It clearly defines all the common games as well as unjustly hidden gems such as Piquet, Setback, and Ninety-Nine. The explanations are spot-on, the tactics are illustrated superbly, and readers will be ready to play immediately. *Card Games For Dummies* is an excellent introductory book."
> — Mike Siggins, Publisher, *Sumo Game Review Quarterly*

"Barry Rigal is already recognized as one of the leading Bridge writers of his generation. In this book he has put together everything you need to know about a host of other card games. His clear and concise explanations provide the perfect introduction to old favorites, such as Oh Hell! and Cribbage, and he also introduces games that deserve to be better known — such as President and Setback. Your only problem will be deciding which game to try first!"
> — Mark Horton, Editor of *Bridge Magazine*

Praise For Deception in Defence by Barry Rigal

"This book is informative, readable and authoritative."
— Ian Reissman, *Bridge Plus*

"This is another of the best books of recent years . . . Each of the sections is full of well thought-out and well presented examples . . . and is very clear and very helpful."
— Roy Dempster, *Bridge Magazine*

"For the aspiring player, both this book and Rigal's earlier work should be compulsory reading. Understanding the concepts contained in these two books will not necessarily make you a better technical player, but it will make you a much more difficult opponent . . . he has made a very promising start down the path to being one of the games leading writers."
— Marc Smith, *Bridge Plus*

"Step-by-step deceptive declarer play . . . this is a scholarly work with all the bases covered and the material well organized."
— David Bird, *The Evening Standard*

"This book concentrates on an aspect of the game largely overlooked by average players . . . there is some very good stuff in it."
— Rob Sheehan, *The Times of London*

Card Games For Dummies™

Quick Reference Card

You keep playing until . . .

Baccarat The banker wins all the player's money, or vice versa.

Barbu All 28 hands have been played. The player with the highest score or lowest minus score wins.

Blackjack The players run out of money.

Bridge One side wins a rubber of two games. The team with the higher score wins.

Canasta A player scores 1,500 points.

Clobyosh A player scores 500 points.

Eights A player scores 250 points.

Euchre One side scores 11 points.

Fan Tan One player has cleaned out all the rest, or everybody has had enough.

Gin Rummy A player scores 250 points.

Hearts A player amasses 100 penalty points. The player with the fewest penalty points wins.

Oh Hell! A complete cycle of hands (starting with 7 cards to each player, then reducing to 1 and back up again to 7 cards) has been completed. The player with the highest score wins.

Pinochle A player or partnership scores 1,000 points.

Piquet Six hands have been played. The player with the highest score wins.

Poker Everyone but one player runs out of money, or the game breaks up.

President Everybody gets bored of humiliating one another.

Rummy A player scores 100 points.

Setback A player scores an agreed number of points, either 11 or 21 points.

Spades One side scores 500 points.

Card game do's . . .

- ✔ Determine the rules of the game before play begins. Most games have several variations, and you need to iron out the rules of the game before you start.
- ✔ Shuffle the cards before each hand. Cut the cards, or arrange for someone else to do so, before dealing them.
- ✔ Make sure that no one can see your cards, both during the deal and during play.
- ✔ Avoid conversation if it gives away information or if the sole purpose of the remarks is to upset or irritate your partner or opponents.
- ✔ Try to remember all the cards that you held at the start of play and recall the salient details of the cards played by the other players.
- ✔ Listen to your partner's bids and watch his plays. He's trying to help you, so don't ignore them.
- ✔ Play each card at the same tempo. The tempo of your play can tell your partner or your opponents a lot about how you feel about your cards.

. . . and don'ts

- ✔ Make any undue efforts to look at anyone else's hand, both during the deal and during the play.
- ✔ Pick up your cards until the deal is finished.
- ✔ Indicate whether you are pleased or unhappy about your hand. In an individual game, you give your opponents information about your hand. In a partnership game, you give your partner illegal information about your cards.
- ✔ Accidentally expose any of the cards while dealing, either by turning a card over or dispersing the cards such that players can see them.
- ✔ Accidentally drop a card on the table (as opposed to playing it). If you do so in an individual game, your opponent has benefited from the sight of part of your hand, which is punishment enough for the error.

  In a partnership game, exposing a card gives your partner unauthorized information about your hand, which leads to penalties.
- ✔ Play or lead out of turn. Pay attention to the game and you won't get caught in this embarrassing position.
- ✔ Criticize your partner. It never accomplishes anything positive. Don't dwell on what has gone wrong; the cards have no memory.

...For Dummies: Bestselling Book Series for Beginners

Card Games For Dummies ™

BUSINESS AND GENERAL REFERENCE BOOK SERIES FROM IDG

Quick Reference Card

Sound like a Card Shark

The following terms apply to many, but certainly not all, card games. Of course, many of the terms have specialized meanings in some games.

bidding: Also known as the *auction*. A preparatory phase before the play of the cards during which players estimate how much their hand is worth in the later stages of the game.

card rank: Each suit in the standard 52-card deck has 13 cards in it. Each card has a rank. The traditional rank, from highest to lowest, is the ace, followed by the king, queen, and jack and then the numeric cards from 10 down to 2.

contract: One player or partnership promises to achieve something in the play of the cards in exchange for determining which suit will have special powers in the hand (see *trump suit*). Bidding typically determines the contract.

cutting the deck: After a player shuffles the deck, another player rearranges the deck one more time by splitting the deck into two halves and then reassembling the two halves.

dealer: The player responsible for parcelling out the cards for a hand. Typically, each player gets a chance in turn to deal the cards during the course of a game.

dealing: The process by which players receive the cards they need to play one hand of a game. In most games, the dealer takes the deck in one hand and uses the other hand to give the top card face down from the deck to the player on his left. Then the dealer does the same for the next player, until all the players receive the due number of cards.

deck: Also known as a *pack*. A standard deck of cards contains 52 cards. The cards should have identical backs. A standard deck of 52 cards does not include any jokers.

declaration: The phase of a game in which the players score points for combinations of cards they hold in their hands, based on a predetermined table of values.

discarding: In games where players must *follow suit*, playing a card in a different suit because you have no cards in the suit that's been led. Discarding means that you can't win the trick.

following suit: Each player must play a card in the suit that's been led, if she has one. For example, if you lead a spade, all the other players must play a spade, if they have one, unless the rules of the game specifically permit otherwise.

hand: The cards a player receives to play a game. Also, if a game requires that several rounds be played in order to complete the total sum of the game, each separate element of that round can be referred to as a *hand*.

lead: The first card played to a trick. The first lead to the first trick is called the *opening lead*.

meld: Also known as a *lay*. Three or four cards of the same value, such as three Ks or four 7s.

revoke: A failure, either mistaken or deliberate, to follow suit, when you possess a card in the suit led.

run: Also known as a *sequence*. A number of consecutive cards in a suit such as the 789 of diamonds.

shuffling the deck: Mixing up the cards by holding them face down and interleaving the cards so that the order of all the cards becomes random and unpredictable.

stock: Also known as the *talon*. If some, rather than all, of the cards are dealt for a hand, a parcel of undealt cards remains. This pile of leftovers is typically placed face down in the middle of the table for use at some later point in the game.

suit: The four separate subgroups that make up a standard deck of cards. Each suit contains 13 cards. The four suits each have a separate identifiable marking; in a standard deck, these markings are spades (♠), clubs (♣), hearts (♥), and diamonds (♦).

trick: The foundation of most card games. A trick typically involves each player detaching a card from her hand and putting it face up on the table. Usually, whoever plays the highest card in the suit which was led collects the cards from all the other players. The winner stacks the cards face down in front of him in a compact unit; this is called the *trick*.

trump suit: The "wild" suit for a hand, meaning that playing a card in the trump suit beats every other card except a card of higher value in the trump suit. The trump suit is typically determined through the bidding. You can normally only play a card from the trump suit on the lead of a card in another suit if you have no cards left in that suit.

...For Dummies: Bestselling Book Series for Beginners

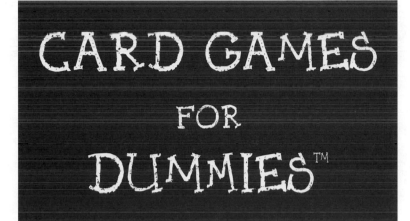

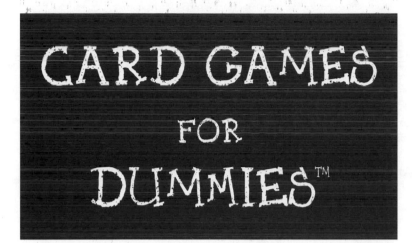

CARD GAMES FOR DUMMIES™

by Barry Rigal

Foreword by Omar Sharif

IDG Books Worldwide, Inc.
An International Data Group Company

Foster City, CA ♦ Chicago, IL ♦ Indianapolis, IN ♦ Southlake, TX

Card Games For Dummies™

Published by
IDG Books Worldwide, Inc.
An International Data Group Company
919 E. Hillsdale Blvd.
Suite 400
Foster City, CA 94404
www.idgbooks.com (IDG Books Worldwide Web site)
www.dummies.com (Dummies Press Web site)

Library of Congress Catalog Card No.: 97-80305

ISBN: 0-7645-5050-0

Printed in the United States of America

10 9 8 7 6 5 4 3 2 1

1E/QZ/RQ/ZX/IN

Distributed in the United States by IDG Books Worldwide, Inc.

Distributed by Macmillan Canada for Canada; by Transworld Publishers Limited in the United Kingdom; by IDG Norge Books for Norway; by IDG Sweden Books for Sweden; by Woodslane Pty. Ltd. for Australia; by Woodslane Enterprises Ltd. for New Zealand; by Longman Singapore Publishers Ltd. for Singapore, Malaysia, Thailand, and Indonesia; by Simron Pty. Ltd. for South Africa; by Toppan Company Ltd. for Japan; by Distribuidora Cuspide for Argentina; by Livraria Cultura for Brazil; by Ediciencia S.A. for Ecuador; by Addison-Wesley Publishing Company for Korea; by Ediciones ZETA S.C.R. Ltda. for Peru; by WS Computer Publishing Corporation, Inc., for the Philippines; by Unalis Corporation for Taiwan; by Contemporanea de Ediciones for Venezuela; by Computer Book & Magazine Store for Puerto Rico; by Express Computer Distributors for the Caribbean and West Indies. Authorized Sales Agent: Anthony Rudkin Associates for the Middle East and North Africa.

For general information on IDG Books Worldwide's books in the U.S., please call our Consumer Customer Service department at 800-762-2974. For reseller information, including discounts and premium sales, please call our Reseller Customer Service department at 800-434-3422.

For information on where to purchase IDG Books Worldwide's books outside the U.S., please contact our International Sales department at 415-655-3200 or fax 415-655-3295.

For information on foreign language translations, please contact our Foreign & Subsidiary Rights department at 415-655-3021 or fax 415-655-3281.

For sales inquiries and special prices for bulk quantities, please contact our Sales department at 415-655-3200 or write to the address above.

For information on using IDG Books Worldwide's books in the classroom or for ordering examination copies, please contact our Educational Sales department at 800-434-2086 or fax 817-251-8174.

For press review copies, author interviews, or other publicity information, please contact our Public Relations department at 415-655-3000 or fax 415-655-3299.

For authorization to photocopy items for corporate, personal, or educational use, please contact Copyright Clearance Center, 222 Rosewood Drive, Danvers, MA 01923, or fax 508-750-4470.

IDG BOOKS WORLDWIDE™ is a trademark under exclusive license to IDG Books Worldwide, Inc., from International Data Group, Inc.

About the Author

Barry Rigal was born with a deck of cards in his hand. Having started with the children's games described in this book, he moved on to Whist, Rummy, and all the Solitaires. He graduated to playing Bridge at the age of 12, and spent the next five years in a generally successful attempt to play cards instead of doing schoolwork. Having taken up Poker at this tender age, he was at least partly responsible for driving the Poker school out of business.

He graduated from Oxford University after having spent four years attempting (successfully he claims) to have earned the title of the laziest man in Oxford, and having captained the Bridge team. After graduating he went to work in accountancy. Highlights of his working career were learning how to play Piquet and Clobyosh in the Tax Department of Thomson McLintock; on his departure, the firm was forced to merge with Peat Marwick. Cause and effect — he'll never know. After four years with Price Waterhouse, supervising the partnership's Bridge team, he went into the world of business.

Barry worked for seven years in the Oil Taxation department of Conoco (UK), and he now believes that his fax and Telex bills were at least part of the reason that the company had to move its London office to Aberdeen. During that time he began a career as a journalist and commentator on card games, on Bridge in particular. Over the course of the last decade, he has traveled extensively in connection with this work, writing for newspapers and magazines, and has written six books on Bridge. He is now a full time writer and his particular interest is in deceiving his opponents.

Barry splits his time between the United Kingdom and the United States, and is currently planning to get married at the end of this year.

ABOUT IDG BOOKS WORLDWIDE

Welcome to the world of IDG Books Worldwide.

IDG Books Worldwide, Inc., is a subsidiary of International Data Group, the world's largest publisher of computer-related information and the leading global provider of information services on information technology. IDG was founded more than 25 years ago and now employs more than 8,500 people worldwide. IDG publishes more than 275 computer publications in over 75 countries (see listing below). More than 60 million people read one or more IDG publications each month.

Launched in 1990, IDG Books Worldwide is today the #1 publisher of best-selling computer books in the United States. We are proud to have received eight awards from the Computer Press Association in recognition of editorial excellence and three from *Computer Currents'* First Annual Readers' Choice Awards. Our best-selling *...For Dummies*® series has more than 30 million copies in print with translations in 30 languages. IDG Books Worldwide, through a joint venture with IDG's Hi-Tech Beijing, became the first U.S. publisher to publish a computer book in the People's Republic of China. In record time, IDG Books Worldwide has become the first choice for millions of readers around the world who want to learn how to better manage their businesses.

Our mission is simple: Every one of our books is designed to bring extra value and skill-building instructions to the reader. Our books are written by experts who understand and care about our readers. The knowledge base of our editorial staff comes from years of experience in publishing, education, and journalism — experience we use to produce books for the '90s. In short, we care about books, so we attract the best people. We devote special attention to details such as audience, interior design, use of icons, and illustrations. And because we use an efficient process of authoring, editing, and desktop publishing our books electronically, we can spend more time ensuring superior content and spend less time on the technicalities of making books.

You can count on our commitment to deliver high-quality books at competitive prices on topics you want to read about. At IDG Books Worldwide, we continue in the IDG tradition of delivering quality for more than 25 years. You'll find no better book on a subject than one from IDG Books Worldwide.

John Kilcullen
CEO
IDG Books Worldwide, Inc.

Steven Berkowitz
President and Publisher
IDG Books Worldwide, Inc.

Eighth Annual
Computer Press
Awards ≥1992

Ninth Annual
Computer Press
Awards ≥1993

Tenth Annual
Computer Press
Awards ≥1994

Eleventh Annual
Computer Press
Awards ≥1995

Dedication

This book is dedicated to Sue, who made the whole project worthwhile and saved my life by fixing all my computer problems.

Author's Acknowledgments

The principal vote of thanks must go to John McLeod, whose e-mail address is John@pagat.demon.co.uk. John provided invaluable assistance for just about every chapter in this book. In addition to his card games site, which offered especially useful data on the basic rules of most games, John gave me essential information when I asked him, and he never got tired of my stupid questions. Thank you, John. (You can find John's card site on the Internet at www.pagat.com.)

In addition I have used the assistance of many other people who have created Web pages on the Internet about card games, and who have been generous with their help and advice.

Thanks are also due to the following people: to Katie Sutton for help on Canasta; to Matt Schemmel and Erin O'Neil for help on Euchre; to Melissa Binde for help on Fan Tan; to Matt Ginsberg and Umesh Shankar for help on Setback; to Mike Block for help on Clobyosh and its variants; to Richard Hussong, Jeff Goldsmith, and Bruce McCosar for help with Eights; to David Dailey for help on Pinochle; to Bruce Blanchard for help on President; to Ernst Martin and Andy Latto for assistance on Poker; to Michael Fosse, Dave Wetzel, and Pat Civale for help on Spades; to Jeff Goldsmith for help on Barbu; to John Hay, David Barker, and Alan Hoyle for help on Hearts; to Carter Hoerr and David Parlett for help on the exact trick games; to everyone else who answered my questions, wrote me e-mail and helped me out, and whom I have accidentally omitted — sorry for not including you here!

Special thanks to Carolyne Krupp for getting me started on this project, and to Mary Goodwin, my Project Editor, for helping me finish it. A tip of the hat also to my excellent Copy Editor, Christine Meloy Beck, and to David Galt for his technical edit.

Publisher's Acknowledgments

We're proud of this book; please register your comments through our IDG Books Worldwide Online Registration Form located at http://my2cents.dummies.com. Some of the people who helped bring this book to market include the following:

Acquisitions, Development, and Editorial

Project Editor: Mary Goodwin

Acquisitions Editor: Mark Butler

Senior Copy Editor: Christine Meloy Beck

Copy Editors: Kim Darosett, Patricia Yuu Pan

Technical Editor: David Galt

Editorial Manager: Mary C. Corder

Editorial Assistants: Darren Meiss, Donna Love, Ann Miller

Production

Project Coordinator: Sherry Gomoll

Layout and Graphics: Steve Arany, Cameron Booker, Angela Bush-Sisson, Elizabeth Cárdenas-Nelson, Maridee V. Ennis, Drew R. Moore, Mark C. Owens, Anna Rohrer, M. Anne Sipahimalani, Kate Snell

Special Art: Shelley Lea, Lou Boudreau

Proofreaders: Chris H. Collins, Christine Berman, Kelli Botta, Michelle Croninger, Rachel Garvey, Nancy Price, Rebecca Senninger, Janet M. Withers

Indexer: Anne Leach

General and Administrative

IDG Books Worldwide, Inc.: John Kilcullen, CEO; Steven Berkowitz, President and Publisher

IDG Books Technology Publishing: Brenda McLaughlin, Senior Vice President and Group Publisher

Dummies Technology Press and Dummies Editorial: Diane Graves Steele, Vice President and Associate Publisher; Kristin A. Cocks, Editorial Director; Mary Bednarek, Acquisitions and Product Development Director

Dummies Trade Press: Kathleen A. Welton, Vice President and Publisher; Kevin Thornton, Acquisitions Manager

IDG Books Production for Dummies Press: Beth Jenkins, Production Director; Cindy L. Phipps, Manager of Project Coordination, Production Proofreading, and Indexing; Kathie S. Schutte, Supervisor of Page Layout; Shelley Lea, Supervisor of Graphics and Design; Debbie J. Gates, Production Systems Specialist; Robert Springer, Supervisor of Proofreading; Debbie Stailey, Special Projects Coordinator; Tony Augsburger, Supervisor of Reprints and Bluelines; Leslie Popplewell, Media Archive Coordinator

Dummies Packaging and Book Design: Patti Crane, Packaging Specialist; Lance Kayser, Packaging Assistant; Kavish + Kavish, Cover Design

◆

The publisher would like to give special thanks to Patrick J. McGovern, without whom this book would not have been possible.

◆

Contents at a Glance

Cartoons at a Glance

By Rich Tennant

"It's called 'Bathtub Gin'. Whoever loses has to take a bath first."

page 7

"Why do I say you're too competitive? For starters, you're playing Solitaire with marked cards."

page 285

"Sure I'll play Fan Tan with you. If you match cards like you match shirts with ties, this should be an easy win."

page 199

"We needed this card to complete our deck, but you can have it back now."

page 133

"No signals that your partner has made a bad bid, please."

page 39

"Well, the first thing old Lucky's gonna do is try to sucker someone into a game of Cribbage, and then he's gonna skunk 'em. And you don't want to be skunked by old Lucky."

page 217

"It looks like you've been playing cards instead of practicing your counting again."

page 321

"Actually Ed, if any of us had been thinking, we'd have asked you to pass on the shuffle."

page 97

"It's jacks or better to open, and the low card in your hand is wild...until my Mom walks in, and then we're playing Fish, got it?"

page 243

Fax: 508-546-7747 • E-mail: the5wave@tiac.net

Table of Contents

· ·

Foreword

Many people think of me primarily as an actor rather than as a card player. In fact, I discovered cards more years ago than I care to mention, and I played Bridge at an international level in the 1960s. Acting may be my business, but Bridge is my passion.

However, it is fair to say that if I limited my card-playing to Bridge, I'd be a much richer man than I am today! I've always been interested in playing card games for high stakes, and over the years, I've collected my fair share of returns from the casinos. At the same time, I've also had my share of losses, and by a course of judicious investment, I've provided many casinos with the wherewithal to refurbish their dining rooms!

Does that mean I'm a bad card player? I hope not. It just means that no matter how often you play, there is always room for improvement in your game. That's where a book like this one proves so useful.

Card Games For Dummies provides an outline to insure that even the beginner can understand the structure of the games under discussion. The book also offers tactical and strategic hints to enable the beginner to improve. I read *Card Games For Dummies* with interest, to see where, if anywhere, I've been going wrong. I know I'll return to the fray with increased confidence.

By covering so many games that are popular today, rather than covering a selection of outdated games like many other books do, Barry Rigal has made a significant contribution to the literature of cards. I look forward to playing many of the games that I read about in this book. I'm sure that you will derive an equal amount of pleasure from it.

Omar Sharif

Introduction

Card games offer the most fascinating challenges that I have ever encountered. In most games, you can manipulate those 52 pieces of pasteboard into infinite permutations and combinations. Working out those combinations is the fun of card games — in almost every game of cards, you don't know what the other players have in their hands. During the course of the game, you use strategy, memory, cunning, and a whole host of other qualities to put together the best hand possible.

At the same time, you don't have to play cards all that well in order to enjoy yourself. Card games allow you to make friends with the people you play with and against. In addition, figuring out the fundamentals of a new card game can bring untold satisfaction.

Why You Need This Book

If you've never played a card game before, you may wonder why you need to buy a book about the subject. Couldn't you just sit down and start playing, picking up a few rules here and there from friends? I would not advise that. Many card games have been in circulation for hundreds of years, generating scores of variations. A reference book not only explains the core rules of a game, but also walks you through how to play the game well.

Card Games For Dummies is different from every other card-game book on the shelf. So many books on cards simply don't talk about the games people play today. The writers of most card-game books are experts in one or two of the games about which they write, but novices at others. They rely on authors of other books on cards to help them out, who were themselves dependent on previous authors. As a result, the games described in the books may not be played any more, or perhaps the games have very different rules. The books, in other words, have lost touch with reality. *Card Games For Dummies* actually focuses on the games that people play today all around the world.

In addition, this book has benefited enormously from a great deal of input from a host of game players who have answered my question about the rules of the games in this book and the regional variations. The net result is that I have captured most of the popular variations to the standard games the way they are really played.

Card Games For Dummies also differs from those other gaming books because it's written in plain English. I eliminate as much card jargon as possible and concentrate on telling you how to get up and going on the play of a game. Of course, some games do involve terms that may be new to you, but don't worry — I tell you exactly what each term means so that you can easily understand it.

Regardless of how much experience you've had with card games, you'll find something in *Card Games For Dummies* for you. Absolute beginners will appreciate that I discuss each game in this book starting at the very beginning. If you've played a few card games before, maybe you'll find a new game. (I can tell you that I have become hooked on several new games since researching this book. I am sure you will have the same experience as I did.)

However, I don't limit my coverage of the games in this book to a description of the game and a summary of the rules. Instead, each chapter offers hints on strategy, so even the experienced player can pick up something to his advantage.

I even tell you where to find information about a game on the Internet and point out places where you can play games online. (If you don't have a computer, or you can't tell the Internet from a hair-net, you won't miss out on anything — I tell you everything you need to know about how to play a game right here in this book.) I've placed all the computer-related stuff in special sidebars, where you can find it easily if you want to read it, or skip over it quickly if you have better things to do.

How to Use This Book

Each game in this book is a self-contained chapter. If you want information on a particular game, you can consult the appropriate chapter and discover everything you need to know about the game.

Besides the Table of Contents at the front of the book, the index at the back of the book can also help you locate the game you want to play without too many diversions along the way. Having said that, one of the more interesting ways to experience this book may be to open the book at random and discover a game that you have never heard of before.

How This Book Is Organized

I've grouped the games into eight parts based on the basic aim of the games. I've also included the Part of Tens, with some valuable tips and hints about card playing.

Part I: Exchanging Cards

In this part of the book, you can discover games in which the players try to improve their hand by taking a card from the deck and letting go of a card from their hand. These games include Rummy and Canasta.

Part II: Trick-Taking Games

For the games in Part II, everyone starts with the same number of cards, and during the play, each player takes a turn to play a card from his hand. Whoever plays the highest of those cards wins them all, or in card-playing jargon *wins the trick*. The games in Part II include Whist, Oh Hell!, Euchre, Spades, and a brief description of Bridge.

Part III: Don't Score Any Points!

The games in this part of the book, which include Hearts and Barbu, go in reverse from most games. Instead of trying to score points, you try to avoid saddling yourself with points.

Part IV: Score As Many Points As You Can!

The objective of all the games in this part is to score points. In many of the games, you score points for having certain combinations of cards. Visit this part to find everything you need to know to start playing Pinochle, Piquet, Setback, and Clobyosh.

Part V: Matching Cards

For Part V, I've brought together Eights and Fan Tan, which are games in which you want to get rid of all your cards as quickly as possible by matching them with other cards and then playing them onto a discard pile.

Part VI: Adding and Climbing Games

You get the lowdown on both Cribbage and President in Part VI. In Cribbage, an adding game, each player attempts to construct as high-scoring a hand as he can, and then he scores points by playing out the cards and bringing the cumulative totals to strategically significant numbers. President, a climbing game, presents another set of challenges; the objective is to get rid of cards by playing a higher-scoring card (or cards) than the previous player.

Part VII: Banking Games

In some banking games, such as Blackjack and Baccarat, the players compete against a central authority figure, the Banker, rather than against each other. In other banking games, everyone competes against one another, as with Poker. I discuss all three games in this part.

Part VIII: Specialty Games

In Part VIII, you get the details on some of the best games in the book. I show you how to play several versions of Solitaire, including Accordion, Clock, La Belle Lucie, and Scorpion. I also present the best and the brightest of children's games from around the world, including Beggar My Neighbor, War, Go Fish, and Old Maid.

Part IX: The Part of Tens

You can't have a ...*For Dummies* book without The Part of Tens, can you? This is where you find tips on how to improve your card-playing skills, by your actions at the table and away from it, and how to help your partner improve his skills, too. I also provide you with a short list of places to look for more information on a game after you finish with this book.

You can find some handy score cards near the back of the book. Feel free to photocopy the score cards as much as you'd like.

Conventions Used in This Book

Throughout this book, I talk quite a bit about specific cards. Instead of saying "the king of hearts" or "the seven of spades" every time I refer to those cards, I abbreviate the cards and suits by using the following symbols:

- **The suits:** I represent each of the four suits in a standard deck of cards with spade (♠), heart (♥), club (♣), and diamond (♦) symbols.
- **The card values:** I use the following abbreviations to refer to specific card values: ace (A), king (K), queen (Q), jack (J), 10, 9, 8, 7, 6, 5, 4, 3, and 2.

When I refer to a specific card in the text, then, you see ♥K and ♠7, rather than "the king of hearts" or "the seven of spades."

I show you entire hands of cards in the figures scattered throughout this book. The figures help you see what a set of cards looks like when you're actually holding it in your hand.

In some chapters, I show you several rounds of play by numerous players in the same hand by using a table that looks like this:

West	North	East	South
♥10	♥Q	♥J	♦Q
♠Q			

Reading the play from left to right, this table shows that West plays first and that he plays the ♥10. North plays directly after West, and she plays the ♥Q. East plays next, followed by South, and then it's West's turn again, and so on until the end of the hand.

Icons Used in This Book

In each chapter, I place icons in the margin to emphasize the following types of information.

With this icon, I point out the wrong way to play a game. Pay special attention to these icons so that you can avoid finding things out the hard way.

This reinforces a point of the game that may be less obvious (or intuitively right) than meets the eye. Nevertheless, I want you to keep these points in mind as you play the game.

I've been playing cards for quite some time, and I use these icons to emphasize some insights that will help make you a sharper player.

Next to this icon, you find a list of all the stuff you need to play a game — I tell you how many players you need, what type of cards you play with, and if you require any other special equipment, such as something to keep score with.

Most of the games in this book have so many variations, I'd have to write a whole library to include them all. Instead, I cover the most popular variations of a game and place this icon next to these digressions from the standard game.

Part I
Exchanging Cards

The 5th Wave   By Rich Tennant

"It's called 'Bathtub Gin'. Whoever loses has to take a bath first."

In this part . . .

The three main games discussed in this part of the book (which include Rummy, Gin Rummy, and Canasta) all involve improving your hand by picking up cards (usually from a stock pile) and getting rid of other cards. You, in effect, *exchange* your cards (or hope to) in order to get the best hand possible.

Chapter 1

Rummy and Gin Rummy

· ·

In This Chapter

▶ Understanding basic Rummy concepts

▶ Plotting some Rummy strategy

▶ Varying the program with Gin Rummy

· ·

*R*ummy? Gin? You may be asking yourself, "Is this *Bartending For Dummies,* or a book about playing cards?" Before you reach for your jigger and shaker, I want to set some things straight. Although the words *Rummy* and *Gin* may conjure up some beverage-related memories — some of them possibly involving headaches — I can assure you that in this book, *Rummy* and *Gin* refer to fun games that you don't have to be over 21 to play.

In this chapter, I show you how to play Rummy and a popular variation of that game called Gin Rummy. After you get the basics under your belt, feel free to call up some friends, throw a party, play some Rummy, and drink the beverage of your choice (gin or not). By the way, before the party, you may want to pick up a copy of *Bartending For Dummies,* by Ray Foley, published by IDG Books Worldwide, Inc.

Rummy

In this section, I show you the ins and outs of the game of Rummy. You master the basics of the game and discover some playing tactics, including how to go for the opponent's jugular, when to minimize the risk of being caught with a number of cards left in your hand, and how to take advantage of other players' strategies.

To play Rummy, you need the following:

▍ ✔ **Two or more players**

> ✔ **A standard deck of 52 cards:** Jokers are optional, depending on whether you want to play with wild cards (see "Playing with wild cards" in this chapter for information). For six or more players, you need a second deck of cards.
>
> ✔ **Paper and pencil for scoring**

Setting up and getting out! The objective of the game

Rummy belongs to the group of card games in which the players try to improve the hand that they are originally dealt. They can do this whenever it is their turn to play, either by drawing cards from the undealt pile (or *stock*) or by picking up the card thrown away by their opponent, and then throwing away (or *discarding*) a card from their hand. In this way, players aim to put their cards into two types of combinations:

> ✔ **Runs:** Consecutive sequences of three or more cards in the same suit
>
> ✔ **Melds:** Three or four cards of the same rank

Figure 1-1 shows legitimate combinations.

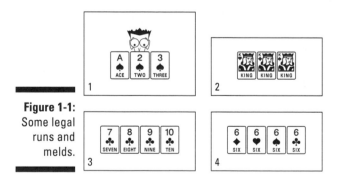

Figure 1-1: Some legal runs and melds.

Figure 1-2 shows an unacceptable combination. This run is illegal because all cards in a run must be of the same suit.

Figure 1-2: An illegal run.

In most Rummy games, unlike the majority of other card games, aces are only low, so runs involving the ace must take the form A23, rather than AKQ. For example, you can't put down ♣A ♣K ♣Q. You have to wait until you pick up the ♣J in order to combine the ♣K and ♣Q in a legitimate run.

The first person who manages to put his whole hand into combinations wins the game.

Dealing the cards and playing

When playing Rummy with two, three, or four players, each player gets seven cards; when playing with five players, each player gets six cards. With more than five players, use two decks of cards and a hand of seven cards. Yes, I promised you no high-level mathematics, but you can cope with a few numbers here and there.

Designate a scorer and a dealer at the start of the game. To determine who should be the scorer, just volunteer the person closest to the pencil and score card. Now you know that you should always be on the other side of the room when someone asks, "Have you got a pencil on you?"

To decide who should be the dealer, everyone takes a card, and the person who draws the lowest card is the dealer for the first hand. The deal rotates clockwise for each following hand.

Deal each player a card, starting with the player on the dealer's left and moving clockwise. When everyone's hand is complete, put the undealt cards face-down in the center of the table as the stock and place the top card, turned upward, beside the stock as the first card of the discard pile.

Pick up your cards slowly; you don't need to play the game with excessive haste, so give yourself time to think about all your possible card combinations before starting play.

Misdeals — accidents in the dealing, such as a card getting turned face-up or too many or too few cards dealt out — generally result simply in another deal, with no penalties.

The player to the left of the dealer plays first. She can do one of two things: She can either pick up the turned-up card or the top card from the stock. If she can put some or all of her hand into combinations, she does so (see "Putting down and adding to combinations" in this chapter). If not, she then discards one card from her hand, face-up on the discard pile, and the turn of play moves to the next player.

The next player can either pick up the last card that was discarded or the top card from the stock pile. He then puts some or all of his cards down in combinations, if he wants to. The play continues clockwise around the table.

If you pick up two cards from the stock by accident and look at either of them, you must put the bottom card back, which gives the next player an additional option. She looks at the returned card and can take it if she wants it. If she doesn't want to take it, she puts it back into the middle of the stock and continues with her turn by taking the next card from the stock.

When you pick up a card from the stock that you don't want, don't throw it away immediately. Put the card into your hand and then extract it. No player, no matter what her skill level, needs to give gratuitous information away.

During the play, players work their way through the stock, taking one card from it (or the discard pile) and discarding a card from their hand. If players completely use up the stock, the dealer reshuffles the discard pile and turns over a new *upcard,* and play continues.

Putting down and adding to combinations

You may only put down a combination when it's your turn to play, and the correct timing is to pick up a card from the stock or discard pile, put down your combination, and then make your discard. The advantage of putting down a combination before you're ready to go out completely is that doing so reduces your exposure if you lose the game (for the details on scoring, see "Going out and scoring" in this chapter). However, you do run a few risks by putting down a run or meld.

The disadvantage of putting your cards on the table is that any player at the table is now at liberty to add to your meld of three of a kind (by adding the fourth card) or to extend your run of cards. Although adding on to your combinations proves very beneficial to your opponents, the longer the game goes on, the more wary you should be of keeping combinations in your hand.

Conversely, of course, you can add to your opponent's combinations — or, if you draw the right card, you can add an additional card to your own combinations. If you want to add a card to an existing combination, first put down any combinations you have, then add to the existing combination, and then make a discard. Your turn finishes with the discard, so make sure that you don't mix up the order of events. If you do, then you can't put down any combinations you may have until your next turn.

If you put down an imperfect run, simply pick up the cards and put them back in your hand. But by doing that, of course, you reveal the cards in your hand to everyone else at the table, making you considerably less likely to get anything useful from the other players. Better put on your glasses and double-check before putting any cards on the table.

Of course, when you have a meld of four of a kind, no one can add a card to the combination, so you're safe to put such melds down immediately. The only reason for not doing so is if you're close to going out and are playing for the extra score (see the section "Going out and scoring" for more information). Additionally, if one of the meld may be used in a run, you may want to retain the combination in your hand until you know how you want to use the cards. For example, you may want to hold some of the cards in Figure 1-3 in your hand until you get some more information.

In Figure 1-3, you could use the ♥9 both in a meld and in a run with the ♥10 and ♥J. Holding the cards for a turn gives you a chance to pick up the ♥Q or ♥8, which would complete the run.

Playing with wild cards

You can also play Rummy with *wild cards,* which represent any card you like. You can add the jokers to the deck, treating them as wild cards, or make the 2s wild.

The cards displaced by the wild cards become wild cards themselves as soon as a combination containing the wild card is put on the table. For example, if you substitute a joker for the ♥4 in a run and then put that run on the table, the ♥4 immediately becomes a wild card.

When playing with wild cards, you may not want to put combinations containing wild cards down as soon as you make them in your hand; you don't want to give anyone else the use of a wild card by letting him make the substitution. Of course, if you feel obliged to put down the meld or run, try to insure that the card your wild card takes the place of has already been played in some other meld or run.

Rummy and Gin Rummy mutate on the Web

Variations of these two popular games abound, and you can find rules to some very exciting games on the Web. For example, you can discover the rules to Literature Rummy, which involves matching novels with their authors, at `edweb/sdsu.edu/courses/edtec670/Literature` `RummyRules.html`. For a Gin Rummy game with a twist, check out the rules to Word Gin Rummy, in which you attempt to construct words in your Gin Rummy hand, at `www.dajam.com/wordup/ginr_rule.html`.

Going out and scoring

The first player to put seven of the eight cards in her hand (including the card that she picks up in her current turn) into combinations *goes out* (places all her cards on the table) and wins. You discard your remaining card as you go out, usually having made the others into one combination of four and one combination of three.

The winner collects points from all the other players. The amount of points she gets is based on the remaining cards in the other players' hands, regardless of whether the cards are in completed combinations or not — which is a good reason to put down combinations as soon as you get them.

At the end of the hand, the players put their cards face-up on the table and call out how many points they have left for the winner. Score the cards according to the following scale:

- ✔ **2s through 10s:** The numbered cards get their face value, meaning that a 5 is worth 5 points.

- ✔ **Jacks, queens, and kings:** The court cards are charged at 10 points apiece.

- ✔ **Aces:** In keeping with its lowly status during the game, the ace is charged at 1 point only.

For example, if you're left holding ♠K ♦K ♦Q ♣A at the end of the game, the winner of the game collects 31 points from you.

Putting all your cards down in one turn is called *going rummy,* which doubles your score; obviously, the availability of this bonus affects your decision to put down combinations earlier rather than later. If you think that you can claim this bonus, you may want to delay putting down your combinations.

If you play with 2s or jokers wild, they count as 15 points if you're left with one of these cards still in your hand at the end of the hand.

The first player to score 100 points is the winner. For a longer game, you can play to 250 points.

Knowing how to play: simple strategy

When you first start playing Rummy, you may find that putting your cards into combinations is quite challenging. Clearly, you want to aim for combinations that have the best chance for completion.

The cards in your hand and on the table can give you information about your chances for completing certain conbinations. For example, if you can keep only two cards from ♠7 ♠8 ♣8, and you're already using the ♦8 in another run, you should keep the spades because you have two chances of success this way — the ♠6 or ♠9. Keeping the two 8s gives you only one possible draw, the ♥8.

Another typical problem is knowing when to break up a pair in order to increase your chances in another direction. For example, imagine that you have to discard from a collection such as the one shown in Figure 1-4.

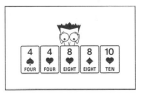

Figure 1-4:
Which one to discard?

The solution to this problem is straightforward: Throw the ♥10 away. Keeping your two pairs gives you a reasonable enough chance of making a three of a kind, and the ♥10 gives you only a single chance of making a combination by drawing the ♥9.

In general, you don't want to split up your pairs. But life (or at least Rummy) isn't always so simple. Suppose that you have the cards shown in Figure 1-5.

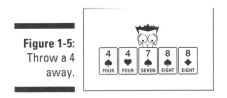

Figure 1-5:
Throw a 4 away.

If you need to throw out one card, throw a 4 away. The ♠7 is a useful *building card,* meaning that it fits well with the ♠8; simple mathematics says that the nest of 7s and 8s gives you four possible cards with which to make a combination (the ♠9, ♠6, ♣8, and ♥8). You have the same number of options if you throw the ♠7 away and keep the two pairs. But the real merit in throwing away one of the 4s is that doing so gives you a degree of freedom on a future discard. By throwing one 4 away, you allow yourself to pick up another potentially useful building card (such as the ♦7) at your next turn, and then you can throw away the other 4. By contrast, throwing away the ♠7 "fixes" your hand and gives you no flexibility.

The odds favor drawing to the run rather than for a meld. When you make a run, you can build on it at either end. A meld, on the other hand, has only one possible draw to help it. For this reason, be careful about which cards you discard. If you must give your opponent a card she may want, try to let her have the melds of three or four of a kind, rather than helping her build runs.

Keeping your eye on the discard pile

When it comes to Rummy, you can't go through the game just thinking about the cards in your own hand — you also need to watch the cards thrown into the discard pile. Watching the discard pile tells you whether the cards you're hoping to pick up have already been thrown away. For example, if you have to keep two cards from ♠7 ♠8 ♣8, consider whether the ♠6, ♠9, or ♥8 have already been discarded. If both spades have already gone, then you have no chance of picking them up — at least not until you work your way through the entire stock, when you may get a second chance at the cards. In such a position, you should settle for a realistic chance, however slim, of picking up the last 8 by discarding the ♠7.

Try to avoid *drawing to an inside run* — keeping, for example, a 3 and 5 in the hopes of drawing the 4. Keeping *builders* (cards that may be helpful elsewhere) is better than relying on a single card coming up.

You're not allowed to review the discard pile for clues. You just have to remember which cards were thrown away — or be very adept at taking surreptitious peeks at the discarded evidence!

Thinking about your opponents' hands

Guessing what your opponent has in his hand helps you make smarter choices about what cards to discard. After all, you don't want to throw away that ♥K if your opponent can use it to complete a run with the ♥Q and ♥J.

You compile a picture of your opponent's hand by reading the negative and positive messages you get from her plays. For example, if you see your opponent throw away the ♥Q, you can be sure that she isn't collecting queens. That information in itself doesn't make discarding any queen safe, though, because she may be collecting high diamonds. But if do you subsequently throw the ♦Q and she picks it up, that action provides you with a positive message; you can safely infer that she is collecting high diamonds.

Making a good discard

Early in the game, beware discarding exactly the same rank of card as your opponent; he may be trying to persuade you to do exactly that. For example, if you hold ♣J ♦Q ♦10, you may be able to persuade your opponent to let her jacks go by tossing your ♣J at the first opportunity. This trick is good strategy — so try it yourself, but be aware that your opponents may be on the ball, too.

Kings are the most attractive discard, followed by queens, because fewer runs involve kings and queens than involve jacks or 10s. (Kings can only appear in KQJ runs, while jacks can appear in runs of KQJ, QJ10, and J109.) Of course, discarding court cards reduces your potential exposure if you lose the game. The higher the card, the more points you may be left with.

Picking up cards from the discard pile

Another critical strategy question in the game is whether to pick up *builder cards,* cards that lend themselves well to combinations, from the discard pile. Say, for example, that you start the hand with the ♠Q and ♦J, and early in the game your opponent throws away the ♦Q. Should you pick it up?

You would automatically keep the ♦Q if you picked it up from the stock, of course — doing so wouldn't give your opponent any clues as to which cards you may find helpful. But if you take a card from the discard pile, you tip off your opponent to part of your hand. If you're playing against a good player who watches your cards, you probably shouldn't take the card. On the other hand, picking up a card that enables you to multiply your options, such as the ♥7 with ♣7 ♣8 ♥8 in your hand, is definitely a good idea, because the ♥7 gives you some flexibility in two directions.

Watch the discard pile. Technically, the cards should be arranged one on top of another, but in real life you can generally see many cards below the top card. Your opponent will be keeping a sharp eye on the pile; so should you.

Try to remember the cards that haven't been discarded as well as the ones that have appeared on the discard pile. When you have almost worked your way through the deck and you see your first 5, it stands to reason that your opponent is probably collecting them — if your opponent wasn't interested in collecting 5s, you probably would have seen a 5 before reaching the end of the deck.

Assume that your opponent is honest until proven to the contrary. If she hesitates on your discard, assume that she is contemplating picking it up; her possible need for that card may affect your future discards. If you subsequently discover that she was simply pausing for effect, say nothing, but remember that she will probably do the same thing next time. You should be able to draw the right inferences after observing her first performance!

Gin Rummy

Gin Rummy is very similar in aim to regular Rummy, but Gin has some additional wrinkles that make it a more interesting and challenging game.

To play Gin Rummy, you need the following:

- ✔ **Two players:** Gin Rummy is for two players only, so if more than two people want to play, you may want to send the extra people out for ice cream or a walk.
- ✔ **A standard deck of 52 cards**
- ✔ **Paper and pencil for scoring**

Getting a fair deal

In Gin Rummy, each player gets ten cards. The dealer makes the rest of the cards a *stock* pile by placing them in the center of the table and turning over the first card. The upcard is offered to the nondealer first. If he doesn't want the upcard, the dealer may take it, and then play continues like in ordinary Rummy except for how the players go out. (For more information on how to play Rummy, see "Rummy" in this chapter.)

The first upcard is a free card; be prepared to take it even if it's only partly relevant to your hand, because the option reverts to your opponent if you don't take advantage of it. If nothing else, taking the card may mislead your opponent about the cards in your hand.

Going Gin, scoring, and knocking

The most difficult (and therefore rewarding) way to go out is to put all your cards into combinations, which is called *going Gin.* If you go Gin, you score 25 points, plus the sum of whatever your opponent has failed to make into complete combinations — her unconnected cards, or *deadwood.*

You must pick up a card, either from the stock or the discard pile, even if you're going Gin.

To help you understand how to score points after you win at Gin (and I do assume that you win, because you've read this great book), take a look at the cards in Figure 1-6.

Figure 1-6:
The winner collects points from the deadwood in the loser's hand.

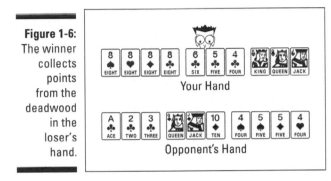

When you go out, your opponent has 18 points left: two 4s and two 5s add up to 18 points; no calculators allowed! Together with the 25 points you get for going Gin, you score 43 points.

You can play to 100 or 250 points, depending on how long you want the contest to last.

Knock, knock! Another way to go out

The most intriguing addition to the rules of Gin Rummy, compared to the standard Rummy rules, is that you have more than one way to go out at Gin. Instead of putting all your cards into combinations, you have the option of *knocking* (which involves literally tapping the table) if you have put almost all your cards into combinations, and the cards that don't make combinations total less than 10 points. If you get to this point, you can knock (just once will do — no matter how happy it makes you feel) and then put your cards down on the table.

After you knock, play stops, and the tallying begins. Your score comes from the deadwood — cards that aren't part of combinations. If your opponent's deadwood exceeds your deadwood, you pick up the difference between your total and his. If your opponent's deadwood doesn't exceed yours, read on to discover the consequences.

Take a look at the cards in Figure 1-7 to get an idea of how to score after you go out by knocking.

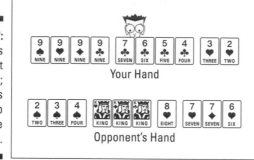

Figure 1-7:
Someone's knocking at the door; someone's racking up some points.

Your Hand

Opponent's Hand

If you count up all the cards in Figure 1-7, you see that your 5 points against his 28 leaves you with 23 points. (If you knock, you don't get 25 points for going out.)

Sometimes your opponent can outdo you when you knock, because he has an additional way to get rid of his deadwood. He can put down his combinations, of course, and those cards don't count toward the score. In addition, he can add his loose cards to your combinations. After your opponent adds any loose cards that he can to your combinations, only his remaining cards count.

Glance at the cards in Figure 1-8 for another example of how scoring can work after someone knocks. Your opponent knocks with 6 points, and you appear to have 11. But your ♦J can be added to her run, reducing your total to 1 and enabling you to *undercut* her by 5. You score 25 points plus the difference (5), so you get 30 points.

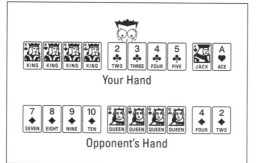

Figure 1-8:
Sometimes you can add cards to combinations after your opponent knocks.

Your Hand

Opponent's Hand

In Oklahoma Gin, which is the most common form of competitive Gin Rummy, the number of the upcard may further restrict your ability to knock. You can knock only if your total of deadwood is less than or equal to the initial upcard. What's more, if the upcard is an ace, you can go out only by going Gin.

Always knock if you can do so early in the game, unless your hand is highly suitable for going Gin. So, for example, if you can knock early in the game with the cards shown in Figure 1-9, go ahead and knock; only three cards can let you go Gin, and the chances of your getting one of those three cards is below the average expectation. If five or more cards can let you go Gin, play for Gin instead. The longer the game goes on, the more wary you should be of knocking.

Figure 1-9:
Go ahead and knock with this hand.

Win, lose . . . or draw?

In Gin Rummy, the hand doesn't have to be played to a conclusion. If the stock gets down to two cards, the hand ends right there. Just throw in the cards and start all over again.

Feeling boxed up: the scoring system

When you reach your game-winning target, you get 100 points simply for winning. In addition, you're awarded bonuses based on the number of hands that you win compared to the number of hands your opponent wins. The bonus comes in the form of a *box*, which is 25 points added to your score for each hand you win minus the number of hands your opponent wins. For example, if you play six hands and each win three, the winner doesn't get a bonus. But if the winner wins more hands than her opponent, the bonus comes into play.

Say that player A and player B play six hands in a game. If A wins four hands to B's two, A scores a 50-point bonus. Here's the scoring of a sample game:

A	B	Notes
52	—	A went Gin with B having 27 points in his hand.
—	26	A knocked with 6 and B undercut with only 5 points.
11	—	A knocked with 3 and B had 14 points.
28	—	A went Gin and caught B with 3 points.
—	27	B knocked with 6 and caught A with 33 points.
41	—	A went Gin and B had 16 points.
124	53	Total
−53		A subtracts B's score
71		The margin of the win
+100		Bonus for winning
+50		The box bonus
221		The total winning score

If you're fortunate enough to reach the winning post, be it 100 or 250 points, without letting your opponent win a single hand, he is said to be *blitzed, schneidered,* or *skunked,* and your final winning score is doubled.

In the Oklahoma variation of the game, you get an additional feature to boost the scoring. If the initial card turned over is a spade, all elements of the scoring are doubled, including the box awards. However, the spade upcard has no impact on the strategy of the game.

Hollywood Gin Rummy produces a much more complex and potentially expensive scoring system. Instead of keeping a single column of scoring for each player, Hollywood Gin uses three columns for each player.

Each of the three columns records different combinations of scores. The first score for each player is recorded in Column 1; the second score for each player is recorded in both Column 1 and Column 2; and the third score for each player is recorded in all three columns.

For example, in the preceding sample game, the Hollywood scoring system would produce the following scores:

Column 1		Column 2		Column 3	
A	**B**	**A**	**B**	**A**	**B**
52		11	27	28	
	26	28		41	
11		41			
28					
	27				
41					
124	53				
(-53)					
71					
50					
121					

The first player to reach 100 points in a column wins that column; the column is then scored as described in "Feeling boxed up: the scoring system."

The Hollywood scoring method increases the chances that a player will blitz his opponent because each player needs to win three hands before they can register a score in Column 3. Hollywood Gin Rummy just provides a way to increase the stakes of Gin Rummy.

Chapter 2

Canasta

. . . .

In This Chapter

▶ Understanding Canasta concepts

▶ Getting into the swing of the game

▶ Varying the program with Canasta for two or three players

. . . .

*O*ne reason for Canasta's widespread popularity may be its use of *wild cards,* which make it a more high-scoring and unpredictable game. Canasta is also one of the few partnership games (other than Bridge) that really works well, although Canasta also functions perfectly well as a two- or three-handed game.

The rules to Canasta may seem a little cockeyed — but bear with me. After you acquaint yourself with a couple of unusual ideas, you will have smooth sailing.

To play Canasta, you need the following:

> ✔ **Four players:** You can also play Canasta with five players (two against three, with one player sitting out each hand) or with six players (three against three, with one of each trio sitting out in rotation).

> ✔ **Two decks of 52 cards, including the jokers in each deck (108 cards in all).** The backs of the cards don't have to be the same, but identical backs do look better.

> ✔ **Paper and pencil for scoring**

Canasta's spicy history

Canasta sounds like a wild South American dance or perhaps an Italian painter — but in fact, the word *Canasta* has slightly more common associations. *Canasta* is Spanish for *basket,* which makes sense because Canasta's roots are in South America.

Canasta started life in Uruguay and migrated to Argentina after World War II. It wasn't until the 1950s that Canasta became a craze in the United States. Canasta's popularity convinced card manufacturers to include the jokers in standard packs!

Your Mission, Should You Choose to Accept It

The object of Canasta is to pick up cards and to fit them into *melds,* or groupings of cards. You score points for the melds, so the more melds, the merrier. The first team to score 5,000 points wins, and if both teams get there on the same hand, the team with the higher score wins.

Putting Your Cards into Melds

You score points by making *melds,* which are sets of three to seven or more cards of the same rank. For a meld to be valid, all the cards in it must have the same number, such as queens, but they don't have to be of the same suit.

A meld of seven, such as seven 9s or seven kings, is called a *Canasta.* Having a Canasta is especially valuable for a number of reasons: You need to make a Canasta to go out, and it also helps your score mount quickly.

Getting wild with wild cards

The 2s and jokers are *wild cards,* meaning that they can have any value you want them to have. Each meld can include one wild card, but a meld must have at least two non-wild cards in it and no more than three wild cards. For example, a meld of three can contain one wild card, and a meld of four can have two wild cards in it. A meld that includes no wild cards is known as a *natural meld.* A meld with one or more wild cards in it is a *mixed meld.*

Forsaking the suits

Suits don't play a role in Canasta (except when it comes to choosing partners); a meld of three queens can consist of two ♣Q and a wild card. The only significance to suits lies in the distinction between red and black 3s, which is explained in "Concerning the ♠3 and the ♣3" and "Putting down the ♥3 and the ♦3" in this chapter.

Looking at some legal melds

Melds take on many different guises, which include the ones shown in Figure 2-1.

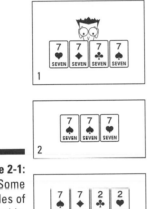

Figure 2-1:
Some examples of legal melds.

But if you try to put down a meld like ♠7 ♣2 ♦2, you won't get too far; this meld is illegal because it contains too many wild cards. Similarly, ♠7 ♠8 ♠9 isn't a legal meld. The only legal melds are groups of the same rank, not runs in a suit.

Calculating the value of your cards and melds

Each card has a scoring value, and these values are important, especially when it comes to putting down the first meld for a partnership. (I discuss the minimum value of the first meld in "Making the first meld for each partnership.") Fortunately, the card values aren't too complicated:

> ✔ **Jokers:** 50 points each
>
> ✔ **2s and aces:** 20 points each
>
> ✔ **Kings through 8s:** 10 points each
>
> ✔ **7s through the ♠3 and ♣3:** 5 points each

You can't use the ♥3 and the ♦3 in melds. See "Putting down the ♥3 and the ♦3," later in this chapter, for more information.

Playing Canasta

In Canasta, the play focuses on making melds, scoring points, and eventually getting out. Canasta is played in partnership, and so the first thing to do is determine the lineups.

Picking partners

You can just pick partners, or you can draw cards, with the two highest cards playing together against the two lowest cards. If two players draw cards with the same rank (two kings, for example), then the rank of the suits decides which card is higher — spades is the highest-ranking suit, followed by hearts, diamonds, and clubs. Partners sit opposite each other.

Dealing the cards and creating a discard pile

After forming two partnerships, each player draws a card randomly from the deck. The person who draws the highest card plays first, and the dealer is the player to his right.

The dealer shuffles the deck, and after an opponent cuts it, he doles out 11 cards to each player one by one in a clockwise rotation. At the end of each hand, the deal moves clockwise one place.

After each player has 11 cards, the dealer turns up one card by the side of the *stock pile* (the remaining cards) to start the *discard pile*. If the card is a 3 or a wild card (a joker or a 2), the dealer turns up another card until he turns over any other card.

Playing around the table

After the deal, the game starts. The player to the dealer's left picks up a card from the stock pile or the discard pile (see "Picking up the discard pile," later in this chapter, for more information; but briefly, you can't pick up the discard pile until you make your first meld). She can then either put down a meld or not. She finishes her turn by discarding a card face-up on the discard pile, covering all the other cards so that her discard is the only card visible.

The play goes in a clockwise rotation, with each player picking up a card, making a meld if he wants to, and then discarding, until someone *goes out* by getting rid of all his cards, which finishes the game.

 Drawing more than one card from the stock pile carries no penalty. However, you must show the card to all other players, and the next player then has the option of taking the returned card or shuffling it into the face-down stock.

Discarding is a critical part of the game; if the discard pile grows to a significant size, one false discard can be disastrous. Err on the side of caution by throwing out what you're sure your opponents don't want. And make the dangerous discards early — the cost of an error is so much less expensive then. How do you know what discards are dangerous? You can work out what your opponents don't want by what they throw away and by what they don't pick up from the discard pile. The longer the play progresses, the more possibilities you can eliminate from your opponents' hand, until you're left with a fair idea of what they're after.

Picking up the discard pile

Players can pick up the top card from the discard pile to make it into a meld. However, if you choose to take the top card, you must then put down a meld immediately, using the card from the top of the pile in that meld.

After you put down your meld, you then take the entire discard pile and add it to your hand. You immediately get a huge hand — and the ability to make many melds and thus score points.

You can't take that top card unless you make a meld with that card or add it to an existing meld or a Canasta — and sometimes not always then! I get to the restrictions in a moment in the section "Freezing the discard pile."

After you pick up the pile, you can make any further melds you want. Then you discard, which ends your turn.

If you pick up the discard pile in error, either as a result of a miscalculation (the meld isn't high-scoring enough for the first meld; see "Making the first meld for each partnership") or because you can't make a meld with the card, you incur a 100-point penalty.

Making a Canasta (a must)

A *Canasta* is a meld of seven or more cards. You or your partner must make a Canasta before either of you can go out; only one Canasta per team is necessary.

A Canasta can start as a meld of three cards that either you or your partner can build into a Canasta.

A Canasta can include wild cards, of course. A *natural Canasta* (which is worth more) has no wild cards, and a *mixed Canasta* includes wild cards. Natural Canastas are worth a bonus of 500; mixed Canastas are worth a bonus of 300.

When you make a Canasta, square up the pile so that only the top card is visible — a red card if it's a natural Canasta, a black one if it's a mixed Canasta. You can still add further cards to it, of course, but it may help your side's strategy to know whether the Canasta is already mixed.

Adding cards to melds

You can add cards at any point to your team's melds, but not to your opponents' melds.

The partnership's assets are joint; you add a queen to your partner's meld of queens, for example, rather than starting a separate pile of your own queens. The player who made the first meld for his side gets to tend the partnership's melds.

If you put down a mixed meld onto your partnership's natural meld, you turn a natural Canasta into a mixed one, thus reducing the Canasta in value. That's life!

Freezing the discard pile

Twos and jokers are wild and can be used for whatever the player wants them to be. Wild cards are also *stoppers* — which simply means that you can't pick up a discarded wild card (and thus the pile as a whole) if the previous player has discarded one of these cards.

If you throw a wild card away (normally an act of desperation), the wild card *freezes* the discard pile — which makes it more difficult for subsequent players, including yourself and your partner, to take the discard pile. Discarding a wild card doesn't make taking the discard pile impossible — just harder, and the next player to have a turn (one of your opponents) can't pick up the pile at all (see "Making the initial meld").

The first player to make a natural meld (a meld with no wild cards) "unfreezes" the discard pile for his side and picks up the discard pile.

Concerning the ♠3 and the ♣3

The ♠3 and ♣3 take some special consideration. You have to keep the following things in mind when you come across one of these cards in play:

- ✔ Like wild cards, the black 3s also freeze the deck, but only for one turn.
- ✔ You can only make these cards into melds on the turn on which you go out.
- ✔ You can't meld these cards with wild cards. If your meld includes a ♠3 or a ♣3, then the meld can't contain a wild card.

The ♠3 and the ♣3 really play no helpful part in the game for the player who picks one up, other than their tactical value to prevent the next player from having a chance to take the discard pile for one turn. Other than that, they're a bit of a drag, because they're so tough to make into melds.

After you or your partner has made the initial meld for the partnership, then whenever it is your turn, you can pick up the top card from the discard pile (and thus the whole pile) and put it down in a meld of three that includes a joker — so long as the pile isn't frozen (no wild cards are in the pile). If the pile *is* frozen, you can only pick up the top card from the discard pile and use it in a natural meld (that is, no jokers allowed).

Don't discard the ♠3 and the ♣3 prematurely. Save these cards for the last possible moment, for when you think that the next player may otherwise take a large discard pile if you put down a helpful discard. As a guaranteed stopper, these cards have significant strategic value in preventing the next player from taking the discard pile, if little value otherwise.

Making the initial meld

Wild cards and the black 3s freeze the discard pile. In addition, the discard pile is automatically frozen at the start of the game until each team makes its initial meld. At the beginning of every hand, you can't pick up the whole discard pile because, as I explain in "Making the first meld for each partnership," you need to make a good scoring play on your initial meld. Until a team makes its first meld, each player on that team can only take cards from the stock pile.

Because the discard pile is frozen, you can't use the top discard (and thus pick up the pile) unless you're going to use it in a meld with two cards of the same rank — in making that meld, no wild cards are allowed unless your set already includes three natural cards.

Bear in mind that after you or your partner has made the initial meld for your side, this restriction is lifted — but when a wild card is discarded by either side, that wild card has the effect of freezing the pile again for both sides.

The chief difference between a frozen and an unfrozen deck is that after you have put down your first meld, you are normally allowed to take any top card (and thus the rest of the pile) by making that top card into a meld of three or more (which may include wild cards) or by adding the top card to one of your already existing melds or Canastas. If the pack is frozen, however, you can only take the top card to make it into a meld, and any meld involving that top card must be a natural one, involving no wild cards.

Discarding a joker or a 2 may seem like a desperate measure, but it may well be worth your while to throw a wild card away to freeze the pack whenever the pile of cards grows to significant size. If your opponents have made their initial meld and your side has not, you may want to freeze the pack for your opponents. Because the joker also acts as a temporary stopper, it, too, has some value in buying some time. If you discard a joker, discard it crossways to the rest of the discard pile so that everyone can see that the pile is frozen. A black 3 freezes the deck but only for one turn, so you don't need to put the card sideways on the pile.

Putting down the ♥3 and the ♦3

The ♥3 and ♦3 are like bonus cards — they play no major part in the strategy of the game, but they can score your side some nice extra points if you're lucky enough to draw these cards. The "Scoring" section discusses just how much they're worth.

As soon as you pick up one of these cards, you must put it face-up in front of you and pick up another card from the stock pile. If you manage to pick up the discard pile and it includes either the ♥3 and ♦3, you must also put the card down in front of you. However, if you pick up one of these cards from the discard pile, you don't need to take a replacement card from the stock pile.

If you pick up a red 3 and forget to put the card down at that time, you can do it at a later turn without penalty. If the game ends, though, and you have a ♦3 or a ♥3 in your hand, you incur a 500-point penalty.

You can remind your partner to put down the ♥3 and ♦3 if he seems to have forgotten.

Making the first meld for each partnership

The first meld for each partnership in a hand must be worth a certain number of points in order for it to be put down. The bad news is that not only does this requirement apply for the first hand, but it also applies for all subsequent hands, too, and the task gets more arduous as the game goes on. The good news is that when one player makes the first meld, he lifts the load from his partner's back simultaneously.

You must meet the following requirements to put down the partnership's first meld of the hand:

✓ The first meld can't contain any wild cards unless the meld contains three natural cards; in other words, two natural cards and a wild card can't make up the initial meld.

✓ The first meld can't contain cards from the discard pile except for the top card. After you have met that initial requirement, however, you can pick up the discard pile and add to the meld by using cards from the discard pile.

✓ You must make the meld on your own — your partner can't help you out.

✓ You can put down more than one meld to make up the required numeric total, but all the cards for the additional melds must be from holdings already in your hand, rather than from cards picked up from the discard pile.

✓ The first meld must be worth a certain number of points, which increases as the game progresses. The value of the melds you put down for your initial meld depends on your team's cumulative total at the start of the hand, as you see in Table 2-1. Refer to "Calculating the value of your cards and melds" earlier in this chapter for more information on assigning points to cards.

Table 2-1	Initial Meld Point Requirements
Your Side's Total Score	*Points to Put Down a Meld*
Negative	0 (any meld will do)
0 to 1,495	50
1,500 to 2,995	90
3,000 or more	120

If you put down an initial meld that doesn't meet the minimum points required, you can put down additional melds on that same turn to make up the required total without penalty. Or you can take back your attempt, but the minimum total you require the next time you try goes up by 10 points. That is quite a severe penalty. Of course, if your opponents don't spot your mistake, you're home free.

After the initial meld requirement is met, if you subsequently try to put down an illegal meld, you get a 100-point penalty. However, if the next player takes his turn without noticing your mistake, then you can't be penalized. For example, if you put down a meld with too many wild cards in it, but the opponents don't notice before the next player takes his turn, the mistake is allowed to stand and there is no penalty.

Bear in mind that you can pick up the top card from the discard pile in the process of making your first meld of the hand. It's better to make your first meld by using that card rather than to make melds purely from cards already in your hand. Even if you can make the initial meld by using only cards within your original 11 cards, doing so is poor strategy; wait to put down melds until you can pick up the discard pile in doing so.

If you put down three queens and three kings from your own hand, for example, you know that the player who discards before you won't throw a king or queen to enable you to pick up the pile, but he may do so if you haven't shown him the melds in your hand. Don't let your opponents know what you're collecting — until it's too late!

Also, the bonus for a Canasta, ♦3, or ♥3 can't be taken into account in the initial meld. That comes at the end of the game, not when you put the meld down.

Going out

You can't get rid of all your cards and go out until your side has made a Canasta (see "Making a Canasta," earlier in this chapter, for the details). In going out, you can either make your whole hand into melds, or you can make a discard as you go out — the choice is up to you. The hand stops as soon as one player goes out.

Trying to go out without first making a Canasta carries a penalty of 100 points.

After picking up your card from the stock pile but before you put down your hand to go out, you can, if you want, ask your partner, "May I go out?" You have to abide by your partner's decision, but you don't need to ask the question.

If you don't abide by the decision or you ask the question after having put down your cards, you're fined 100 points, and your opponents can stop you from going out — if they want. Similarly, if your partner gives you permission to go out and you can't, that costs you 100 points.

Asking the question gives your partner the chance to tell you "No" and then put down the melds in her hand on her next turn, so as not to be caught with too many unnecessary points when you go out on your next turn. If she doesn't have too many cards left, don't worry about asking her, because your opponents may benefit more than you by unloading their melds as quickly as possible and not keeping the cards in their hand and being caught for a penalty.

During play, you can ask the other players how many cards they have left. The answer can help you decide whether to go for a big pick-up of the discard pile; you may not want to be left holding the baby if a player from the other side is about to go out.

In Canasta, you try to kick your opponents when they're down; you go for as big a hand as you can when you have made melds and they haven't. Conversely, you try to cut your losses, if it seems that they have all the cards, by terminating the game as quickly as possible.

If the whole stock is used up, the game essentially comes to a stop. But it may continue for a very short while longer. That is because the player who has taken the last card of the stock throws away a card, and if the next player can take this card and add it to one of his existing melds, he must do so — and take the discard pile, too, of course. Then he discards a card, and the same thing applies to the next player. As soon as the next player can't use the discard, the game is over, and the usual scoring takes place. If the last card of the stock is a ♦3 or a ♥3, the game ends at that point.

The *force-play* involves forcing the next player to take the pile of cards by giving him something he *must* pick up. The reason for creating a force-play is to land the next player with a big pile of cards that he can't get rid of. The play has an element of danger to it, but if the player has only a few cards in his hand, you can sometimes be relatively confident that this strategy can succeed.

Conversely, if you think that the next player wants to pick up the pile, prevent him from doing so by making your last discard a black 3 or a wild card, which, as you know, he is not allowed to pick up.

Scoring

At the end of the hand, as soon as one player goes out, the scoring starts. Each player scores as a negative the points left in his own hand (refer to "Calculating the value of your cards and melds"). Then you add up the points for the melds and subtract the negative points from that score.

Then you get to add in any bonuses you may be eligible for:

- ✔ You get a 100-point bonus for going out.

- ✔ You get a 200-point bonus for going out *concealed,* which means going out without first putting down any melds. If you can go out with a concealed hand after your opponents have just taken a large pile, you may go some way toward reducing the damage caused by the points in your partner's hand. But going out concealed isn't a recommended strategy, because it carries a great deal of danger with it.

- ✔ Every ♥3 or ♦3 your team has is worth 100 points. If you have both ♥3s and both ♦3s, you get a 400-point bonus for 800 points in all, rather than 400 points. If your side hasn't made a meld, you subtract the values of the ♥3s and ♦3s from your score.

Playing Canasta with Two Players

Canasta works perfectly well as a two-handed game, and the rules are almost identical to the four-handed variety (refer to "Your Mission, Should You Choose to Accept It") — except, of course, that all partnership elements don't come into play. The major differences when playing with two players are

- ✔ Each player gets 15 rather than 11 cards.

- ✔ When it's your turn, you can either take the top discard or draw from the stock. But if you draw from the stock, you take *two* cards and discard only one. Your hand grows fast, effectively speeding up the game.

- ✔ You need two Canastas to go out.

Most of the penalties are eliminated in this variety of the game, because you don't have a partner who can benefit from any unauthorized information.

Playing Canasta with Three Players

The three-handed game, which is often called Cut-Throat Canasta, is very similar to the two-handed variety except for the following differences:

- ✔ Each player gets 13 cards.

- ✔ The first player to pick up the discard pile plays against the other two in tandem for the rest of the hand. At the end of the hand, the lone player gets a score just for his hand, but the partnership gets a collective score in every respect but one — that of the red 3s.

- ✔ The ♥3s and ♦3s only count for the person who turned them up, not for the team, even though in all other respects the team's scores are identical.

- ✔ You traditionally play to 7,500 points.

Part II
Trick-Taking Games

The 5th Wave   By Rich Tennant

"No signals that your partner has made a bad bid, please."

In this part . . .

The title of this part contains a word that may be new to you: *trick*. Don't worry if you don't know what a trick is — I'll explain it to you when I start discussing a game.

Besides picking up some new vocabulary words (I promise, I don't use too many fancy-schmancy words), you can also come to this part of the book to get the lowdown on such games as Whist, Oh Hell!, Euchre, Spades, and Bridge — all of which revolve around tricks.

Chapter 3
Whist

• •

In This Chapter

▶ Discovering Whist basics

▶ Plotting some Whist strategy

▶ Varying the program with Knock Out Whist, German Whist, and Three-Handed Whist

• •

*T*his chapter should come with a warning label: Whist is a highly addictive game. After you figure out the fundamentals, you may find yourself spending more time at the Whist table than you ever thought possible. If your non-Whist playing friends complain that they never see you anymore, you may want to consider taking up another hobby.

To play Whist, you need only the most basic equipment:

✔ **Four players**

✔ **One standard deck of 52 cards (no jokers):** You may prefer to have a second deck to speed up the dealing a bit. One player can shuffle one deck while another player deals the other deck.

✔ **Pencil and paper for scoring**

What's Whist All About?

In Whist, the object is to score points by winning *tricks.* During the play of a trick, each player at the table plays a card. One player plays first, or *leads,* a card; the rest of the players are honor-bound to play a card in that suit (or *follow suit*) if they can. The player who puts down the highest card in the suit that was led wins the trick and collects all four cards.

Each team scores points for the tricks it wins. The first team to score 7 points wins (see "Scoring" for more information on winning the game).

Playing with a Trump Suit

In Whist, the cards rank from the ace (highest) to the 2 (lowest). However, one type of card, a *trump card,* can beat any other card in any other suit.

The *trump suit* acts as the master suit. If you play a card in the trump suit on a card from another suit, the trump card wins the trick (unless someone else plays a higher card in the trump suit). You determine the trump suit in one of three ways (agreed on in advance):

- ✔ **Cut the second deck, if you have another one, and make the suit of that card the trump suit.**

- ✔ **Cut your only deck before the deal starts and make the suit of that card the trump suit.**

- ✔ **Turn the dealer's last card face-up and make the suit of that card the trump suit.** This method gives the dealer the advantage of possessing a trump card and the disadvantage of everyone knowing one of the cards in his hand.

You can't simply play a trump card whenever you feel like it — the rules of Whist require you to follow suit at all times if you can, meaning that you must play a card in the suit that's been led, if you have one.

If you have no cards in the appropriate suit, you have the option of playing a trump card or *discarding* (throwing away) any card that you feel like getting rid of. Naturally, you don't want to play a trump card when your partner has just led an ace or followed suit with an ace, because you're playing as a partnership, and your partner is already making a pretty fair stab at taking the trick. Therefore, save your trump cards for a more valuable moment. But you do want to take a trick if you can, and sometimes playing a trump card is the only way to win the trick.

Be careful about following suit whenever you can; the penalty for *revoking,* or failing to follow suit, is three tricks. You lose the tricks, and the other side is credited with them. For example, if you revoke, and then end up winning all 13 tricks, your opponents score 3 tricks, and your side only scores 10 tricks.

Dealing and Playing the Cards

You can either play in arranged partnerships or cut the deck for partners. If you cut the deck, the players who turn up the two highest cards play against the players with the two lowest cards. After you determine partnerships, the partners sit opposite each other.

Whist on the Web

Whist players of every kind can find something of interest at the Card Players' Web Site located at members.aol.com/sharksinc/sites/index/html. You can download a shareware version of Ultimate Bid Whist, a computer program that lets you play against your computer at either a novice or expert level. (The program is for Windows 3.1 and Windows 95; to install the shareware, just follow the directions at the site.) If you want to join a new Whist club forming in your area, or if you want to form your own Whist club, click the e-mail link available at the site for more information. The site also offers a page of links to a host of card-game sites, including the Internet Gaming Zone, the Netplay Game Club, and other non-Whist specific sites.

You next cut for the deal, and the lowest card (with aces low) deals the first hand. Thereafter, the deal passes clockwise around the table.

The dealer deals out all 52 cards, face-down, one by one, clockwise, starting with the player on her left.

The player to the left of the dealer plays the first card of the trick. Then play proceeds clockwise around the table, with each player contributing a card. Whoever wins the first trick (either by playing the highest card in the suit led or by playing the highest trump card) leads to the next trick, and so on, until all the cards have been played.

You must play a card in the suit that's been led if you have one. If you don't, you can play a trump card or simply discard a card in another suit.

One player in each partnership (it doesn't matter which player) takes care of the tricks for his side; he stacks the four cards that make up the trick neatly in front of him, so that at the end of the hand each side can see how many tricks they have won. At the end of the hand, unless something has gone horribly wrong, the two sides have 13 tricks between them.

After the hand is scored (see "Scoring" for the details), the players move on to the next hand.

Scoring

After the last trick has been played, each team counts its tricks. Then the time of reckoning is upon you.

Scoring trick points

The first six tricks won by your side count for nothing. After the sixth trick, any additional tricks score your team 1 point each. For example, if your side wins 11 tricks, you score 5 points.

The object of Whist is to score 7 points before your opponents. If you make that magic 7, you score a *game*. Scoring two out of three games wins you the whole contest, also known as a *rubber*.

Playing to 7 points is standard in the United States. In the United Kingdom, players commonly play to 5 points.

Scoring honor cards in the trump suit

If neither partnership *scores game* (scores 7 points) after counting the tricks won by each side, you have a further chance to register points: You get to look at the trump-suit honor cards in your pile of collected tricks.

The *honor cards* in a suit are the ace, king, queen, and jack.

The side with the most trump-suit honor cards gets to score 1 point apiece for those cards. For example, if your side has all four honor cards, you get 4 points; if your side has three honor cards, you score 2 points (because you have two more honor cards than your opponents have), and if each side has two honor cards, no points are scored. (By the way, this is where the phrase *honors are even* comes from.)

If you get to score your trump-suit honor cards, you first record the trick score, and then you add on the honor points and move on to the next hand.

Honor points aren't universally recognized (they're always scored in the U.K. and sometimes in the U.S.), but you should know how to score them — just in case. Be sure to clarify at the start of a game whether your group wants to score these cards.

You can't win the game with honor points if you need just 1 point to win. If you have 6 points at the start of the hand, you can't *reach game* except by scoring trick points. The honor points are simply ignored in that case. You can win with honor points if you have 5 points at the start, though.

If trick points get one side to game, then the other side doesn't get to count its honor card points. For example, say that your side has 5 points and your opponents have 4 points. You then win eight tricks (worth 2 points), but your opponents have 4 points for honor cards. Who wins? You do, of course — you don't think that I'd let you lose!

Scoring the rubber

You carry forward your point total from the previous hands until one side or the other reaches the magic figure of 7, in which case both sides start again from the beginning. Whichever side wins two games first wins the rubber, whereupon you have the *final reckoning,* or scoring, when you calculate the precise margins of victory and defeat.

The winners subtract the losers' score from their own at the end of the rubber, and the difference is the margin of victory.

Playing to Win: Basic Whist Strategy

You can play Whist purely socially, without putting any special work into the play of the cards. You don't have to try to remember the cards your partner plays, or what suit she leads initially. If you play Whist in this manner, you may find the game an enjoyable pastime — even if you find that you don't do especially well at it!

Remembering the cards

One vital aspect to your winning strategy is remembering the high honor cards on each hand. Hopefully, you can easily recall what cards you started the hand with, but also try to recall the salient high cards as they appear during the hand. Remembering which high cards have been played tells you which ones are still out there, just waiting to take your tricks.

Also make note of the suit your partner leads. Your partner probably has good cards in that suit, and she'll probably want you to lead that suit if you get the lead.

The leading role

The first card that is played to every trick is the *lead.* Of all the leads in a hand, the lead to the first trick (the *opening lead*) is the most important, because it may dictate the way that the rest of the play advances. All subsequent leads may thus be affected by it. So the question is, what suit should you lead, and which card in the suit should you play?

If the dealer gives you a sequence of honor cards, lead the top card from that sequence. So from KQJ, you lead the king, and from QJ10, you lead the queen. However, if the sequence starts with the ace, lead the lowest card; from an AK combination, lead the king, and lead the jack from AKQJ.

If you have to make a lead early in the hand and you don't have a comfortable suit from which to lead, such as one that includes a sequence of honor cards at its head, think about using one of the following reasonable alternatives:

- ✔ **Lead a small card from a long suit of four or more cards, particularly one in which you have high cards, such as the king, queen, or jack.** By leading a long suit, sometimes you can force the opponents to use up their trump cards prematurely to take the trick — cards with which they may win a trick anyway.

  If you lead from a suit in which you have length, lead your fourth-highest card, which gives your partner some general perspective on your hand. For example, if you have the ♠Q ♠9 ♠7 ♠5 ♠2, lead the ♠5. Leading low from a suit in which you hold a few fairly-high cards creates the chance that all the other highest cards in the suit will get played at once (because everyone must follow suit). If this happens, then your fairly-high cards become the new highest cards left in that suit. Of course, your partner doesn't know exactly what you have in the suit, but he may be able to guess that your lead of a small card suggests that you have some length in the suit, maybe a high card in the suit.

  From ♥K ♥9 ♥5 ♥2, lead the ♥2. Your partner can work out that you have only four hearts. Why? Because if you had five hearts, your fourth-highest heart couldn't be the 2, could it?

- ✔ **Lead a singleton (a holding of just one card) in a suit that isn't the trump suit.** The next time someone plays that suit, you won't have any cards left in it, so you can play a trump card and win the trick.

  Don't consider this lead if you have good trump cards, because you may win tricks with those trump cards anyway. A better move may be to lead your long suit or even to lead a trump card.

- ✔ **Lead a trump card.** Seriously consider this lead if you have five or more trump cards. If your highest trump cards are in a sequence, lead the highest card in the sequence; otherwise, lead your smallest trump card.

  You should also lead trump cards early if you have a bunch of high cards but only two or three small trump cards, cards that you're not likely to win a trick with if someone leads the trump suit; by leading trump cards, you take out the opponents' trump cards, which stops your side's high cards from being trumped.

You may find that some of this advice contradicts itself. You can't find the right lead on every hand by applying formulas to it. No hand exactly fits one pattern, and hands come in many different shapes. These leads are only suggestions, not a guaranteed route to success. What makes Whist such fun is that you need to apply your brain and take chances.

Although this section is all about opening leads, let me throw in a piece of advice that applies to making subsequent leads. When in doubt, play a card in the suit that your partner leads at his first opportunity. Your partner will play a card from a strong suit for his opening lead, so playing a card in that suit gives him a chance to play a card from his strong suit. This move has the great advantage of retaining partnership harmony. After all, your partner can hardly blame you for following his advice!

Playing second to a trick

If you're the second person to play to a trick, play a low card (preferably your lowest card) in the suit that's been led, unless you have a good reason to do otherwise. The logic is to save your firepower for later. Because your partner still has to play on the trick, you hope that she can take care of things for your side.

However, you may have some good reasons not to play your lowest card:

- ✔ **You have a sequence of honor cards in the suit that's been led.** If you have such a sequence, play the *lowest* card in the sequence. Thus, when you have the QJ1094, play the 9, the lowest card in the sequence.

- ✔ **You have the ace in the suit that's been led.** One very awkward decision as second hand is whether to play the ace in a suit other than the trump suit, if you have it. You should play the ace if you have five or more cards in the suit or if the card led is an honor card — the king, queen, or jack.

  The strategy of second hand playing low is to let your partner, who plays last to the trick, have the chance to play a significant card on the trick. If you play low, the third hand still needs to put out a high card to give her side a chance to win that trick. But when you have the ace in the suit led, you may not want to risk losing it, because one opponent may be able to trump the next round of the suit. When an honor card has been led, and you know that you can capture a high card in the process of playing the ace, it is very tempting — and probably right — to do so.

Playing third to a trick

When you play third to a trick, or *third hand,* you have the benefit of seeing which card your partner leads to the trick, giving you valuable information about playing your hand.

When you play third hand, you usually play the highest card in the suit your partner leads. Clearly, you don't want the opponents to win a trick with a lower card than is necessary, so force them to win the trick with a high card — if they can.

When you have a sequence of honor cards, follow suit with the lowest card in your sequence, which can help give your partner a clearer picture of what's going on. When your partner sees you play a 9 and the fourth hand captures your 9 with an ace, he has a fairly good idea that you have a number of cards in the middle, because the fourth hand would have won the trick with the 10 or jack if he could, instead of wasting his ace unnecessarily.

Playing fourth to a trick

When you play fourth to a trick, you're entirely on your own; win any trick that your partner hasn't already won for your side.

If you have an ace in your hand and don't play it at the first opportunity to take the trick, who knows what fate that ace will suffer? Maybe the rats will get it; one opponent may trump your ace on the next round.

If you can't win the trick, play your lowest card.

Finessing (nice and easy does it all the time)

In the real world, *finesse* refers to tact, diplomacy, and the ability to behave properly at cocktail parties. In the world of cardplaying, a *finesse* is an attempt to win a trick without using the highest possible card in your hand in the process. In a finesse, you save your highest card for later.

When you play your medium-sized card, you hope that your opponent who plays after you can't beat your card. If she can, your finesse fails.

Figure 3-1 shows you a finesse in action. The figure looks only at the clubs in everyone's hands; they have other cards, too.

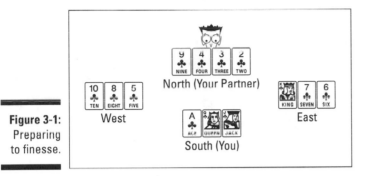

Figure 3-1:
Preparing
to finesse.

Your partner, North, leads the ♣2. If you play the ♣A, you win the trick. You can play the ♣Q now, but the opponent on your right plays the ♣K, winning the trick.

But notice the difference if you play the ♣J initially. If you play the ♣J at your first turn, it wins the trick. Now if you tackle another suit, you hope to let your partner lead the club suit when he gets the lead again. You can put in the ♣Q when it's your turn to play. With the ♣A still to come, you collect three tricks without losing one. You exploited the good fortune that it was East, not West, who had the ♣K. Playing the ♣J (or ♣Q) attempts to win a club trick with a lower card than your top one (the ♣A).

If your highest and second-highest cards in the suit led are separated by one card, consider not playing the very highest card you have if you play second or third to a trick. For example, consider playing the jack from a holding including the KJ or the queen from a holding including the AQ. Playing your second-highest card may give you the chance of exploiting the favorable distribution of the opponents' cards to win the trick and save your highest card for later.

Making discards

When somebody leads a suit in which you have no cards left, you have two options:

- ✔ You can try to win the trick by playing a trump card.
- ✔ You can throw away (or *discard*) a card that you feel no need to keep.

Throwing away a card is called *discarding;* if someone leads a trump card and you have none (bad luck!), you have no choice but to discard.

Raising the blue peter

When Whist was at its most popular in the early 19th century, it was a game almost exclusively for the aristocracy, who had a great deal of time to devote to the game — time which, in a different era, is wasted on such inessentials as how to pay the mortgage.

One of these nobles, Lord Henry Bentinck, came up with an imaginative idea to signal whether his partner's lead was successful or not. (Bear in mind that, according to the unwritten etiquette of the game, smiling and scowling are not acceptable ways of conveying that message.)

Bentinck suggested that if his partner led an honor card, he would play a high card — say,

the 7, 8, or 9 — as the third hand to indicate that he liked the opening lead.

Bentinck likened the maneuver to *hoisting the blue peter,* which is the traditional flag that indicates readiness to sail. The English abbreviated the term to *peter;* Americans refer to the process as an *echo* or *come-on.*

You raise the blue peter to give your partner the go-ahead to play the suit again. For example, if you possess a high card or if you have only two cards in the suit, you can play your higher card when your partner leads the king to say that you can trump later rounds of the suit.

When you make a discard, you want to throw away losers and keep winners — that may sound obvious, but you may be surprised at how often even experienced players seem to forget this!

In general, discard small cards rather than high ones. Doing so also helps your partner see which suits you have no interest in. If your partner knows that you discard this way, then she can plan the rest of the hand around that information.

Three-Handed Whist

Two perfectly playable versions of Three-Handed Whist exist: One involves three players and a *dummy* hand (a hand that all the players can see), and one just involves three players.

Playing with a dummy hand

You begin by dealing 13 cards to all three players and the dummy hand, which is situated opposite the dealer. You determine the trump suit in the standard fashion (see "Playing with a Trump Suit" in this chapter), and the player to the left of the dealer plays the first card. At that point, one player (it doesn't matter who) turns over the dummy hand and exposes it to the light of day. That player then sorts the dummy hand and lays it out on the table.

From this point on, the dealer chooses the plays of both his hand and the dummy hand. Play progresses in the standard clockwise fashion (refer to "Dealing and Playing the Cards" for more information), and the other two players team up together, with one of them playing before the dummy hand and one after it. At the end of the hand, the deal moves clockwise, and the new dealer takes on the other two players, again with the aid of the dummy.

The game is scored the same as traditional Whist (refer to "Scoring" in this chapter). Both players record the score for the partnership as their own score; the players compete against each other in the scoring even though they score points as a team. The first player to score 7 points wins.

Playing with three hands

This variation may involve less skill, but it creates more excitement.

Deal the four hands and then determine the trump suit for the hand (see "Playing with a Trump Suit" in this chapter). The dealer looks at his own hand, and the other two players do likewise. If the dealer dislikes his hand, he has the option of exchanging his hand with the fourth hand — an irreversible decision.

If the dealer decides to exchange his hand with the fourth hand, he should take care to memorize the hand before switching.

If the dealer doesn't want to make the switch, the option goes to the player on his left and then to the third hand. If the dealer does switch his hand, either of the other players can exchange her hand with the discarded hand.

Swapping your cards for the dealer's discarded hand is truly an act of desperation, but sometimes the only way is up! Of course, if you do exchange your cards, one of the other players knows your hand precisely, which should prove a big advantage to him, but if your cards truly reek, you may decide to take the risk.

If you're the dealer and you have two or fewer aces and kings and fewer than four trump cards, you should definitely exchange hands, because the bonus for knowing an extra 13 cards proves very valuable. Even if your hand is slightly better than normal in terms of aces, kings, and queens (you can expect to have about one of each, on average), you may still feel that the tactical merits of exchanging hands may be worthwhile.

When the swapping is complete, the game is then played as a three-handed game, in that the discarded hand takes no part in the play. Everyone plays on her own, against the other two players (see "Dealing and Playing the Cards" for more information). Your score is simply the tricks you manage to take, converted into points. For example, if you win 6 tricks, you score 6 points.

You can play to a finite number of hands, or the first to 50 points wins. Honor cards aren't scored at all.

German Whist (Two-Handed Whist)

German Whist is a game for two players, which may explain why the game is also occasionally referred to as Honeymoon Whist. If you decide to play this game on your honeymoon, you must be very devoted cardplayers.

The dealer deals 13 cards to each player and turns over the top card of the remaining 26 cards, the *stock*. This card defines the trump suit for the whole hand (refer to "Playing with a Trump Suit" for more information).

The game falls into two stages: the preparation stage and the actual play of the hand — although the nature of the two stages may seem pretty similar.

Improving your hand

During the preparation stage, you attempt to improve your hand by playing out cards and receiving cards in return. The two players are fighting for the right to pick up either the upturned card or the face-down top card of the stock. Depending on whether the face-up card is a good or bad card, both players try to win the trick or lose it.

The nondealer may lead any card in her hand, to which the dealer must follow suit (play a card in the suit if he has one). The winner of the trick takes the upturned card; the loser takes the face-down card from the top of the stock. You then turn up a new card and repeat the process; the winner of the previous trick leads. Repeat this process 13 times.

This procedure is all preparation; these 13 tricks don't count for anything toward the scoring of the hand. They just set you up for the finale.

Playing the hand

Now the serious part of the game begins. During this final stage, you want to win as many of the 13 tricks as possible. You keep the same trump suit as for the first 13 tricks, and you simply play out the cards, one at a time. The player who won the last trick of the preparation phase leads a card, and the other hand must respond by playing a card, following suit if she can. The winner of one trick leads to the next trick, and so on for all the 13 tricks.

The game offers a great test of memory as you try to keep track of what happened in the initial phase of the game and who ended up with which cards. Try to keep track of all the aces, kings, and queens at the very least, so that as the preparation stage comes to an end, you can lead middle cards out and force a high card out of your opponent's hand.

For example, say that the top card you're about to play for is the ♣7, and clubs are the trump suit; if you have the ♥10 and the ♥9, and the ♥K and the ♥Q have already been played, leading the ♥10 may force your opponent to relinquish her ♥A if she wants that trump card. Of course, she may have the ♥J, or she may not.

Don't try to win tricks in the initial phase of the game unless you want the top card. Try to weigh how good the card you led is as compared to the top card. Don't, for example, lead an ace just to get a king in that same suit, because you have simply exchanged a good card for another one. This move also gives your opponent a chance to throw a card of his choice in the suit led — and who knows, perhaps also to pick up something good in exchange?

You may want to lead trump cards in the early stage to *kill,* or reduce the effectiveness of, your opponent's hand. This tactic may prove particularly relevant if you can see that your enemy has trump card control as the first stage of the game runs down. You may also want to leave yourself with a suit (other than trumps) in which you have no cards at all in the early part of the game, so that you can trump when your opponent leads that suit and win a key card.

Knock Out Whist

Knock Out Whist is simple in structure. The game doesn't require a high degree of skill, but it does allow for some element of calculation.

Technically, the number of players of the game is unlimited, but you may find that the game works best when the players start out with seven cards each, which limits the number of players to seven.

The dealer deals seven cards face-down to everyone and then turns over the top card of the stock to determine the trump suit (see "Playing with a Trump Suit" for more information). The player to the dealer's right leads to the first trick. If you can, you must follow suit. If not, you can play a trump card, if you want, or you can discard a card from another suit.

The highest card in the suit led or the highest trump played wins the trick, and whoever won that trick leads to the next trick.

At the end of the hand, the deal progresses clockwise.

Anyone who takes no tricks on any hand is eliminated immediately. The last player left in is the winner.

In a fun variation of the game, players who haven't won any tricks get a sort of second chance, picturesquely named "a dog's life." While everyone else gets seven cards, the player who lost out on the last hand gets just one card. Play progresses normally — except that the canine player has the opportunity to play his card on any trick he chooses. When it is his turn to play, he can play, or he can pass by knocking the table. If the player would have been first to lead to the first trick, he can do so or knock. If the player actually succeeds in winning his trick, the player to his left leads to the next trick. The lucky player is then brought back into the game in normal fashion.

After each hand, the dealer gives one fewer card to each of the players until the deal gets down to one card. Whoever takes the most tricks on the previous hand gets to choose the trump suit for this last hand. If two players tie for the most tricks taken, those players cut the cards, and whoever draws the higher card gets to choose the trump suit. The usual suit order (spades, hearts, diamonds, clubs) applies if both players cut the same value card.

If you want to play Knock Out Whist for money, each player left in at the end of every hand simply puts in a chip at the start of each hand. The winner takes all.

Chapter 4

Oh Hell! and Other Exact Bidding Games

. . . .

In This Chapter

▶ Discovering Oh Hell! basics

▶ Planning strategy at Oh Hell!

▶ Varying the program with Ninety-Nine and Romanian Whist

. . . .

*O*h Hell! (the game is always given its exclamation point) is ideal both for children and adults, in that it requires sufficient skill to make it an enjoyable challenge for everyone, and it involves just enough luck that everyone stands a reasonable chance of winning — or at least of not losing by too much. (If you lose to your children, you can emphasize the luck factor; if you win, you can console them with the thought that as they get older, they will be able to beat you one day.)

To play Oh Hell!, you're certainly not required to bring any devil-worshipping paraphernalia with you. Instead, you just need the following:

✔ **At least three players:** Oh Hell! is best played with four players, but it can be played with up to eight players.

✔ **One standard deck of 52 cards**

✔ **Paper and pencil for scoring:** You may want to construct a score sheet set out in columns, with a column for each player.

Oh Hell!

Oh Hell! is based on taking *tricks*. During the play of the cards, players take turns extracting one card from their hand and putting it face-up on the table. The person who plays the highest card wins and collects all the played cards — that's one trick. The player who wins the trick plays the first card to start the next trick. The process is continued until all the cards are played.

Like most games where trick-taking is an element, the players in Oh Hell! score points for winning tricks. However, winning at Oh Hell! is more than just a matter of winning tricks. Before the actual play of the hand, the players must estimate *precisely* how many tricks they will win in the hand.

The relative importance of predicting your trick total accurately far outweighs the reward for actually winning tricks — so picking up a bad hand is not, in itself, a problem. Indeed, a really bad hand may be easier to judge accurately than a really good one.

The strength of Oh Hell! as a card game is that you don't need a good hand to succeed at it. Making good estimates about your hand, rather than having good cards, determines your success at the game. Luck isn't a factor in the quality of your hand, which is a very satisfying ingredient for a card game.

Dealing the cards

The players cut the cards to determine the dealer, with the player who draws the lowest card dealing the first hand.

The dealer deals out as many cards as possible, depending on the number of players, starting with the player on his left and giving everyone the same number of cards. The cards are dealt face-down. The dealer then puts down the remaining cards and turns over the top card to determine the trump suit (see "Playing with a trump suit" for more information) for that hand; the other undealt cards play no further part in the game. In a four-player game, in which all the cards get dealt out, cut the deck to determine the trump suit before dealing out the first hand.

Playing with a trump suit

You must play a card in the suit that's been led if you have a card in that suit. That is, you must *follow suit,* if you can. But if you don't have a card in that suit, you may play a card from the *trump suit,* which automatically wins the trick — unless someone plays a higher trump card than yours.

The smallest trump card beats even the ace in a *side-suit* (any non-trump suit). If you can't follow suit, you can also play a card from another side-suit. Doing so is often called *throwing away* or *discarding* that card.

Oh Hell! by any other name

Oh Hell! goes by a wide variety of other names. You may know the game as Pshaw, Blackout, Up the Creek without a Paddle, and the rather less-exciting Nomination Whist.

Bidding: You have to hit your mark

The *bidding* starts with the player to the left of the dealer, who can bid any number of tricks that she likes up to the maximum, which is the number of cards received by each player. Your bid represents the number of tricks you intend to take in the course of the hand.

How much you bid is determined by your high cards, your trump cards, and by what everyone else is bidding! The bidding continues clockwise until it comes back to the dealer, who has the final bid. Nothing stops the players from contracting, as a group, for too many tricks or too few tricks, and any player can try for no tricks at all.

Everyone but the dealer can bid for as many tricks as they think they can take. One of the little peculiarities of Oh Hell! that can lead to much pleasurable aggravation (if you aren't the unfortunate dealer) is that the total number of tricks contracted for can't equal the number of tricks available. In other words, if five cards are dealt to each person, then the total number of tricks bid can't be five. So if the first three players bid one, two, and one, respectively, the dealer can't contract for one trick because doing so would make the total five.

Having the number of tricks contracted for equal the number of tricks available allows for the possibility that everyone makes his contract — a situation which is inherently unsatisfying, I suppose. Whatever the reason, the smaller the number of cards, the more potentially arduous this rule can be, and on the round when only one card is dealt, it can produce particularly irritating results for the dealer, who bids last.

Not everybody plays the rule that dealer is restricted by the number of tricks available. I think it spices the game up, but not everybody sees it the same way.

The scorer writes down the bids on the score sheet as the bids are called out, before the hand starts, so that he can check afterwards who has made her contract and so that he can tell the dealer what *call* (bid) is forbidden to him.

WARNING!

If you make a bid out of turn, the bid stands and other players can take advantage of it, in that they can make their decision based on more information. However, if the dealer makes a bid out of turn, it can't be accepted, because the disadvantage of bidding last must go to the dealer.

TIP

Don't bid too high; when in doubt, bear in mind that playing to lose a trick is generally much easier than playing to win it. Look at the hand in Figure 4-1 to see what I mean.

Figure 4-1:
A hand with plenty of potential — but no guarantees!

Suppose that four people are playing, and you hold this hand as first to bid. Hearts are the trump suit. You can see that you may, on a very good day, win all four tricks — you're virtually certain to win at least one, if not two. In fact, all four of your cards *might* win a trick. However, you're much better advised to bid two rather than three, and then listen carefully to the rest of the bidding to determine your play strategy based on everyone else's bidding.

Playing the cards

The player on the dealer's left leads to the first trick, and play continues clockwise. Cards rank in the standard order with aces high, and you have to follow suit (play a card in the suit that was led) if you can. If you can't follow suit, you have the choice of throwing away a card (playing a card in a non-trump suit) or trumping by playing a card from the trump suit.

TIP

In the early phases of the game when you have plenty of cards, initially leading a suit in which you have only one card can be a good idea. Depending on whether you win or lose that trick, you can be more flexible in your strategy in other suits.

At the end of the hand, each player announces how many tricks she took, and the scorer writes down the scores for each player (see "Scoring the game" for more information).

REMEMBER

You're allowed to check the bids during the hand to remind yourself of what you and other people are shooting for.

If a player exposes a card by playing it out of turn or by dropping it, it becomes a *penalty card* and must be played at the first legal opportunity. If a player errs by failing to follow suit, he may correct his mistake before the next trick is started. His *revoke card* (the card that he played by mistake) becomes a penalty card to be played on his next turn, and all the other players who played after him on the previous trick may change their cards if they want. If the revoke isn't spotted in time, the deal is canceled, and the revoker suffers a 10-point penalty.

Scoring the game

For every trick that you get on each hand, you score 1 point. If you make your bid, you get an additional 10 points.

The rise and fall of the Oh Hell! empire

After a hand is over with and scored up, the deal passes clockwise for the next hand, and that player deals out the cards as before. But this time, she deals one fewer card to every player, and that reduction continues on each subsequent hand until each player has only one card. On the next hand, the number of cards goes *up* by one, and the sequence progresses until it reaches the maximum again. The game ends after that maximum hand, and the winner is the person who finishes with the highest total.

Some people start with one card, work their way up to the maximum, and then come back down to one card. Either way is possible, and which way you choose really doesn't matter.

If two players tie for the lead at the end of the game, the deal passes on, and everybody plays one more hand with the maximum number of cards. Additional deals with the maximum number of cards continue until the play determines a winner.

Romanian Whist

The main variation on Oh Hell! is called Romanian Whist, for the surprisingly good reason that it comes from Romania. In fact, the game is just called Whist in that country.

To play Romanian Whist, you need the following:

- ✔ **At least three players:** The game can be played with up to eight players.

- ✔ **One standard deck of 52 cards:** At the start of the game, the deck is pared down so that you have eight cards per player in the deck, using only the highest-ranking cards. If you have three players, for example, you use a deck that has only the ace through 9 in it — in other words, a 24-card deck. If you have six players, a 48-card deck is used, which means that only the 2s are excluded to get the numbers right. With eight players, play a six-card deal.

- ✔ **Paper and pencil for scoring:** You may want to construct a score sheet set out in columns, with a column for each player.

Dealing the cards

The players cut the deck to determine the dealer. The dealer then gives each player the appropriate number of cards, dealing clockwise, starting with the player on the dealer's left.

This game differs from Oh Hell! in that you start with one card, work your way up to eight, and then work your way down again. More importantly, the progression is a rather labored one. Instead of going up one card at a time, every player takes a turn to deal a hand with one card each. Thereafter, the deal progresses normally until you get to the round of eight cards. At that point, everyone takes a turn at dealing again, and then the progression retreats back down to one again for another complete round.

Choosing the trump suit, bidding, and playing

In Romanian Whist, you determine the trump suit by turning over the top card of the undealt cards, except that when you play the eight-card round, the hands are played with no trump suit at all (refer to "Playing with a trump suit" in this chapter for the details on trump suits).

The normal Oh Hell! rules apply to the bidding (refer to "Bidding: You have to hit your mark") and playing the cards (refer to "Playing the cards").

Scoring the hand

If you make your contract exactly, you score 5 points plus 1 point each for the tricks you take. If you make fewer tricks than you contract for, you lose the value of your bid. If you make more tricks than you bid for, you lose the value equivalent to the tricks you took.

That scoring routine sounds complicated, but it really isn't. Look at how the scoring applies to the four-handed game shown in Figure 4-2, with three cards each and clubs as the trump suit. North deals.

Figure 4-2:
Scoring a hand.

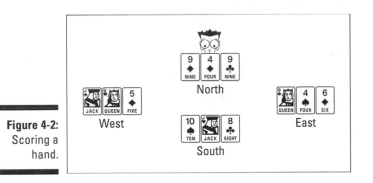

East bids zero, South bids one, West bids one, and North bids zero — rather unhappily. A bid of two is a valid option here, but the diamond suit just seems too unlikely to be able to generate a trick.

East leads the ♠4 and South plays the ♠10, West wins the trick with the ♠J, and North throws away the ♦9.

West leads the ♦5, North plays the ♦4, and East plays the ♦6, creating a problem for South. If he trumps this trick and leads the ♥J, he may well win the last trick. Because discarding now has the added bonus of defeating East in her contract, he throws away his ♥J, giving East a trick she didn't want. North wins the last trick because her ♣9 is the highest trump card left.

The scoring goes like this: West, who makes his bid, scores 6 points. East, who underbid, loses her tricks, 1 point. South, who overbid, loses his bid, 1 point. North, who underbid, loses 1 point, too, her trick total.

One highly entertaining variation to the last full cycle of one-card games is to hold your card on your forehead so that everyone but you can see your card. You then have to make your bid in the usual fashion, without knowing your card, based on the bids that everyone else is making.

Ninety-Nine

Ninety-Nine combines the skill of Oh Hell! with some other attractive features. The objective of Ninety-Nine is to predict how many tricks you will take, but the method of doing so is very original and adds a great deal of spice to the game.

To play Ninety-Nine, you need:

- ✔ **Three players**
- ✔ **One standard deck of 52 cards:** Use only the top 36 cards (ace through 6 in each suit) together with a joker or, alternatively, the ♣2 if you don't have a joker.
- ✔ **Paper and pencil for scoring**

Dealing the cards and determining the trump suit

Deal out the pack and turn over the last card in the deck to establish the trump suit for the hand (refer to "Playing with a trump suit" in this chapter for more information on trump suits). If the card turned over is the joker or a 9, the hand is played with no trump suit.

The game consists of a *rubber* of exactly nine hands, with the deal passing clockwise at the end of each hand. The winner is the player who scores the most points overall.

Ninety-Nine marks its place in time

Most of the card games I describe in this book have a fairly well-established pedigree. However, Ninety-Nine is a very modern game, and unlike most of the other games, which evolved over the passage of time, this game was specifically invented by David Parlett in 1968. It's an outstanding game, and one of my absolute favorites.

Bidding for tricks

Now comes the second most interesting part of the hand, which is determining how many tricks you will take. Although you get 12 cards, you use only nine of your cards; you discard the other three cards before the hand starts, and in discarding those three cards, you make your bid as to how many tricks you will win with the remaining nine cards.

The suits of the three cards you discard signal your bid. It works like this:

- ✔ **For every club you discard, you undertake to win three tricks.**
- ✔ **For every heart you discard, you undertake to win two tricks.**
- ✔ **For every spade discard, you undertake to win one trick.**
- ✔ **For every diamond you discard, you undertake to win no tricks.**
- ✔ **If you discard the joker, it stands in for the turned-up card.** The joker represents the number associated with the upturned card. So if the turned-up card was the ♠7, discarding the joker represents one trick.

The cumulative total of your discards represents your bid. For example, discarding a club, a heart, and a diamond represents five tricks, as do a club and two spades or two hearts and a spade.

You discard your three cards face-down, so none of the other players know what you're aiming for.

Determining the right cards to discard

Say that you get the cards in Figure 4-3 and that spades are the trump suit.

Figure 4-3:
Aces and trumps — a strong combination.

The way to look at this hand is to concede that taking more than five tricks is unlikely; too many aces and trumps are in the other players' hands. Can you discard, say, a club, heart, and diamond to leave you with a realistic chance of five tricks? Probably not; the other players aren't going to be bidding all that low because not so many diamonds are out. So they will probably stop you from winning five tricks. All right, how about going for four, discarding two hearts and a diamond? Not bad. Three looks too low as a possible target because you have too many aces and kings, so go for four.

After you decide to discard two hearts and a diamond, you must decide which ones. Discard your middle cards for flexibility. Getting rid of the ♥Q, the ♥10, and a high diamond is probably the right move here. You want to get the lead early and find out whether your *side-suit* (that is, suits other than the trump suit) winners will win tricks. If so, lead low trump cards at each opportunity. If not, lead high trump cards.

You often find that the trump suit gets in your way of bidding what you want, even if you have cards in all the suits. For example, look at the hand in Figure 4-4, in which clubs are the trump suit.

Figure 4-4:
Lots of clubs — but no convenient discard.

You have the potential to win seven tricks out of nine, but to bid seven tricks requires discarding two clubs (you can't discard two hearts and a club because you have only one heart). If you discard two clubs, you don't have enough winners left. It looks best, therefore, to discard a club, a heart, and the ♠Q and go for six tricks.

When diamonds are the trump suit, you frequently find that you see most of the diamonds discarded, because that tactic gets a player to a low number while reducing her hand's strength simultaneously. Bear in mind that when diamonds are the trump suit, if you leave yourself holding a single middle diamond, it's much more likely to win a trick than, say, a middle club.

Again, though, a bad hand without diamonds can cause you severe problems. Imagine that you're dealt the hand in Figure 4-5 with spades as the trump suit.

Figure 4-5:
Diamonds may be a girl's best friend, but not here.

This hand surely won't win more than a trick — if that. But the minimum bid you can make is for two tricks, by discarding two spades and a diamond. Do so, therefore, and hope for the best.

One other strategy is possible, although it's a council of desperation. You may reasonably say that you have no chance of two tricks with this hand; if so, perhaps your optimum strategy on this hand is to mess up the other players' chances: Discard your high cards and try to make the other two players go over the top on their bids. Here, you can discard the ♦J, the ♥Q, and the ♥8 and then try to lose every trick and make the others go too high. I like this approach — anything that can irritate the other players has to be a good policy.

Discarding middle cards if you can is nearly always good strategy, leaving yourself with sure winners and sure losers. So in normal circumstances, if you have the ace, jack, and 7 in a suit, throw the jack — unless you're trying to avoid winners at all costs, in which case you throw the ace.

Playing the hand

Unless anyone wants to make a premium bid (see the section "Making premium bids," later in this chapter), everyone leaves his bids face-down on the table, and the player to the left of the dealer leads to the first trick. The normal rules of cards apply: You must follow suit if you can, or else you can play whatever you want.

At the end of the hand, all the players announce their tricks taken and whether they have succeeded in their contracts.

Scoring

After you play the hand, you score it up. Each player scores the number of tricks he has taken, at a point each, and on top of that adds a bonus if he makes his contract. The bonus varies depending on whether he is the only player to succeed in making his contract:

> ✔ **If you're the only player to succeed, you get an extra 30-point bonus.**
>
> ✔ **If two players make their contracts, they each get 20 points.**
>
> ✔ **If everyone succeeds, they all get an additional 10 points.**

You're allowed to consult your bid during the course of the play, to remind yourself of what you bid and which cards you discarded. Make sure that you don't mix your bid into your tricks taken or switch a trick with your bid!

Instead of playing nine hands and having the winner determined by the highest score at the end, you can also score by reference to games. A game is 100 points, and the first player to reach two games wins. As soon as a player reaches 100 points, he gets a bonus of 100 points, and a new game starts again. A *rubber* is the best of three games.

This form of scoring is less affected by the scramble at the end to overtake the hand in the lead by desperate declarations or revelations. I think that I prefer the simple scoring, because everyone has a chance to win to the end.

Making premium bids

Occasionally, you're dealt a hand that is so clear-cut that you can afford to play for higher stakes and *declare* your bid by showing the bid to the other players.

The consequence of declaring your bid is that if you succeed, you get a further 30-point bonus on top of what you would normally have scored, but you must give an extra 30 points to each opponent if you fail. You need to be quite confident to try it out — or quite desperate toward the end of the game.

The same warning applies even more strongly to the second, more extreme alternative. If you have a really sure thing, you can declare your bid and reveal your hand to the opponents by turning it face-up. If you succeed, you get 60 points on top of what you otherwise get; if not, you give 60 points to each of the other players. This is known as *revealing,* although in practice, you're both revealing your hand *and* declaring your bid.

If you fail in a premium contract, you still get your trick score.

Only one player can make a premium bid on each hand. The player to the left of the dealer gets the first chance to declare his bid or reveal his hand. If he opts to reveal, he wins the bidding; if he opts to declare, then the player to his left or the dealer can outbid him by revealing their hands. If the first player opts to pass, the second player gets the same options, and finally the choice is up to the dealer.

Don't automatically assume that trying to defeat a premium contract must be in your best interests. Say that the player on your left declares her bid when she's 60 points behind you. The player on your right is 12 points in front of you. Even if the premium bid comes home, you'll still be comfortably in front of the bidder, so long as you make your contract. So concentrate on beating your real opponent by making your contract, and let the player who declared succeed if she can.

Well, I declare!

Take a look at the sort of hand that may make a declaration. In the hand in Figure 4-6, spades are the trump suit.

Figure 4-6:
Low cards and aces, a potent combination for a declaration.

The decision to declare on this hand is by no means cast-iron, but think about how likely you are to make exactly one trick if you discard the ♠Q, the ♦K, and the ♦Q. Discarding those cards represents a bid of one trick, and you hope to win the ♥A, lose the lead with the ♠7, and find a way to avoid winning a trick in any of the other suits. This strategy isn't a lock to succeed, but you do stand a pretty good chance.

Another example is shown in Figure 4-7. Hearts are the trump suit.

Figure 4-7:
Sure tricks and sure losers.

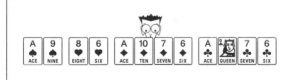

Again, nothing is certain in life except death and taxes, but discarding the ♠A, ♠9, and the ♦10 and going for two looks reasonable. I advise leading the ♦A and hoping that it wins the trick. If it does, I'd take the ♣A and then get off lead with the ♣6.

The ♦A in the preceding example is by no means sure to win — someone could have discarded all his diamonds. But discarding those diamonds means that player intends to bid low, and thus he may not want to trump your trick anyway. Any of the other aces is more likely to get trumped, because by discarding cards in another suit, you're representing yourself to take tricks, unlike in the case of discarding a diamond.

Revealing choices

Hands on which you may choose to reveal your hand have to be fairly cut and dried, I think. Again, of course, circumstances alter cases; if you're not playing for stakes, desperate measures may be called for toward the end of a rubber. Keep in mind that you play nine hands in total in a contest, which makes up one rubber.

In any circumstances, the hand in Figure 4-8 qualifies for a revelation. Suppose that hearts are the trump suit in this case and that you're the first player to bid.

Figure 4-8:
Nearly a
sure thing.

Can you see that you have a virtual lock on zero tricks if you discard your three diamonds and lead the ♥7? Unless someone started the hand with and has kept all four outstanding spades (keep in mind that each suit has only nine cards), you're safe, because your low spades will ensure that you can avoid taking a trick in the suit.

One variation of revealing the hand is to allow the player who reveals or declares to choose her own trump suit — which has the possible defect of making the bids a little too easy to attain. Limiting this option to when you reveal your hand only may be less disruptive. In this variation of the game, a player who reveals his hand is also allowed to choose 9s as the trump suit. Here, a separate trump suit is created of the 9s, ranking in descending order: clubs, hearts, spades, and diamonds.

Incidentally, if you reveal your hand and announce that you're going for all nine tricks and succeed when no one else makes her contract, you score 99 points — hence the name of the game.

Chapter 5

Euchre

- -

In This Chapter

▶ Understanding the card values in Euchre

▶ Determining how to bid and how to play Euchre

▶ Planning strategy at Euchre

- -

*E*uchre is an excellent card game, simple in concept but with a high degree of subtlety in the play. The game also offers myriad variations, because it can be played with any number of players and as a long or short game.

To play Euchre, you need the following:

✔ **Four players**

✔ **A standard deck of 52 cards:** You don't need all the cards, however. Take out the ace through the 9 in each suit, making a deck of 24 cards, for the game.

✔ **Paper and pencil for scoring:** You can also keep score by using some of the remaining playing cards, if you prefer that method. See the sidebar "Keeping score with playing cards" in this chapter for more information. To save a little time, you can play with two separate decks. The partner of the dealer shuffles the second pack while his partner deals, and then he puts the shuffled deck on the dealer's right, ready for the next hand.

Acquainting Yourself with Euchre

Euchre is a trick-taking game. A *trick* results when each player plays a card; the player who plays the highest card in the suit of the first card played or the highest *trump card* (see "Determining the Trump Suit") collects all the cards together and stacks them in front of him — he takes the trick.

Playing Euchre on the Internet

If you yearn for a Euchre game at all times, day or night, visit the home of WebEuchre at www.webdeck.com/webeuchre.html; the site lets you download WebEuchre, a program written by Michael Riccio, for all types of computers. Just follow the WebEuchre Wizard's instructions at the site, and you'll soon join other Euchre fans online for live games. If you want to play Euchre on the Net, this is the place to go.

In Euchre, you win a hand and score points for taking the majority of the tricks in a hand, which means winning three or more of the five tricks available (Euchre is a five-card game). You get a special bonus if you manage to take all five tricks.

You play the game with partners, but under special circumstances, a member of a partnership can elect to go solo — if she thinks that going alone is worthwhile. See "Playing for Bigger Stakes (The Lone Arranger)" for the details.

Picking Partners

You play Euchre with four players, either with prearranged partnerships or with partners selected by cutting the deck. If you cut the deck for partners, the two highest cards take on the two lowest cards.

After you determine partners, the partners sit opposite each other. In partnership games, partners almost always sit across from each other, probably to keep the players from one another's throats.

Getting a Fair Deal

You can select the dealer at random. Or you can deal out the cards until a jack appears. Whoever gets the jack is the dealer.

The dealer shuffles the cards and offers them to the player on his left to cut. That player can cut the deck or tap (*bump*) the cards to indicate that no cut is necessary.

The dealer deals clockwise. Just to make things interesting, the dealer deals out five cards, face-down, in packets of two to each player and then three to each player. Go figure. After dealing the cards, the dealer turns over one card and places it in the middle of the table. The rest of the deck plays no further part in the hand.

At the end of each hand, the deal rotates clockwise.

A *misdeal* can occur in any of several ways, but, for the most part, no serious consequences arise from a misdeal. If the deal is flawed for whatever reason — because a card is turned over on the table, the deck has a face-up card in it, or the deck contains the wrong number of cards — the deal is simply canceled, and the hand is redealt.

If a player deals out of turn, and someone notices this fact before the top card is turned over, the deal is simply canceled. But if the top card is turned up before anyone notices, the deal stands, and whoever missed her deal simply loses out. (As you see later, dealing carries an advantage with it, so you don't want to skip the deal.)

If a player is dealt the wrong number of cards and discovers this fact before the first trick is started, then a redeal takes place with no penalties. If the error isn't corrected in time, play continues, and whichever team has a player with the wrong number of cards can't score on that hand. The moral of the story is — count your cards!

Determining the Trump Suit

After each player has received five cards, the dealer places the remaining four cards in the center of the table with the top card turned face-up. This upcard determines what the *trump suit* is for the current hand. The remaining three cards play no part in the current hand.

The trump suit represents the boss suit, meaning that a card in the trump suit beats any card in any other suit. In Euchre, you have to *follow* to the suit that has been led (play a card in the same suit), but if you can't follow suit, then you may play a trump card and win the trick (unless someone plays a higher trump card than you).

The dealer can add the turned-up card to his hand in exchange for a discard of his choice — under certain circumstances. I talk about this option in "The Bidding: A Short Acceptance Speech."

Jacking It Up (Ranking the Cards)

When you pick up your hand, you first sort it into suits. The standard order of the cards applies — within each suit, the ace is high, and the values descend to the lowly 9.

The only exception to this rule lies in the fact that the *trump suit* (the suit of the upcard in the middle of the table) ranks as follows:

- ✔ The highest trump card is the jack, often referred to as the *right bower* (rhyming with *flower*).

- ✔ The second-highest trump card is the jack of the suit the same color as the trump suit, often called the *left bower.* This card deserts its own suit and becomes a trump card for the hand; it counts as a trump card for the purposes of following suit, rather than as a card in its own suit. So the ♠J ceases to be a spade when clubs are the trump suit, and it becomes a club.

- ✔ The remaining five cards in the trump suit are the ace, king, queen, 10, and 9, ranking from highest to lowest in that order.

For example, if clubs are the trump suit, the cards have the rank shown in Figure 5-1. Diamonds and hearts rank from the ace through 9, as you expect.

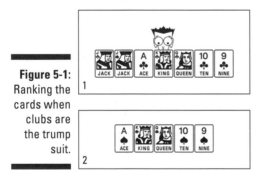

Figure 5-1: Ranking the cards when clubs are the trump suit.

The Bidding: A Short Acceptance Speech

After the players pick up their cards and sort them, it's time for the bidding. Everyone has seen what card has been turned over for the trump suit; the question is whether anyone wants to bid to take three or more tricks with that suit as the trump suit. Each player gets the chance to take on that assignment — or refuse the invitation, in which case the bidding goes into a second phase (see "Knowing what to bid" later in this chapter). Therefore, you first need to value your hand for play in the trump suit.

Because the second phase of the game involves playing with the trump suit of your choice, you also have to look at your hand and value it for play in a new trump suit. Players decide in turn whether they want to play with the determined trump suit. Later, they may get a second chance to pick a trump suit — if no one wants to take on the challenge with the initial trump suit.

Starting the bidding

Each player in turn, starting with the player on the dealer's left, can agree to play in the trump suit of the upcard in the middle of the table (the card that defines the trump suit of the hand) on behalf of his partnership, or he can pass. If any one of the four players accepts the suit of the upcard as the trump suit in the first round, the dealer adds the face-up card to his hand and throws one card away from his hand face-down.

The partnership that makes the decision to take three or more tricks (as opposed to passing) are referred to as the *makers* and the other side are the *defenders*. The players follow these protocols during the first round of bidding:

1. **The first player either plays with the predetermined trump suit, saying "I order it up" (meaning that he is asking the dealer to take the upcard), or he passes, saying "I pass."**

2. **The second player, the dealer's partner, can pass, or she can accept the turned-up suit as the trump suit by saying "Partner, I assist."**

3. **The third player follows the pattern for the first hand by ordering it up or passing.**

4. **The dealer accepts the choice of the trump suit by saying "I take it up" and picks up the card to add it to his hand, or he rejects it by saying "Over," or "I turn it down."**

   If he rejects the trump suit, he takes the upcard and puts the card face-up at right angles to the deck below the other three cards, to indicate what suit isn't acceptable as the trump suit for the second round of bidding (see "Entering the second phase of bidding" for more information).

Knowing what to bid

The most delicate strategy in the game hinges on deciding whether to accept the trump suit and make a bid or not. As a general rule, you can expect your partner to help you get one trick in addition to the tricks that you can take from your own hand, so holding two sure tricks is enough to consider bidding, and holding any three trump cards is definitely enough to make a bid.

You must also consider whether a different trump suit may work better for you. If no one wants to play in the initial trump suit, someone has a chance to select her own trump suit, so evaluating your hand for both purposes is important.

You're rewarded if you succeed in your bid and are penalized if you fail, so you want to get it right if you can. If you fail, it's called being *euchred* — hence the name of the game.

Each member of the partnership who didn't deal the hand — and are thus first to speak on both the first and second rounds of bidding — needs a relatively better hand than the dealer's side to accept on the first round. They really shouldn't accept the trump suit without at least three probable tricks at the start of the game (before tactical considerations of the state of the match enter into the equation). This is because their side gets first crack at selecting the trump suit on the second round of bidding if everyone passes. In addition, the fact that the dealer picks up a trump card tilts the odds in his favor — and pushes his side toward making an aggressive bid to select the trump suit in the first round.

Keep in mind that the left bower (the second-highest jack) may be of more use to you on the second round of bidding, particularly if you aren't the dealer. So if you have the left bower, consider not picking the trump suit on the first round, but passing, and then selecting the suit of the same color on the second round. That way, the dealer doesn't get to take the upcard to improve his hand, and your left bower becomes the boss trump card, the right bower. Of course, there won't be a second round of bidding if someone accepts the initial trump suit, but that is a risk you have to take.

A variation to the bidding is played widely in Australia, England, and Canada. If the partner of the dealer accepts, he must accept on his own (thereby playing solo; see "Playing for Bigger Stakes [The Lone Arranger]," later in this chapter), rather than accepting for the partnership.

Entering the second phase of bidding

If all four players pass, the top card is turned down, thereby eliminating the dealer's inherent advantage. On the second round of bidding, players may again accept the responsibility of trying to go for three tricks, naming any other suit as the trump suit.

Again, the bidding goes around the table, starting with the player on the dealer's left, who can pass or name the trump suit. If she passes, then the next player has the same choices, and so on. Whoever first selects a trump suit wins the bidding — now all she has to do is make her bid good. If all four players pass, then the hand is thrown in, and the next player deals a new hand.

Don't forget your jacks; they can become very valuable all of a sudden. And also remember to value the jack in the suit of the same color as the trump suit. As soon as you or someone else nominates a new trump suit, a previously irrelevant jack suddenly becomes very powerful.

If the dealer doesn't accept the face-up card, it normally implies that he doesn't hold a bower (jack) in the trump suit or in the same color. (If he did, he may well have gone for the original suit as the trump suit). If you're in doubt whether to bid and what suit to select as the trump suit, the nondealers should go for the suit of the same color as the initial trump suit, while the dealer's partner should go for a trump suit of the other color.

On the second round of bidding, you can't bid the suit of the original upturned card. That suit is only a possible trump suit on the first round. If a player on the second round calls the same trump suit as the upturned card, his side may not participate in the bidding.

Ending the bidding

At the end of the bidding, one side or the other has elected to go in partnership for at least three tricks. If the bid was made on the first round, then the dealer has picked up the upcard and put it in his hand. If the acceptance was made on the second round, then whoever chose the trump suit has announced it, and the dealer has left the upcard alone. Is that all? Not quite. . . .

Playing for Bigger Stakes (The Lone Arranger)

If any player (not just the declarer's partner; see the earlier variation) has a particularly good hand, she can raise the stakes by opting to play the hand on her own. The player who selects the trump suit has the option of going alone. As soon as she indicates her intention of doing that, her partner puts his cards face-down, for this hand alone, and the game becomes a three-handed one.

A hand with the top three trump cards is a sure thing for going alone, of course. Two of the top three trumps and an ace on the side may be enough, but you may want a little more as insurance.

Some play that one player from each side (either defender) may also opt to go alone, whether or not the maker (the hand that accepts the choice of the trump suit) has decided to do so. (In other words, you could be looking at a game for only two players.) However, it's common to play that a defender can't play alone.

When a player goes alone, the hand on his left leads to the first trick. If both a defender and a maker go alone, then the defender leads.

Why would you want to play alone? The only reason for doing so is if you have a guaranteed three tricks with a serious chance of making five tricks in your own hand. If you make three or four tricks, the game is scored the same as if you were in partnership (see "Scoring" in this chapter for details). But if you make all five tricks, either as maker or defender, you score twice as many points as you would otherwise have done.

Some people play that the penalty for being euchred when going alone is doubled, too — making the decision to play alone an even more problematic call, because failure becomes more expensive.

Going alone has no real advantage unless you have a reasonable chance of making five tricks on your own; otherwise, you simply increase the chance of a penalty without any chance of increasing the rewards. With three sure winners in your hand, the critical question is whether your remaining cards give you a practical chance of a clean sweep. If not, play in partnership, and hope that your partner can come through with the goods.

For example, say that you're the dealer's partner, the ♣9 is the turned-up card, and you have the hand in Figure 5-2.

Figure 5-2:
A highly promising hand — but for how many tricks?

This hand isn't even assured of winning three tricks, technically, although it's heavily favored to do so. However, if the ♠J is in your partner's hand or is one of the three face-down cards, or if it's in your opponents' hands without any other trump cards accompanying it (and you can see three trump cards out of the seven already), you stand a fair chance of making five tricks — though only a fair one. Still, the odds on your partner making the vital difference are almost nonexistent, because you can either win the tricks on your own or not at all. The hand in Figure 5-2 is an excellent hand to go solo on.

By contrast, consider the hand in Figure 5-3.

Figure 5-3:
Caution!
Help
wanted!

Now you're almost sure to have four clear winners in your hand, but the ♦10 isn't a favorite to win the last trick unless your opponents discard poorly. Of course, their poor discarding is by no means impossible! I'd go for all the tricks with my partner's help rather than bidding on my own.

The Play's the Thing

After the bidding, the player to the left of the dealer plays the first card (unless a solo bid is made; see "Playing for Bigger Stakes [The Lone Arranger]" in this chapter). If one player is playing alone, the player to his left leads. If two players are out of the game, the defender leads.

The play goes clockwise around the table. You must *follow suit* (play a card in the suit led) if you can, but if you can't, you can throw off any card or play a trump card as you see fit. Whoever plays the highest card of the suit led or the highest trump card wins the trick.

Failure to follow suit when you can do so is called a *revoke.* You must correct a revoke before the winner gathers in the trick. If a revoke is identified, the innocent side may add 2 points to its score or deduct 2 points from the other side. If a lone player revokes, the penalty is 4 points (see "Scoring" for more information).

Only limited advice can be offered in the play of the cards. Part of the game lies in memorizing the cards played. You have to know who may have what cards left to determine what to lead — and what to throw away, when you have a choice. Obviously, the turned-up card is one that you want to try to remember; if the dealer has added it to his hand, don't forget it.

If you have the opening lead and you have two or more trump cards, consider leading those trump cards. Otherwise, lead from a sequence if you have one. Start with the highest card in the sequence to help out your partner, so that he doesn't waste his high cards unnecessarily.

Unlike some other card games, saving a winner for a rainy day in Euchre generally has no advantage. Take your tricks while you can, or you may never get them.

Scoring

The team who chooses or accepts the trump suit and then wins three or four tricks simply scores 1 point. If that side gets all five tricks, it's called a *march* or a *sweep,* and the team scores 2 points.

Three tricks are necessary to fulfill the obligations you assume when you determine the trump suit.

If the makers fail to fulfill their obligations, the defenders score 2 points (whether they get three, four, or five tricks), and the makers are said to be *euchred.* However, the biggest score comes if you go solo and make all five tricks; then you score 4 points.

The first team to 10 points *reaches game* and wins. You can also play to 5 points for a shorter game.

Keeping score with playing cards

You don't necessarily need to write down the scores to keep track of the running totals. Serious Euchre players use playing cards, placed one on top of another, to keep their own totals. Specifically, you need an extra 2 and 3 card to keep score with playing cards.

To indicate one point, you turn up the 3 and put the 2 face-down to cover all but one of the spots. Showing 2 and 3 are easy, of course. For 4, you put both cards face-up with the 3 partly over the 2. If you're playing to 10 points, use an additional 2 and 3 card, and put the two cards crossways to add 5 points to what is showing.

Chapter 6

Spades

● ●

In This Chapter

▶ Understanding how to play Spades

▶ Exploring strategy in Spades

● ●

A great deal of creative energy is still being exercised on the rules of Spades — which, in turn, implies that the game is likely to improve as these modifications are tested and either incorporated or discarded. However, the many variations of the game create a problem: Because the rules are so fluid and no rules are *official,* everybody seems to have his own variation on what you can or can't do, and the scoring system is a nightmare.

The rules that I set out in this chapter may not correspond exactly to the rules that your friends play by — because everybody follows his own version of the game — but they do cover the basics of the game and allow you to play along with others or even teach your friends to play by "your" rules.

To play Spades, you need the following:

✔ **Four players**

✔ **One standard deck of 52 cards:** In some variations, you need the jokers, too.

✔ **An efficient scorer with pencil and paper**

Grasping the Basics of Spades

Spades is traditionally a game for exactly four players, played in partnership (the partners sitting opposite each other). The players take turns playing out one card from their hands; all the players must play a card in whichever suit is played first (or *led*) if they can, which is called *following suit.* The four cards played constitute a unit of play called a *trick.*

Playing Spades on the Internet

Spades players from around the world have embraced the Internet with open arms — there are no less than three places where you can pick up a game of Spades on the Internet. Spades is among the best-represented games in Cyberspace.

For a free game of Spades, visit the infamous Internet Gaming Zone at www.zone.com/spades.html; you'll find players of every skill level waiting to take you on in a game.

You can also play live over at WebSpades (www.webdeck.com/webspades.html) using the WebSpades program designed by Michael Riccio. Or you can play via telnet with the software available at NetSpades (www.cris.com/~Cdrom/dnload.shtml); an account with CRIS, which apparently sponsors the site, currently costs $10.00 a month.

If you have no cards in the suit led, you can play anything you like; if you play a spade on the lead of a heart, diamond, or club, you win the trick, because spades are the master (or *trump*) suit; even the smallest spade is higher than the ace in any other suit. The person who plays the highest card or the highest spade collects up the four cards played and wins the trick.

In Spades, the object (up to a point) is to win as many tricks as possible. However, in Spades, each of the four players must estimate in advance of the start of play just how many tricks he or she is going to win. This estimate is called a *bid*, and your bid can include opting for no tricks or up to 13 tricks.

However, the peculiarity of Spades is that, although both sides can join freely in the bidding, this auction is not competitive — both sides get to make a bid and then pursue their target (unlike some games, in which only one side gets to make a bid and then the other side is totally occupied with stopping them).

Each side independently names and then chases its own specific number of tricks. If they succeed, they are generously rewarded; if they fail to meet their target, they are equally heavily punished. But that is not the end of the story. Spades is an *exact trick* game: If you make more tricks than you bid during the auction at the beginning of the hand, you are also heavily punished at some point down the line. So the trade-off between valuing your hand correctly in the bidding and then making your contract exactly (rather than making too many tricks or making too few tricks) is a very fine line indeed. All these factors make Spades a fascinating game.

Getting Started

Before you can play the hand, you need to be aware of a few things and take care of some minor chores.

Choosing partners

The partnerships in Spades are frequently fixed, but you can alternate lineups at the end of a contest, or *rubber* (see "Mastering the Scoring" for more information about rubbers).

Ranking the cards

The cards rank from aces on down to 2s. So if you decide to play without adding in any wrinkles, ranking the cards is no big deal.

However, if you like wrinkles, you can use a number of variations when ranking the cards. One common variation is to add two jokers to the deck, with separate markings to distinguish the Big and Little Jokers. The two jokers become additional trump cards, ranking as the highest and second-highest trump cards, making the trump suit 15 cards. Because the game can only sensibly be played with each player having 13 cards, the options are either to remove the ♥2 and ♦2 or to deal 15 cards to the dealer. The dealer then removes two cards from his hand and leaves them face-down; those two cards play no further part in the game.

Getting a good deal

The dealer is selected at random by cutting the deck; the person drawing the highest card deals. The traditional Bridge custom of having the player on the dealer's left shuffle the cards and the player on the dealer's right cut them is as good as any.

Starting with the player on the dealer's left, the dealer distributes the deck card by card, face-down to each player, so that everyone has a 13-card hand. The deal progresses one place clockwise after each hand.

Being the dealer is clearly a significant advantage, because you get to hear the other players commit themselves to a number of tricks before you have to decide on a bid.

Bidding Your Hand Accurately

After the hand is dealt out, the players begin a single round of bidding, when everybody gets to estimate the number of tricks that they personally intend to take, and then the partnership's bids are added together. A partnership then seeks to make that number exactly.

In the constantly evolving world of Spades, even the question of who bids first generates controversy. Some people say that the dealer is the first to speak, but normally the bidding starts with the player to the left of the dealer, or the *Elder Hand*.

Two distinct styles of bidding are also currently played. I treat the more Spartan style as the norm and consider the second one to be a variation, but both schools have many followers.

The first school assumes that each player has one bid and one bid only. At his turn, each player can opt to bid any number of tricks between zero and 13. After his opponent bids, his partner does likewise and makes an estimate, and the combined total for the side is the number of tricks that the partnership needs to take to fulfill its *contract* for the hand.

The partnership registers its tricks as a unit — it doesn't matter whether it is you or your partner who takes the tricks; the important thing is that your side gets them. So if you bid 2 and your partner bids 3, then whether you get 5 or your partner gets 5 is irrelevant; if you get 5 tricks between you, you make your contract.

The second school of bidding is much more lax about the restrictions on communications between the two partners. Starting with the non-dealer's side, the two players are allowed to have a brief and non-specific conversation about the trick-taking capabilities of their side. The first player of each partnership may provide clues along the following lines: "I have a hand with three sure tricks and the possibility for up to five or even six tricks."

Let's call the whole thing off: the misdeal rules

Some variations of Spades allow a player to call for a misdeal before the bidding if his hand satisfies certain conditions. For example, a player may call for a misdeal if he holds one or no spades, holds a *side-suit* (that is, not spades) of seven or more cards, or doesn't hold any court cards (the ace, king, queen, and jack).

In these situations, the player should ask his partner if they want a misdeal before the bidding commences; however, his partner's reply isn't binding.

Thereafter, the second player may make her bid with some idea about what her partner has in terms of potential tricks that he hasn't included in his bid.

Players are allowed to talk about "half-tricks" and "maybes" but they're not allowed to talk about their precise holdings in a specific suit or whether they have *length* (several cards) or *shortage* (few cards) in a specific suit.

For example, with the hand shown in Figure 6-1, you bid two or three tricks, counting one trick for the ♥A and one for the spades, if you're allowed to make only a single bid. If you're allowed to pass along some hints, you can say something like "I am reasonably confident of two tricks, but I might get as many as four on a good day."

Figuring the value of your high cards

Your success at bidding rests largely on knowing how to value your cards. As a simple rule, count all aces as being worth a trick to start with. No surprise there. Count kings as worth about two-thirds of a trick, unless they're backed up by the ace in that suit; if you have the ace as well, treat the pair as two full tricks. However, be aware that the ace-king in a *side-suit* (a suit that isn't the trump suit, spades) of more than five cards is potentially vulnerable (because the danger of a high card being trumped by the opponents increases).

Queens are difficult to value unless they're supported by other honor cards; they are worth something — but not much. With an ace, treat the combination as $1\frac{1}{2}$ tricks; with a king, treat the pair as worth a full trick. Otherwise, treating a queen as about one-third of a trick is about right, unless the queen is in a side-suit of more than five cards, in which case you may discount it altogether.

Valuing jacks, unless combined with other high honors, is a very risky business. Because the jack is unlikely to win the first or second round of a suit and because someone may be out of the suit by then and able to trump your winner, counting jacks at all is pretty optimistic.

Building your bidding picture

Potentially, the most testing area of Spades is to evaluate your hand correctly for the bidding; as you see in "Mastering the Scoring" later in this chapter, the consequences for a miscalculation in the bidding are almost equally severe whether you overestimate or underestimate your call. So getting your bid right and drawing the right inferences from other people's bids can gain you a large number of points — not to mention your partner's undying affection.

As soon as the bidding begins, each subsequent bidder can build up more and more of the picture, and using your judgment becomes easier as bidding proceeds.

Depending on whether you believe them or not, you may be able to include in your calculations not only other people's bids but also the comments that they make. Those clues can help you work out just how good your hand really is and can help you make an accurate assessment of its worth.

Hands generally fall into one of two categories: *balanced* hands, which have two to four cards in each suit, or unbalanced or *distributional* hands, which have some suits with plenty of cards in them (a *long suit*) and some suits where you have very few cards (a *short suit*). The more distributional your own hand (that is, the more really long and short suits you have), the more danger that your high cards in the side-suits won't score tricks. As you can see, if you have the ♥A and only one other card in the suit, everybody else is likely to have at least one heart. But if you have five clubs, including the ♣A and ♣K, counting both as sure tricks is dangerous, because one of your opponents may have only one club and trump your winner by playing a spade on it.

Trump cards (any spade card) are valuable in themselves; count any trump card after your first three as worth a full trick. All trump honor cards, such as the ace, king, or queen of spades, should be valued at a full trick.

Whatever the suit they're in, all high honor cards (KQJ) in a very short suit become even less valuable, because your flexibility is impaired. A king on its own (also called a *singleton*) and a *doubleton* queen (one in a two-card holding) may both be wiped out very easily. That's because when someone leads out her ace in that suit, for example, you have to play your king under it if you have only one card in the suit.

Here goes nothing!

You can bid for zero tricks if you think your hand really stinks. A bid of _Nil,_ (also known as _Nill, Null,_ or _Nillo_) carries additional liabilities and benefits. The concept is to make no tricks at all, and it carries a generous bonus for success — with an equally heavy penalty for failure.

Because _going Nil_ is such a difficult feat to achieve, a player making the call gets the edge of being able to exchange a certain number of cards with his partner in order to improve both players' hands for their various purposes. The number of cards swapped depends on the rule structure you play; some variations allow three, some two, some one card, and some don't allow the exchange at all. If your partner goes for Nil, then she passes you the cards face-down, allowing you to look at her cards before you choose which cards to give her.

Normally, the two players in a team combine their bids to form a total contract for their side. The exception to this rule is a call of Nil; if you bid for no tricks, then your success or failure depends on your own personal performance. While your partner does his best to help you by overtaking any high cards that you play, it's up to you, and you alone, as to whether you make your Nil bid.

Assuming that you play the rule permitting you to exchange three cards, the potentially unpromising hand in Figure 6-2 qualifies for the Nil bid.

Figure 6-2:
With a hand
like this
one, bid Nil.

You can exchange the high trump cards and the ♥K and hope to pick up low cards in the other suits from your partner to protect you a little from the danger of winning a trick with your high cards in diamonds or clubs.

Turning the tables, your partner may bid Nil when you have the hand shown in Figure 6-3.

Figure 6-3:
Adjust your bid if your partner bids Nil.

You probably intended to bid for three tricks because of your aces, kings, and queens. But if you're playing by the two-card exchange rule and you hear you partner bid Nil, you increase your bid, expecting to receive at least one sure trick from your partner. Say that you bid five tricks and receive the ♣A and the ♠J. Getting those cards argues for passing the ♦4 and the ♥5, because you can be pretty sure that your hearts can overtake any high card that your partner has in the suit.

See "Mastering the Scoring" for the details on scoring successful and unsuccessful Nil bids.

Additional options in the bidding: the games people play

Most variations of Spades have to do with the bidding. Here are some of the most popular options:

- The combined totals of the tricks bid for by both teams may not equal 13, in order to ensure that someone must fail in her bid, even if it is only to the extent of taking overtricks. It obviously becomes the dealer's responsibility, as the last bidder, to prevent the total from equaling 13.

- A number of specific bids, allowed by some groups, can attract large bonuses or penalties. A call of "ten for two" means that the partnership intends to get at least ten tricks (or exactly ten tricks, in certain hard-line schools). This bid scores 200 points if the partnership meets it and costs 100 points if it fails.

- Some people play that winning all the tricks wins the game, even if the bid for all the tricks was not actually called. A bid for all 13 tricks is called *Shooting the Moon, Moon,* or *Boston*. (Moon normally wins the game outright if called and achieved, but it can be scored as 500, a scoring difference that is only significant if the team has a negative score at the time. If no ten for two bid is permitted, Moon may score as plus or minus 200.)

✔ If both partners don't look at their hands, they have the option of making *Blind bids.* Blind bids by a partnership for seven or more tricks count double, but such calls may only be permitted when the team making them is more than 100 points behind.

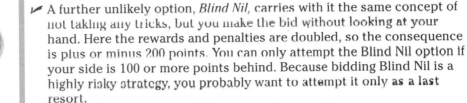

✔ A further unlikely option, *Blind Nil,* carries with it the same concept of not taking any tricks, but you make the bid without looking at your hand. Here the rewards and penalties are doubled, so the consequence is plus or minus 200 points. You can only attempt the Blind Nil option if your side is 100 or more points behind. Because bidding Blind Nil is a highly risky strategy, you probably want to attempt it only **as a last resort.**

Bidding Blind is a good way to randomize the proceedings if you're losing the game heavily; desperate situations demand desperate remedies.

✔ If both players go for Nil and achieve it, that Double Nil scores either 500 or an automatic win. Beware — Double Nil is considerably more difficult to achieve than Nil; you always have your partner protecting you on a Nil call by taking tricks if you appear to be winning them, but you have no one to come to your rescue on a Double Nil call. Also, you don't exchange cards on Double Nil.

Playing the Cards

The scorer writes down the bids on the appropriate line of the score sheet after the bidding is over. A single digit for the team's score is usually sufficient, unless a Nil or a Blind bid has been made, in which case the scorer notes that element of the bid. Then the play starts.

The play of the cards goes clockwise, starting with the player to the dealer's left. He puts a card face-up in the middle of the table, and then all the other players contribute a card in turn. You must *follow suit* (play a card in the same suit as the first card played out) if you can. Each player plays one card, and whoever plays the highest card in the suit that was *led* (the suit of the first card played to the trick) or the highest trump card (if someone can't follow suit and plays a trump card instead) takes the trick.

At every trick except the first, the player who won the previous trick is free to lead anything she likes with one exception, which I come to in a minute. However, the opening lead has significant restrictions; in fact, the play has no flexibility at all: Everyone must play his lowest club. If you can't follow suit, you must discard a heart or a diamond — no trumping allowed.

As you can see, the need to sacrifice your low clubs at the beginning may impact your strategy for Nil; if you're forced to release your lowest club at the start of play, you may need extra protection in that suit in the form of low cards. A holding such as ♣K ♣9 ♣8 ♣2 may be considerably more dangerous than it appears when the ♣2 is immediately lost, because you have to sacrifice your only low club, and now you may win a later trick in the suit.

As with almost every other element of the game, the first trick rules can vary significantly. Some versions say that the opening leader (either the dealer or the player to his left) can lead any card except a spade. Some authorities allow a player to trump the first trick if she has no clubs. Yet another variation is that after the ♣2 is led, all players can then play any club they want, not just their lowest club.

Whoever wins the first trick leads to the next trick, and play continues with no further restrictions — except that, although you may lead any suit at any time, you can't lead spades at any point in the game until the suit is *broken*. The breaking spades rule means that the suit is off-limits until someone trumps the lead of a side-suit or until a player on lead is down to all spades left. Thereafter, you may lead spades at any time.

Mastering the Scoring

Those of you familiar with Whist (see Chapter 3) and Bridge (see Chapter 7) may think the scoring follows predictable paths — but beware the sting in the tail that comes with overtricks!

If you bid and make your contract, either exactly or with *overtricks* or *sandbags* (tricks over your bid), you multiply your bid by ten and score that total. Any overtricks count one each. So bidding seven and collecting nine tricks scores 72 — not all that much different, you may think, from bidding eight and scoring nine tricks for 81 points or actually hitting the nail on the head with a bid of nine for 90.

Scoring Nil bids

If you bid Nil and make it, you score 100 points; bidding Nil and failing costs you 100 points. (See "Here goes nothing!" for the details on bidding Nil.)

If you fail in a bid of Nil, the rules vary as to what happens to your tricks. Some versions play that your tricks count toward helping your partner make his bid; some variations say that your tricks are ignored for that purpose. The simplest rule, in my opinion, is to ignore those tricks.

Scoring revokes

The failure to follow suit (or failure to follow with your lowest club on the first trick) is a serious crime. Both lapses can be lumped together under the heading of *revoking* or *reneging* and carry a serious consequence. One rather kind possibility is to award the non-offending side a 15-point bonus and abandon the hand. This approach is too lax, in my opinion. The alternative penalty structure — that the offenders are deemed to have failed in their contract(s) and the other side scores their contract — may be generous to the innocent parties, but it does help to remind the guilty players of the gravity of their offense.

Getting sandbagged with overtricks

You may see little reason to be cautious in the bidding — because a slight underbid hardly seems to matter — but that is before you experience the true joy of sandbags.

Now for the shock to your system: When you get to ten overtricks, you automatically get 100 points deducted from your total, and the clock starts again. In the standard version of the scoring, the 10 overtrick points are canceled out altogether, rather than increasing your score by 10 points, although some versions allow you to rack up your 10 as you lose 100. But the mainstream approach is that if you are at 458 points, bid five tricks, and make seven, your score becomes 400, not 410 (458 + 52 – 100 – the 10-point overtrick deduction = 400).

You can also play without the overtrick rule altogether or just take off 1 point for each overtrick, but that approach defeats the main purpose of the game, in my opinion. You can achieve the same negative values for overtricks by counting each of them as –10. This accounting method simply gives you an immediate deduction for the sandbags rather than a delayed impact. (*Bags on* or *bags off* is the "in" way of referring to whether the overtrick rule applies.)

Some people play that you get an additional bonus for making your contract exactly by winning the last trick with a high trump card (a spade higher than the 9). In fact, if you win the last two or three tricks with high trump cards, you get a bonus of 20 or 30 points, as the case may be. This situation happens surprisingly often, because the prohibition on playing spades before they're broken quite often results in the high spades remaining unplayed until the end of the game.

Dealing with undertricks

If you fail in your bid, no matter by how many tricks, you lose ten times the value of your bid. If you bid ten and fail, for example, you lose 100 points. Let me emphasize that the degree of failure is irrelevant; no matter how many tricks you fail by, you still lose 100 points.

A less popular version of the scoring treats the overbidding penalty as 10 points for every trick that you overbid. So calling ten and making eight tricks costs you 20 points, not 100.

Finishing the game

You play until someone wins the *rubber*. Each rubber is made up of several hands, on which either side can record a positive or negative score. Usually, the first side to get to 500 points wins the rubber. If both sides go past the winning post of 500 points on the same hand, the higher score wins. The game is also playable to 300 or 400 points.

Chapter 7

Contract Bridge

*I*n my (admittedly biased) opinion, Bridge is far and away the best card game ever invented. Having said that, you may be surprised and rather disappointed to discover how little of this book I devote to Bridge.

I have an excellent reason for keeping my coverage of the game at a minimum: My friend and world-renowned bridge player Eddie Kantar wrote *Bridge For Dummies,* published by IDG Books Worldwide, Inc. I can't recommend *Bridge For Dummies* more highly; it provides the absolutely definitive guide to the game, and it has already won awards as a great tool for getting to know the game.

At the same time, I want to tell you a little bit about this exciting game, if only to give you an appetite for Bridge. After reading this chapter, pick up Eddie Kantar's book. You won't regret it.

To play Bridge, you need the following:

- ✔ **Four players**
- ✔ **One standard deck of 52 cards (no jokers)**
- ✔ **A pencil and paper for scoring**

Getting Ready to Play the Game

Bridge is built on the concept of taking *tricks.* A trick is created when all the players take a turn to play a card from their hands. Whoever plays the highest card in the suit that was *led* (the suit of the first card played in the trick) takes all the cards and wins the trick. If you're playing a game that has a *trump,* or boss, suit and you have no cards in the suit originally led, you can play a trump card and win the trick that way. If more than one player plays a card of the trump suit, whoever plays the highest trump card wins the trick.

Bridge is a partnership game, in theory, with partners sitting opposite one another — for the principal reason that they can only hurl verbal abuse at one another from that relatively safe distance and can't resort to physical violence. The players are traditionally allotted compass directions to distinguish them; therefore, North and South take on East and West, as you see in Figure 7-1.

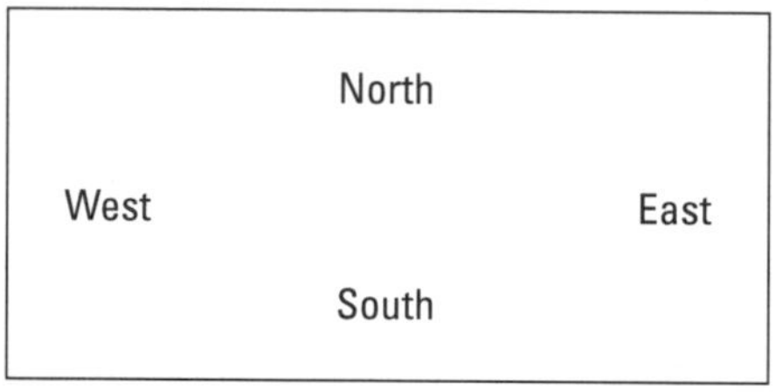

Figure 7-1:
Each player
is assigned
a direction.

```
                    North


   West                            East


              South
```

The two partnerships vie against each other, trying to win as many of the 13 tricks available on each hand as they can. Ultimately, the team that most accurately predicts the number of tricks that they will win on each hand scores points that go toward winning the contest.

If you successfully make as many tricks as you promised to, the points you get go toward a *game* (see "Understanding the Scoring" for more information). The first partnership to win two games wins the *rubber.* After a rubber, the players can either quit or start another rubber.

Bidding the Cards

The bidding phase of the game, which is sometimes called the *auction,* resembles those scenes you see on television where dealers in a stock market shout out competing prices. In Bridge, the process is marginally more decorous; the players take turns calling out their bids. Speaking out of turn is just as much a faux pas in Bridge as it is in other walks of life.

During the bidding, the players hope to win the right to determine which suit is the *trump suit,* or the "wild" suit for the hand. Determining the trump suit is very important because playing a trump card automatically wins the trick (unless someone else plays a higher trump card). Unlike most trump games, Bridge has a perfectly viable fifth option: Either side can elect to play the hand at *notrump,* in which case there is no trump suit.

The bidding also determines how many tricks a partnership hopes to take in a hand.

The minimum starting bid is for seven tricks (just more than half of the 13 tricks available). In Bridge, the first six tricks are taken for granted; for example, a bid of 1♠ is Bridge shorthand for "I intend to take seven tricks with spades as the trump suit."

After the first bid is made, the other players in turn may, if they want, make a higher bid, just as in an auction; or they can discreetly stay out of the battle by passing. Unlike the common perception of an auction, you don't need to fear that a severe nervous tic may force you to bid more than you intended.

A higher bid can either be for a higher number of tricks or for the same number of tricks in a higher-ranking suit. In Bridge, the suits are ranked as follows, from lowest to highest:

- ✔ **Clubs**
- ✔ **Diamonds**
- ✔ **Hearts**
- ✔ **Spades**
- ✔ **Notrump**

To keep the ranking of the suits straight, just remember that the first letter of each of the suits corresponds to the order of the alphabet. Clubs, for example, is the lowest-ranking suit, and *c* comes before *d* in the alphabet, with *d* being the first letter of the next higher-ranking suit, diamonds. Of course, notrump doesn't quite fit into this handy mnemonic device; you just have to force yourself to remember that notrump outranks all the suits in the deck.

The bidding ends when three players in a row pass. The last bid (passing is not considered a bid) becomes the *contract* for the hand; the contract determines what the trump suit is for the hand and the number of tricks that the successful bidder must win in order to make good on her bid.

Bridge builds popularity over time

No other sport's genesis has been so well-documented as Bridge, probably because the game was developed almost entirely in the 20th century. If you contrast Bridge with soccer or golf, you find that the origins of the latter games are almost wholly shrouded in antiquity.

Auction Bridge, an early precursor to Contract Bridge, was born out of three other games, Khedive (an Egyptian game), Biritch (a Turkish-Russian game), and Plafond (a French game) in the 19th century. Auction Bridge featured a limited amount of bidding, in that only the dealer and his partner were allowed to bid, and they had only one bid between them.

Toward the end of the 19th century, the rules of Auction Bridge were codified by The Portland Club of London. In fact, the centennial of this event a couple of years ago gave the current Bridge authorities in England a chance to amuse and bemuse the tourists by hiring an open-top carriage and parading down the center of London in full Victorian dress.

In the 1920s, Harold Vanderbilt, multimillionaire and uncle of the famous Gloria Vanderbilt, took a cruise to Havana. During his trip, he whiled away the journey by explaining to his companions his personal variations to Auction Bridge, based most directly on the French game Plafond. Vanderbilt used his trip to codify the rules and the scoring system of what eventually became Contract Bridge.

When Vanderbilt returned to New York, he dropped a copy of his rules at the desk of the Knickerbocker Club, a then-famous card club. Vanderbilt's rules precipitated an obsessive craze.

Bridge grabbed the public by the throat (metaphorically) and has never really let go. Some Bridge enthusiasts say that more people play Bridge than any other sport in the world (except for fishing).

Playing the Hand

Whichever member of the partnership of the successful bidders named the trump suit first — even if he didn't make the final winning bid — gets the fun of playing the hand. This lucky player is called the *declarer*.

The partner of the declarer is known as the *dummy;* the dummy puts her hand face-up on the table as soon as the player to the left of the declarer leads to the first trick. The declarer then gets to play both his own hand and the dummy's hand.

The dummy is a spectator; if you're the dummy, you get to watch your partner doing his best to win tricks, and you can't interfere and tell him about his mistakes until after the hand is over.

In Bridge, as in most card games, you must play a card in the suit led if you possess one — hence the phrase *to follow suit.*

The play of the hand goes around the table, with the three players playing out cards, until all 13 tricks have been played. If the partnership who made the final contract wins the number of tricks that they said they would make, then they score points. If the partnership doesn't make the specified number of tricks, then the other guys score points.

Understanding the Scoring

A further complexity comes from Bridge's labyrinthine scoring system, which affords a greater prize for bidding your cards accurately. Therefore, you always want to try to contract for the number of tricks your side can make, because the tricks you bid for successfully go toward scoring *game*. Game means a total of 100 points, and you can get that many points by contracting to take nine tricks in notrump, ten tricks in hearts or spades, or 11 tricks in clubs and diamonds.

Just as you play tennis for the best of three sets, and wrestling divides into the best of three falls, a Bridge contest is divided into three games. To *reach game,* your partnership must score 100 points. The partnership that makes two games first wins the *rubber.*

If you and your partner successfully bid and take 12 tricks (a *small slam*) or all 13 tricks (a *grand slam*), you not only score enough points to reach game in one hand but you also get an additional bonus, the *slam bonus.* So as a player with a good hand, you want to get your side to try to bid for a game contract if possible, or maybe even a slam to get that bonus, too.

What's all the fuss about?

Until you've dipped your toe into the sea, you can't really imagine how deep the water is. Similarly, until you play a little and really get addicted to this great game, it may be hard for you to understand why people (including me) get so excited about Bridge. Allow me to explain.

The bidding phase of the game is especially difficult (and rewarding) to master, because it requires experience — to visualize your partner's hand — and skill — to combine the two sets of assets to arrive at the best contract.

What I love about the game is the constant struggle for perfection, which is almost impossible to meet. So many unknowns come into play that getting everything right all the time is almost impossible. But at the same time, that quest for perfection is what makes the game so challenging.

The other intriguing aspect, from my perspective, is that however good a player you are, you need to play the game as a partnership. You can't do it all alone; you must help your partner along the way, too.

Part III
Don't Score Any Points!

The 5th Wave   By Rich Tennant

EDWARD SCISSORHANDS AT A CARD PARTY.

"Actually Ed, if any of us had been thinking, we'd have asked you to pass on the shuffle."

In this part . . .

Points are the hot potato in this part of the book. The games focus on not winning particular cards that rack up points. In some games the bad news is limited to a certain suit in the deck; in other games different cards are chosen to be the plague carriers at the start of every hand by the dealer, at his discretion.

Included in this part are such classics as Hearts and Barbu.

Chapter 8

Hearts

- -

In This Chapter

▶ Understanding the basic concept of Hearts

▶ Planning strategy at Hearts

▶ Varying the program with Black Maria, Honeymoon Hearts, and other Hearts variations

- -

*H*earts is a game of skill; to a certain extent, you're under the sway of whether you receive helpful or unhelpful cards, but good card-sense and, especially, a good memory make an enormous difference at this game. Keeping track of how many cards have been played in each suit helps you to master this game, and practice and experience have no substitute.

To play Hearts, all you require is the following:

> ✔ **Three or more players:** Four is ideal, but you can play sensibly with any number up to seven.
>
> ✔ **A standard deck of 52 cards**
>
> ✔ **A pencil and paper for scoring**

Getting to the Heart of the Matter

Hearts is a cut-throat game, meaning that it normally isn't played in partnerships, whatever the number of players.

The game revolves around *tricks*. In a trick, everyone takes turns playing one card. Whoever plays the highest card in the suit led (the suit of the first card played) picks up all the cards played. The person who wins the trick leads anything he likes from his remaining cards to the next trick, and the process repeats itself until all the cards have been played.

The object of Hearts is to avoid scoring points, rather than to accumulate points. More specifically, the aim of Hearts is not to win tricks that contain certain cards that score you points.

Hearts on the Web

WebHearts (www.webdeck.com/webhearts.html), gives you a chance to practice your Hearts play and strategy using a program designed by Michael Riccio. You can also find live Hearts play at ClassicGames.com (www.springerspan.com/); after a short registration process, you can match your Hearts wits against other Hearts enthusiasts.

The name of the game may have tipped you off that the problem suit in this game is the hearts suit. The ♠Q has a particularly unpleasant role in the game, too. Whoever wins a trick that includes one of these 14 *danger cards* picks up a penalty in the process; the details of the point-scoring are discussed in "Scoring: the day of reckoning," but bear in mind that the ♠Q is as bad as all the hearts put together.

You play Hearts to a set penalty-score, and the winner of the game is the player who has the lowest score at the point when someone else goes over the top. Alternatively, you can play a set number of hands and stop the game at that point, with the lowest score winning.

Dealing the cards

At the start of the game, cut for seating rather than just for the deal — the seating positions matter in Hearts. Arrange the seating from highest to lowest, with the player who cut the lowest card dealing the first hand; the players stay in the same seats for the whole game. The dealer shuffles and passes the cards to the opponent on his right to cut.

Deal all the cards out in traditional fashion — one card at a time, face-down, and clockwise. If the number of players doesn't allow for an even distribution, take out enough of the 2s and 3s from suits other than hearts to even out the deck. At the end of every hand, the deal passes to the left to the next player.

Misdeals can arise in a number of ways. If a card is turned face-up in the deck, or the wrong number of cards are dealt out, or if the dealer turns over anyone else's cards, the hand is immediately redealt with no penalties. If the dealer manages to turn over one of her own cards, the deal stands, with the only consequence being that the other players have a little extra information about one of the hands.

If no one spots that some players have the wrong number of cards before play begins, the deal stands, but the penalties are very severe. Play continues until the last possible valid trick, when the players with the wrong number of cards pick up the penalties for the unplayed heart cards as if they had won the trick with those cards in it.

Passing your cards: left, right, and center

After you pick up and sort your cards, you get to pass some of your cards to your opponents. This passing stage of the game gives you a chance to get rid of some cards that you think may score points.

Getting rid of your bad cards involves a cycle of four passes:

- ✔ On the first hand, players pass three cards to their left-hand opponent.
- ✔ On the second hand, players give three cards to their right-hand opponent.
- ✔ On the third hand, each player passes three cards across the table.
- ✔ On the fourth hand, players retain their hands without a pass-on.

Two common additions to the cycle of passing on cards (to make it a six-way cycle) are to pass one card to everybody — the *scatter* — and for each player to put three cards into the middle of the table, shuffle the cards, and then redistribute them at random — the *smoosh*.

To pass your cards properly, select your three cards, put them face-down in front of you, and then pass those cards before looking at the cards that you're about to pick up.

One alternative rule allows you to pass along the cards that you receive to the next player as long as you don't look at those cards first. This procedure can result in getting back the cards you passed on, particularly if you're switching with the player opposite you.

When it comes to passing on cards, you should think carefully about the nature of your hand before making your move. You may assume that because hearts and the ♠Q score the points (and, by extension, the ♠K and ♠A are likely candidates to capture the ♠Q), these cards are the hot potatoes, so you would want to pass them on immediately; but this assumption isn't necessarily so.

Certainly, on some occasions you want to pass your hearts and your top spades; particularly if you're short in either suit, you want to unload the high spades (♠A, ♠K, or ♠Q only, of course) and your top hearts. However, if you have plenty of spades — say, at least five in the four-player game — you can safely hold on to your high spades.

Similarly, if you have a series of low hearts, you don't need to pass any of them on. Instead, throw away all the cards in a side-suit so that you can play whatever you like when someone else leads the suit, and thus give something unpleasant to your opponents. (You call the act of dumping an unwelcome present on an opponent *painting* a trick.)

By the third of fourth time diamonds or clubs are led, you're just as likely to collect the ♠Q or a bunch of hearts by winning a trick in diamonds or clubs as you are from leading hearts or spades.

So, for example, if your hand looks like Figure 8-1, the spades are dangerous, but the hearts are not, because you have so many of them. You should get rid of the ♠A, the ♠Q, and the ♣J in the pass.

Figure 8-1:
Keeping
your hearts
may be the
wisest
decision.

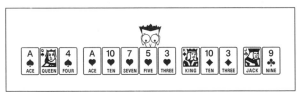

Alternatively, with the hand in Figure 8-2, the spades look safe enough, but you may want to get rid of all your hearts. Or you may keep the hearts and throw the ♦A, ♦Q, and ♣10 to create suits in which you have no or few cards.

Figure 8-2:
The spade
suit spells
safest
policy.

Focus on what cards you get from your opponent. Doing so may help you guess at what sort of hand she has by virtue of what she has let go — and thus what her intentions are for the hand. You can usually infer what her possible danger suits are, too.

As soon as the cards have been appropriately passed, the play of the hand starts.

Starting to play

The player on the dealer's left starts by playing whatever card he likes.

The alternative version is for whoever has the ♣2 to lead it. If you play this variation, remember that having only a very few clubs or even passing all of your clubs before play begins may allow you to discard critical cards early in the game when a club is led.

In Hearts, the cards rank in regular fashion, from ace to two, with the ace high. You must *follow suit* (play a card in the suit led) if you can, and if you can't, you can play whatever you want.

Each player throws in a card, and whoever plays the highest card in the suit led wins the trick. Each player stacks the tricks she has taken in front of her to facilitate the scoring at the end of the hand.

After the opening lead, where a club lead may be compulsory in some variations of the game, you have only one other vital restriction on which cards can be played and when — and this condition is much more restrictive. Unless the heart suit has been *broken* — that is, a heart has been discarded on an earlier trick — you can't lead a heart unless it's the only suit you have left in your hand.

Some play that the discard of the ♠Q allows you to lead hearts thereafter, and some versions of the game allow you to lead hearts at any time.

If you have the ♠Q, you may want to get rid of it as quickly as possible. Or you may want to try to pass it on to the opponent who's winning the game, or to the closest pursuer behind you, or even to someone whose face you don't like! Either approach is fine, unless you play that you must pass on the card as quickly as possible.

As a general rule, the right approach in Hearts is judicious self-preservation first, spite and malice next. Throw the dangerous cards in your hand away first before painting tricks with hearts that your opponents win. If you never score any points yourself, you're pretty sure to win, so try for that goal first and wait to upset your opponents until you feel safe.

Leave yourself with low cards in each suit for the later rounds of play — the third and even maybe the second round of a suit. Doing so allows you to lose tricks late in the game when everyone is trying to unload their hearts and the ♠Q. Avoid playing on your safe suits (the ones where you have 2s and 3s and thus won't win tricks) until the end of the hand — but be aware that your opponents are doing the same thing.

Hearts may not have the complex rules that other games have, but it does have rules. Keep yourself out of trouble by following these guidelines:

- Playing out of turn (when it was someone else's turn) has no formal penalty. If a trick in which someone led or played out of turn is finished and turned over, then the game simply continues. But a player who still has to play on a trick in which someone has slipped up can demand that the lead and all the other cards played to that trick be taken back.

- Failure to follow suit is called a *revoke*. A player may correct a revoke at any point until the trick ends. After that point, if someone draws attention to a revoke, the player who didn't follow suit takes all the penalty points on that deal, and no one else gets any penalty points at all.

Scoring: the day of reckoning

At the end of the hand each player collects all the cards in his trick pile, and the arithmetic begins. The simple version of the game doesn't tax your math skills unduly. Each player gets 1 point per heart-card in his tricks, for a total of 13 penalty points possible in each hand. However, when the ♠Q is involved, things become more expensive.

The ♠Q, which is also called the Black Lady (or Black Maria, Black Widow, Slippery Anne, or Calamity Jane), costs you 13 points on her own. Not surprisingly, therefore, you need to gear your strategy of both passing and playing to avoid taking this card. For that reason, you pass the ♠A and ♠K, and also the ♠Q before play begins.

Of course, passing on low spades before the play starts may be a tactical blunder, because that may help a player guard the ♠Q and thus not have to play the card when the suit is led.

Because the penalty associated with the ♠Q outweighs that of the hearts, leading spades early (if you can afford to) is often right, to ensure that someone else takes in this card — not you. By leading spades early (but not the ace and king, of course), you hope to flush out the ♠Q and let someone other than you pick her up. With the ♠Q out of the way, you can't be too badly hurt on a hand, even if you do win a number of hearts. So long as you don't have either the ♠A or ♠K, leading spades early is usually safe.

You do have one rather unlikely escape if you get a really terrible hand stuffed full of high cards. If you manage to take all the penalty cards and thus collect 26 points, you finish up doing remarkably well: You have the option of reducing your own score by 26 points or charging everyone else 26 points. This accomplishment is called *shooting the moon,* and it's a great deal easier to do in theory than in practice. The right hand rarely comes along for it, because if anyone sees you trying to take all the tricks, they'll save a heart or two for the end to allow someone else to share the penalty points and prevent you from achieving your aim.

Shooting the moon is more dangerous than it may seem; in my experience, more points are lost in unsuccessful attempts to shoot the moon than are gained by making it.

You play to 100 points when 26 points are at stake.

Scoring variations in Hearts flourish as thickly as weeds on a lawn. Here, listed in descending order of frequency, are some of the most common additional rules about scoring. They can all be played simultaneously or not at all:

✔ *Shooting the sun,* as opposed to the moon, involves taking all the tricks as well as all the penalty points. You get a 52-point bonus for shooting the sun.

✔ Counting the ♦J — or, in some circles, the ♦10 — as a bonus card is quite common. Winning the trick with that card in it has real merit because it reduces your penalty points by 11 (or 10, in the case of the ♦10).

If you're playing the rule about shooting the moon, you generally don't need to take the ♦J to shoot the moon, but some versions of the game require that you win this card, too.

Playing the rule about the ♦J influences which cards you decide to pass on. You may want to keep the top diamonds in order to try for the prize. However, you may find capturing the ♦J is easier if you pass it on, rather than trying to use it to take a trick. In high-level games, you're unlikely to find players winning tricks in diamonds early on with this card. In practice, because players rarely get the chance to take an early diamond trick with this card, it tends to get discarded at the end of the hand.

✔ If you manage to score exactly 100 points, your score is immediately halved to 50 points. Some versions play that if you avoid scoring any points on the next hand, your score is further reduced to zero.

✔ The ♣10 can be a potentially lethal card if you play the rule, common in some circles, that the card doubles the value of the penalty points for whoever takes it. For example, capturing the ♣10 and three heart cards costs you 6 points, not 3.

✔ The ♥A may be charged at 5 points, not 1.

✔ Occasionally, the ♠Q carries a penalty of only 5 points, not 13.

✔ Anyone who avoids winning a trick in a hand may be credited with –5 points.

✔ In Spot Hearts, all the heart cards are charged at their face value rather than at 1 apiece. The ♥K, ♥Q, and ♥J are 13, 12, and 11 points respectively, meaning that the deck contains 104 penalty points if the ♠Q counts for 13 points. Now, playing a game to a score of 500 or so becomes sensible.

Playing with Three or Five-Plus Players

The rules of the game for three or for more than five players differ from those for four players only because the deck can't be divided equally among everyone (refer to "Getting to the Heart of the Matter" for more information about playing with four people). But you can correct this problem simply by removing one or two surplus cards. For example, the ♣2 — clubs being traditionally the lowest suit — comes out in the game for three players, and the ♣2 and the ♦2 are removed in the game for five players, to even out the deck at 50 cards, making the deck divisible by five.

More interesting, however, is to start the deal with a full deck and to deal an even number to each player. You then leave the extra cards face-down on the table as a *kitty*. Whoever wins the first trick has to add the points in the kitty to his total at the end of the hand. He is permitted to look at the cards without showing anyone else until the end of the hand. This rule makes losing the first trick a very good idea!

A more generous alternative is to permit whoever wins the first trick to add the cards in the kitty to her hand and then to discard an equivalent number of cards. Because this version can result in some significant cards playing no part in the hand at all, this rule seems unnecessarily generous to me.

This rule about forming a kitty has occasionally been extended to the four-player game — where, of course, it isn't strictly necessary. The idea is that each player is dealt only 12 cards, with the remaining four cards forming a kitty.

Clearly, the rules about passing on cards change depending on the number of participants. You can work out for yourself that the cycle of possible ways to pass and receive cards must expand with every additional player added into the game. You can add additional passes so that you exchange cards once with each of the other players — or whatever takes your fancy.

Hearts for Two Players (Honeymoon Hearts)

Each player gets 13 cards, and then the remaining stock of cards is put in a pile with the top card turned over. The nondealer leads a card, the dealer (who must follow suit if he can) plays a card in turn, and the winner takes the face-up card and the loser takes the top face-down card. Then the new top card is turned over, and the sequence continues for 13 rounds until the stock is used up.

At the end, when the stock is exhausted, the players play out their remaining cards and score them up as a regular game of Hearts (refer to "Getting to the Heart of the Matter"). Only the last 13 cards count for this game; the first 13 tricks are just an attempt to build up the hand.

Black Maria

This game, which was invented and popularized in the 1920s, is the most popular English variation of Hearts. Black Maria works well for three or a higher number of players and contains all the traditional Hearts rules (refer to "Getting to the Heart of the Matter"), but it has some additional penalty cards in the spade suit.

In this version of the game, the ♠A, ♠K, and ♠Q are charged respectively at 7, 10, and 13 points, making the spades more dangerous than the hearts.

This change makes tackling the spade suit a priority for someone who doesn't get the ♠A, ♠K, or ♠Q. Admittedly, she may pick up a heart or two along the way, but in playing repeatedly on the spades, she eliminates the danger of a severe charge to herself later on in the hand.

Cancellation Hearts

If a large number of players, say six or more, want to play Hearts, playing with one deck means that the players don't have enough cards. When each player has only eight cards, the risk of players having unbalanced hands, with only one or even no cards in a suit, becomes too high, and playing skillfully is difficult. To solve the problem, you can play Hearts with two decks, but that solution introduces a different question — what happens when two players play the same card on a trick? The solution is an intriguing one: These cards can cancel one another out. When two identical cards are played on the same trick, both cards are treated as not existing. A trick which goes ♠2 ♠7 ♠7 ♠4 ♠4 ♠3 is won by the ♠3; the 4s and 7s cancel each other out.

Canceling cards allows for some interesting turns in the play. For example, with six players at the table, player number one leads the ♦2. The ♠Q is discarded on this card, and the next player tries the ♦4. Player four also plays the ♦4, player five puts on the ♦3, and player six, who has both the ♦2 and the ♦3 left, has the choice of torturing either player one or player five by canceling out one player's card and saddling the other player with the ♠Q. What a nice position to be in!

If a whole trick is canceled out, then any penalty points associated with that trick are carried forward and go to the winner of the next trick.

Chapter 9

Barbu

*I*f you can play Barbu well, you probably won't have trouble with just about any other card game in the world. The skills that you need to be a good Barbu player can carry you successfully through any other challenge a deck of cards has to offer. Does that mean that Barbu is difficult to play? No, but it isn't necessarily easy to play *well*.

Barbu is actually comprised of several different games, and judging which hands are best for which games presents an interesting challenge. It's a game of strategy, where a good memory for the cards is a big help.

To play Barbu, you only require

✔ **Four players**

✔ **A standard deck of 52 cards**

✔ **A large sheet of paper, with four columns drawn on it**

✔ **A scorer with neat handwriting**

Don't try to play Barbu on a train or in a car; some of the phases of the game require a tabletop on which to lay out the cards.

Can You Barbu?

When you play Barbu, which rhymes with *canoe,* you actually play seven different games. Barbu consists of a *rubber* of 28 hands, each player dealing seven hands. The dealer for each hand has initial control of the hand; after the cards are dealt, the dealer looks at his hand and gets to choose which of the seven games he wants to play — the only requirement being that he must select each of the seven games once and once only.

The object of Barbu is to avoid scoring penalty points in most of the games and to score positive points at the relatively rare moments when winning points is possible.

A complete rubber of 28 hands takes about two hours or so, so long as everyone moves at a civilized pace. In fact, the most difficult aspect of the game is the scoring. Keeping score involves recording each player's result on each deal and who has chosen what game. The winner is the person who finishes up with the highest plus total or the least-negative score.

Playing Barbu

Barbu may be complex in that it offers seven different games to choose from, but you may find that the actual mechanics of the game are more than easy for you to conquer.

Dealing the cards

All the games involve the same start: You cut for the deal on the very first hand (the person who draws the lowest card deals), and then the dealer deals out all 52 cards, in the traditional clockwise fashion, starting with the player to her left and dealing out the cards face-down one at a time.

 Customarily, each player deals seven consecutive hands, during the course of which he makes his seven choices about which games to play when. But you don't always need to follow custom. Alternating the deal may actually help to keep everyone focused. When the deal rotates, it moves clockwise around the table.

Doubling and redoubling

When you think that you have a better hand than some (or all) of the players, you can *double* those players, which is like an extra contest between you and those players. If you make a double against a player and win by doing better in the game than she does, you find the difference between your score and hers and then add that difference to your score. The loser of the double, on the other hand, has to subtract the difference from her score.

For example, if you double a player who finishes up losing 10 points on the hand, whereas you only lose 4 points, you get 6 points, and he loses an additional 6 points. You finish with a positive 2 points, and the loser finishes with a negative 16 points.

Each player must double each dealer at least twice during the course of the 28 games, and you can double more often if you like. In fact, you can double any other player any time you like.

The player to the left of the dealer always gets the first chance to double one or all of the other players, and then the opportunity passes clockwise around the table.

The dealer or another player can *redouble* if he thinks that the doubler has misjudged the situation. If a player redoubles, then the difference between the score is doubled. In the preceding example, if the player you doubled had redoubled you and he lost 10 points and you lost 4, he would lose an additional 12 points and you would gain 12 points. You would finish with a positive 8 points and he would finish with a negative 22 points.

Be conservative as first to speak when it comes to doubling. You can be more aggressive about doubling the players who have passed already on the opportunity. You can trap people by "sandbagging" them if you want to. Pass at first, looking depressed if you're a good actor, and then redouble the people who double you.

Similarly, when considering doubling the dealer, try to do so on hands where other players have implied a good hand by doubling him themselves. Conversely, be happier to double the other players when they haven't doubled the dealer.

Choosing from the seven games

The dealer has seven different games to choose from — which sounds like an awesome prospect, doesn't it? But cheer up; if you've glanced through the chapters of this book, you may have encountered some of these games, or very similar games, before. The Hearts you play in Barbu, for example, resembles the game I discuss in Chapter 8; Fan Tan appears in Chapter 15; and the game of Trumps is like Whist (see Chapter 3).

In two of the games, you can score positive numbers; in the other five games, you try to avoid accumulating penalty points.

The positive games are

- **Trumps:** Choose the trump suit and take as many tricks as possible.
- **Fan Tan:** Try to get rid of all your cards as quickly as possible.

The negative games are

- **Barbu:** Avoid winning the trick with the ♥K in it.
- **Hearts:** Avoid winning tricks with hearts in them.
- **Nullo:** Avoid winning tricks altogether.
- **No Queens:** Avoid winning tricks with queens in them.
- **No Last Two Tricks:** Avoid winning the last two tricks.

All the games except Fan Tan feature taking tricks. The concept of a *trick* involves one player *leading* a card, and then each player must *follow suit* by playing a card from the suit led. Whoever plays the highest card in the suit led takes up all four cards (the trick), stacking it in front of him and, in some cases, collecting any penalty cards appearing in that trick.

One game, Trumps, has a *trump suit*. A trump suit is a boss suit, meaning that a card in the trump suit beats every other card except a higher card in the trump suit. Whenever you can't follow suit because you have no cards in the suit led, you must play a trump card or play a higher trump card than any previously played.

After you decide which game you want to play, just say the name of the game once and then begin play. At the end of each game, the cards are redealt, and the dealer then chooses the game for that hand. The process continues until all the players have chosen each of the seven games.

Trumps

In Trumps, you try to win tricks to score points. The dealer should consider choosing this game if she has six or seven cards (or more) in the same suit that she can use as a trump suit.

The dealer specifies that she has chosen Trumps and names the trump suit. The dealer can name any suit she wants as the trump suit.

It's very unusual for a player to double the dealer when he chooses Trumps, but with three sure winners in your hand, doubling the other players makes sense.

The dealer leads to the first trick, and the dealer has no obligation to lead a card in the trump suit at the first trick.

Players are required to follow suit by playing a card in the suit led, with aces high. If they can't follow suit, they *must* play a trump card or *overtrump* by playing a higher trump card than the previous player, if they can. If they can't play a higher trump card, they can *throw away* or *discard* whatever card they want by playing it on the trick.

The winner of each trick can lead whatever she wants to the next trick.

Each trick is worth 5 points, so 65 points are up for grabs during the course of the hand. After all the tricks have been played, the players count up their tricks and give themselves 5 points for each trick.

Just to show you how a game of Trumps progresses, take a look at an example hand in Figure 9-1. West is the dealer, and he chooses diamonds as the trump suit.

North gets the first chance to double. North passes, East passes, and South daringly doubles North and East but not West, who has a good hand. South expects to get at least two tricks (from the ♠A and ♦A), and he hopes to squeeze out more tricks by doubling North and East. Because West is likely to get at least six tricks, the double is a fair gamble. No one redoubles.

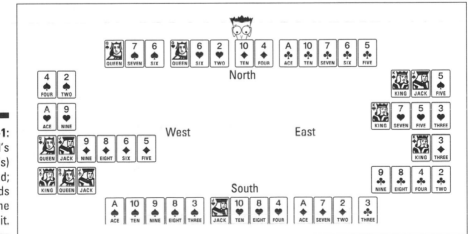

Figure 9-1:
A girl's (and boy's) best friend; diamonds is the trump suit.

West leads a diamond to get the trump cards out of everyone else's hands. That way, he ensures that he wins his tricks in the club suit, without letting anyone else trump those tricks. Keeping in mind that each player must play a higher trump on a trump lead if he can, West's correct play is to start with the ♦8. North plays the ♦10, East the ♦K, and South the ♠A. A good start for West, because the rest of his diamonds will now all be winners! However, South now decides to lead a club. On this trick, West plays the ♣J, and North takes the trick with her ♣A. Next, North leads a trump card; she might have led a club if South hadn't doubled her, but she thinks that South wants clubs led (after all, South played the suit). It isn't in North's interest to help someone who has doubled her by leading the suit that he wants. North, therefore, leads a diamond, and West wins this trick and goes on to lead every one of his diamonds but one. Then West plays the ♣Q and ♣K. The hands now stand as shown in Figure 9-2.

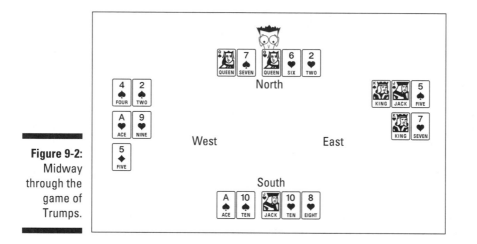

Figure 9-2:
Midway through the game of Trumps.

North

West   East

South

West leads his low spade, which brings out the ♠7, ♠J, and ♠A. South then leads the ♥8, on which the others play the ♥9 and ♥K. East then leads her ♥7, and West wins the trick with his ♥A. On the next trick, West plays his winning ♦5, and he concedes the last trick to East's ♠K.

West finishes with eight tricks, giving him 40 points. North finishes with one trick for 5 points, and South and East finish with 10 points each. The players score a total of 65 points among them. However, before the players enter those scores, they must remember that South doubled North and East. Both North and South have to look at their performance relative to South's. North scored 5 points and South 10, meaning that North loses 5 points to South. Because South and East both scored 10 points, those players don't need to adjust their scores.

The final scores for the hand are West 40, North 0, East 10, and South 15.

Fan Tan

Fan Tan, or Dominoes, is discussed in great detail in Chapter 15. Please refer to Chapter 15 to discover the fundamentals of the game.

The version of Fan Tan played in Barbu differs from the traditional game in a few important ways:

- In this version of the game, the dealer can start all four of the suits from the number of his choice, rather than always starting from the 7. For example, he may choose to start all the suits from the 5 rather than from the 7.

- Aces are always low.

- The winner scores 40 points, the second-place player 25 points, the third player 10 points, and the fourth player –10. But the doubles and redoubles may make life more complicated.

Because you can generally muddle through Fan Tan whatever your hand looks like, you may want to save this game for the end of your turn as dealer. Hands without the cards at the extremes of the suits, namely the aces and kings, may make especially suitable hands for the game.

To see how a game of Fan Tan unfolds, imagine that West chooses this game on his last turn and has the not-especially suitable hand shown in Figure 9-3.

West, the dealer, has to decide where to start the Fan Tan from. He has more high than low cards, so he picks a high number, the queen.

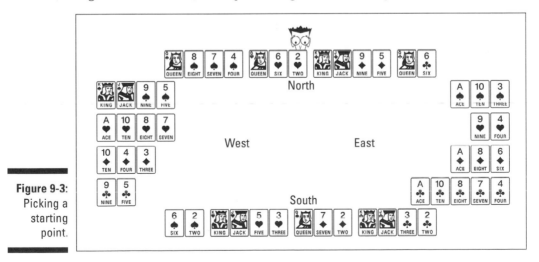

Figure 9-3: Picking a starting point.

When choosing which card to start the Fan Tan on, choose a card you don't have many of, because doing so forces other players to put down that card, and thus they're unable to block you out. The more choices other players have, the more likely they are to be able to frustrate you.

North, with virtually no low cards, doubles all the other players by saying "Maximum." East passes mournfully, and South doubles East. Despite South's many low cards, he has no aces and thus can't lose. West doesn't redouble North.

The play for the hand shown in Figure 9-3 appears in the following table, P meaning that the player has no legal move and passes.

West	*North*	*East*	*South*
P	♥Q	P	♦Q
P	♠Q	P	♥J
♥10	♦K	♥9	♥K
♥8	♣Q	P	♣J
♥7	♥6	♣10	♣K
♠K	♦J	P	♥5
♦10	♦9	♦8	♦7
♠J	P	♠10	♥5
♠9	♠8	♦6	P
♣9	♠7	♣8	♠6
♠5	♠4	♣7	P
P	♦5	♠3	♠2
♦4	♣6	♠A	P
♦3	P	♥4	♦2
♣5	P	♣4	♣3
P	P	♦A	♣2
P	P	♣A	♥3
P	♥2	♦A	—
♥A			

A remarkable result: West loses despite having only one end card because East manages to hold on to the ♥4 for a remarkably long time. The fact that East is unable to play for four of the first six tricks works dramatically to her advantage, in that when she can play, she manages to exert some control.

Always play on the suits in which you have end cards as quickly as possible and hold off on playing on suits where you don't have end cards. Notice, for example, that East plays on clubs (the ♣4) as soon as she can, rather than making a neutral move by playing an end card.

The score is as follows:

✔ South, who wins, had been doubled by North and had doubled East, so in both cases the difference between his score and theirs is added in to his score. He gets 40 points for winning, plus 15 points from North (the difference between 40 and 25) and 0 from East (the difference between 40 and 10) for 85 points total.

✔ North, who finishes second, gets 25 points for taking second place, loses 15 points to South, picks up 15 points from East (for the difference between 25 and 10), and takes 35 (the difference between 25 and –10) from West for 60 points total.

✔ East wins 10 points for third place but loses 15 points to North and 30 points to South for –35 points total.

✔ West loses 10 points for finishing fourth and loses 35 points to North for –45 points total.

The four scores add up to 65, as they should.

Barbu

The namesake of the suite of games involves avoiding the ♥K. Whoever takes the trick that contains ♥K (*Le Barbu,* "the bearded one," because in the standard French playing deck, the ♥K has a beard) loses 20 points. That sounds simple, doesn't it? And indeed it is, for the most part. Of course, there has to be a catch, and here it is: No one is allowed to lead hearts unless he has nothing but hearts in his hand.

After the dealer announces that he wants to play Barbu, he then leads a card, and everyone must play a card in that suit. If a player doesn't have a card in the suit that the dealer leads, then that player may play any card he likes. Although no one may *lead* a heart until he has nothing but hearts left in his hand, a player may *play* a heart if someone leads a suit in which he has no cards.

The highest card played on a trick wins the trick, and the winner leads to the next trick. When the ♥K appears, play stops after that trick.

Barbu is an excellent game to choose if you have the ♥K in your hand — because as soon as someone leads a suit in which you have no cards, you can always play the ♥K and ensure that someone else takes the card. And because you have the ♥K, no one else can pass it on to you — although you may be forced to win the card if someone leads hearts at the end of the game. The only way you can end up with the card is if you reach the end of the game and someone gets to lead hearts at you, or if you get stuck with the lead at the end of the game. Conversely, you may not want to choose this game if you don't have the card but you do have some danger suits. In this context, a *danger suit* is any suit in which you expect to win the third or subsequent round of the suit, because you have plenty of high cards and no small cards.

You should double at this game if you feel that you can avoid winning the second and third tricks in clubs, diamonds, and spades. Beware doubling the dealer — he may stick you with the ♥K!

Keep a watchful eye out for non-hearts suits in your hand that may allow your opponents to discard their hearts. For example, in Figure 9-4, you may think that the hand looks safe from winning the ♥K because you *have* the ♥K, and you should be able to give it to someone else when a diamond or club is lead.

Figure 9-4:
Is this hand safe for Barbu?

But if your opposition makes you win a spade trick by leading the suit after you have no cards left in clubs or diamonds, you're forced by the rules of the game to lead all your spades before you can play hearts. On the lead of all those spades, the opponents may be able to throw all their hearts away. If you decide to play Barbu with such cards, you would lead the ♠A and hope that someone contributes the ♠K. Then you could extract everyone else's spades right at the start of the game and then lose the lead by playing the ♦Q and then the ♣3.

Figure 9-5 shows a hand that may be suitable for playing Barbu.

Figure 9-5:
A bad hand for everything?

Playing Barbu, you may be able to clear away the spades and clubs early and find someone leading a black card to let you throw the ♥K away. You have aces, which is important because you can thus hope to control the play by winning tricks and dictating which suit is played.

Now look at the hand in Figure 9-6.

Figure 9-6:
A good hand for Barbu.

You don't have the ♥K, and you should be able, with a bit of luck, to avoid collecting it when someone leads a club, diamond, or spade. The ♥Q and ♥10 are two bad cards to have, but no other player will be able to throw away the ♥K on the lead of a heart. Barbu proves a great game to play if you hold this hand.

The hand in Figure 9-7 is a bad hand for Barbu.

Figure 9-7:
Don't play Barbu with this hand.

You may find that someone can throw the ♥K on the third round (or earlier) of spades or diamonds, and that you may be forced to win that trick.

I want to walk you through a full hand of Barbu so that you see how the play may go. Check out the way the hands are dealt in Figure 9-8.

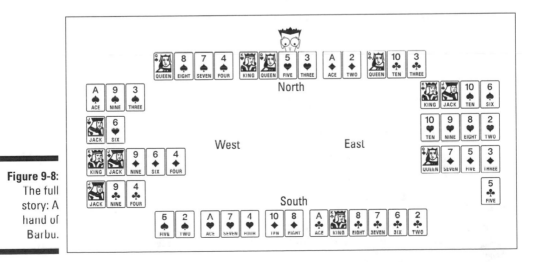

Figure 9-8:
The full story: A hand of Barbu.

North is the dealer; her possession of the ♥K persuades her to go for Barbu. East wants to double, but she has a dangerous spade holding (plenty of spades and no small ones); still, if the game is close to the end and she needs to double the dealer (she must do so twice, remember), this may be the hand on which to do so. South has a favorable hand for the game. When deciding whom to double, he may double the *family* — that is, the other two nondealers (East and West), also known as the *flanks*. West passes, and North has no one to redouble, because no one doubles her.

The dealer can only redouble someone who has doubled her; she can't double the other players.

North leads to the first trick, and the play goes like this, with the winning card in each trick underlined.

West	North	East	South
♠<u>A</u>	♠8	♠K	♠5
♣J	♣Q	♣5	♣<u>A</u>
♦9	♦<u>A</u>	♦Q	♦10
♠9	♠7	♠<u>10</u>	♠2
♦6	♦2	♦7	♦<u>8</u>
♣9	♣<u>10</u>	♠J	♣6
♠3	♠<u>Q</u>	♠6	♥A
♣<u>4</u>	♣3	♦5	♣2
♦<u>4</u>	♥K	♦3	♥7

West collects the ♥K, for which he loses 20 points, and he loses an additional 20 points to South, who doubled him, for −40. (South's double of East is irrelevant, because both avoided the ♥K.) South collects 20 from West, and the other two players score zero.

The total of the points scored by all the players must come back to −20, whatever bets have been made.

Hearts

The Hearts played in Barbu differs from the traditional game (which I discuss in Chapter 8) in the following ways:

✔ You don't have the complications of the ♠Q or other diversions. What you do have is a penalty of 2 points per heart taken, and a 6-point penalty for winning the ♥A.

✔ A total of 30 points can be awarded, regardless of the doubles and redoubles.

Just like the traditional game of Hearts, you can't lead hearts until the suit has been *broken* — until a heart has been discarded.

Consider choosing Hearts if you have six or more cards in the heart suit. No one can lead hearts until the end of the hand; even if your hearts aren't low, with six or more hearts in your hand, you should get the chance to throw away hearts near the end of the hand. Conversely, avoid choosing Hearts if you have a clubs, spades, or diamonds suit without the 2 or 3; you may find yourself leading the suits and collecting hearts by the handful.

Look at the sample hand of Hearts in Figure 9-9 to see how the doubles may work out. North is the dealer and has a fair number of games left — which means that she doesn't have to pick Hearts unless she wants to.

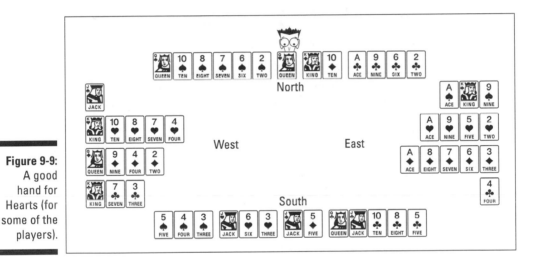

Figure 9-9:
A good hand for Hearts (for some of the players).

North picks Hearts, and East passes discreetly (hoping that no one doubles her). You aren't supposed to mislead people by your tempo of passing or doubling — but many people do! Note that East would have a far better hand if she had the ♦2 instead of the ♦3 because she would then be more likely to lose the lead at the right moment. South has a fair hand in all respects but one, the long clubs, without any small cards in that suit; as a result, South is in danger of getting landed with quite a few hearts via his club suit. South could reasonably double East but probably shouldn't even do that. West doubles South and East and doubles North, too, because he needs a double. North redoubles West, and the play starts.

The plays are shown in the following table, with the winning card in each trick underlined.

West	North	East	South
♦Q	♦K	♦<u>A</u>	♦J
♠J	♠10	♠<u>K</u>	♠5
♣K	♠Q	♠<u>A</u>	♠4
♥K	♠8	♠<u>9</u>	♠3
♣7	♣<u>A</u>	♣4	♣Q
♦9	♦<u>10</u>	♦8	♦5
♣3	♣<u>9</u>	♥A	♣8
♥10	♣<u>6</u>	♥9	♣5
♥8	♣2	♥5	♣<u>10</u>
♥7	♥Q	♥2	♣<u>J</u>
♥<u>4</u>	♠7	♦7	♥3
♦2	♠6	♦<u>6</u>	♥J
♦<u>4</u>	♠2	♦3	♥6

North tries to extract the diamonds from the other players' hands on the first trick, to avoid winning a trick in that suit toward the end of the hand. Conversely, East tries to kill off the spades as quickly as she can for the same reason, and does so very successfully. West, meanwhile, pitches his dangerous ♣K quickly — a wise move, as it turns out. North finds herself rather unluckily forced to win two club tricks, but after South gets the lead with only clubs and hearts left, the rules of the game compel South to lead his clubs first. Fortunately for South, West has to win the ♥4 and lead diamonds on the 12th trick. East plays her ♦6 at the 12th trick and forces West to take the last trick.

The scoring is as follows:

- ✔ East escapes with –4, which may look surprising, given her high cards. In fact, aces in long suits aren't necessarily such a disaster; what tends to hurt you is having no 2s or 3s in a long suit. In addition, East picks up 2 points from West because of the double (West has 6, East has 4; the difference is 2), so East finishes with –2.

- ✔ South loses 10 points and loses 4 to West (10 minus 6) for –14.

- ✔ West has –6 in trick points. He loses 2 to East, gains 4 from South, and gains 8 from North (10 minus 6 multiplied by 2, because of the re-double) for 4 points.

- ✔ North has –10 and loses 8 to West to finish –18.

The totals of all four players scores adds to –30.

Nullo

In Nullo, the object is not to win tricks at all. The penalty associated with each trick is 2 points, so a simple –26 points are at stake.

Use the following rule to decide whether to play Nullo for a particular hand: Low cards are good, high cards (aces, kings, queens, and jacks) are bad. If you have high cards, you want them in your long suits, preferably with 2s or 3s.

The players must follow suit (play a card in the suit that's been led) if they can. Whoever plays the highest card in the suit that's been led wins the trick and leads to the next trick. There is no trump suit in Nullo.

Try to lose every trick, unless you can see that the play may come back to haunt you by leaving you with more than one trick later on in the hand. Don't sacrifice high cards to win the first round of a suit if you can make the play on the second round of the suit. By that time, someone else may have played a higher card.

Conversely, in some situations, you need to leave yourself with low cards. Say that you have to lead from a suit such as Q9753; leading the 3 is a serious blunder — you need to keep both the 5 and 3 for later play in the suit. On the other hand, the 9, or preferably the 7, is the right starting card; someone else is sure to take the trick. Leading the Q may make you win an unnecessary trick, one that you could have avoided.

Nullo is a game where having the lead can frequently be a severe disadvantage — but you're going to have to pick the game at some point, come what may! It's best to make your mind up about the lead before deciding to choose Nullo; a middle card from a long suit or any short suit lead tends to work out best.

In this game, taking two tricks or so is a good result, so if you're doubled, assume that the doubler has expectations of scoring less than that — which, in turn, suggests that redoubling should only be done with a realistic expectation of collecting one or no tricks.

If two players double you and you expect to take two tricks, a redouble may work, because it's unlikely that they will both beat you.

Figure 9-10 gives you a chance to see a game of Nullo in action. East is the dealer, and she chooses Nullo.

South has such bad clubs that he might not consider a double on this hand, and West's hearts are even more dangerous, so he passes, too. North has too many aces and kings to be happy with a double, although when East and South pass, a case can be made for doubling them both. In any event, everybody passes.

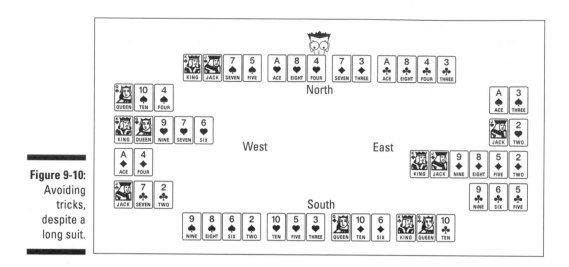

Figure 9-10: Avoiding tricks, despite a long suit.

East leads the ♣6, and the play record proceeds as shown in the following table. The winning card in each trick is underlined.

West	North	East	South
♣J	♣8	♣6	♣<u>Q</u>
♠4	♠7	♠3	♠<u>8</u>
♠Q	♠J	♠<u>A</u>	♠6
♣7	♣4	♣9	♣<u>K</u>
♠<u>10</u>	♠5	♣5	♠9
♥7	♥<u>8</u>	♥2	♥5
♣2	♣3	♥J	♣<u>10</u>
♦A	♠<u>K</u>	♦K	♠2
♥Q	♥<u>A</u>	♦J	♥10
♥<u>9</u>	♥4	♦9	♥3
♦4	♦<u>7</u>	♦5	♦6
♥K	♦3	♦2	♦<u>10</u>
♥6	♣<u>A</u>	♦8	♦Q

South finishes up with six tricks but is more hurt than surprised by that result. The fact that he does so badly in clubs and diamonds is a little unlucky — but only a little. His score is –12. Not so painful! West gets away with winning only two tricks because nobody leads hearts consistently, which is sheer chance. West loses 4 points. North wins four tricks, as expected, for –8. East escapes with one trick for –2. The total of all four players' scores is –26.

No Queens

In No Queens, your goal is to avoid winning tricks with the queens in them.

No Queens is one of the more difficult games to judge when to call, because bad things can happen to you in completely unexpected ways. All you have to do is avoid winning a trick with a queen in it — but you find the queens being discarded on other tricks as many times as you find them winning a trick in their own right or falling under an ace or king. For that reason, finding a good hand for No Queens is very difficult. In general, the more unevenly distributed your own hand (the longer your long suits), the less likely you can predict the play. Avoid choosing this game when you have a short suit headed by an ace, king, or queen. But a long suit without small cards can produce equally painful results!

 In No Queens, you can't wait for the perfect hand to come along; if you escape with having won only one queen, you haven't done so badly. If you're doubled at this game, you should have realistic (maybe even confident) chances of escaping with no queens to redouble. You should redouble when you have one or two low cards in all the suits (for example, 2s, 3s, and 4s) and no aces and kings that you may be forced to play earlier than you would like. Either that, or you have to know that the doubler is an optimist — they abound in Barbu. Each queen is worth 6 points, so 24 negative points are to be awarded one way or another.

An example hand is shown in Figure 9-11.

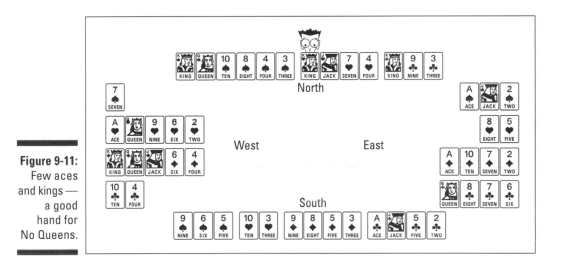

Figure 9-11: Few aces and kings — a good hand for No Queens.

The dealer, South, calls No Queens, having already used up Nullo and Hearts (although this hand is fine for either of those games). West decides to double everyone, including the dealer (because of his low cards in long suits), a fairly aggressive play, and North, thinking that East must have a bad hand as everyone else appears to have a good hand, doubles East — again, a fairly speculative play.

South leads the ♥10 (a lucky move, because his other choice, the ♦8, might be unsuccessful, because North might have given him the ♠Q!).

The following table shows the play of the hand, with the winning cards underlined.

West	North	East	South
♥<u>A</u>	♥K	♥7	♥10
♠7	♠K	♠<u>A</u>	♠9
♥9	♥<u>J</u>	♥5	♥3
♦Q	♠4	♠<u>J</u>	♠6
♥Q	♠3	♠2	♠<u>5</u>
♦<u>K</u>	♠Q	♦10	♦5
♣10	♣9	♣8	♣<u>A</u>
♣4	♣K	♣Q	♣<u>J</u>

The play stops when a player wins the fourth queen.

In this example, everyone wins one queen, so the doubles become irrelevant, and everyone loses 6 points.

West tries to get the lead as early as possible so that he can lead his short suits and be ready to throw his queens away soon after that. When South gets the lead at the sixth trick, he plays a diamond, and West doesn't expect someone both to have no diamonds and to have a queen to throw. He logically plays the ♦K, but it probably costs him 24 points (6 points for the queen and 18 points in doubles). But, and this is a big but, North doesn't have to throw the queen at that point. Because it's in her interest to make West end up with points (because of the double), she could save up the queen for West. That is one of the risks in doubling; you make enemies easily, and players choose whom to throw their queens to!

No Last Two Tricks

This game involves trying to avoid winning the last two tricks. Nothing else matters. No Last Two Tricks may be the most difficult game to master in Barbu, because to play it well you have to try to remember what is going on in all four suits. Not an easy task! What makes a good hand — and what makes a bad one — isn't obvious in No Last Two Tricks, either.

Figure 9-12 shows a pretty good hand for No Last Two Tricks. It has quite a few high cards that let you win the lead when you want, so clearing out all the high cards and leaving yourself with all the 2s and 3s for the last four tricks are easy matters. (Aces are high in No Last Two Tricks.)

The hand in Figure 9-13 is terrible for No Last Two Tricks. This hand can only follow other people's leads and will probably be left with a winning card in three of the four suits at the end. It has no low cards, and the absence of low cards is the killer, not the presence of high cards.

Figure 9-12:
Plenty of 2s
and 3s
are great
for No Last
Two Tricks!

Figure 9-13:
No low
cards and
no aces —
disaster for
No Last
Two Tricks.

 It isn't just the number and location of your high cards that matter at this game; the *distribution* of your suits (the number of cards you have in each suit) is also important. The worst possible distribution in your hand is a 4-3-3-3 pattern — four cards in one suit and three in each of the others. This sort of arrangement almost guarantees that you have to follow suit at the end of the hand and are thus left to play on a suit that you may not want to lead. A 4-4-4-1 shape is equally unattractive, because, again, the odds are that you have little flexibility in terms of discarding early in the hand.

You should double the other players, including the dealer, whenever you have no suits in which you think you may win the third trick, or whenever you know that you can lead any danger suits early enough and often enough to eliminate the danger.

The penalty for taking the last two tricks is severe. The next-to-the-last trick is worth 10 points and the last trick 20 points, so trying to keep track of what cards have been played is definitely worthwhile. (If it is any consolation, I have never seen a hand of this game where all four players were happy with their performance in retrospect.)

Check out the hands in Figure 9-14 to see how a game of No Last Two Tricks could progress. West is the dealer, with a fair number of games left to choose from. He has a clear call, in that although you can see that he may not like developments in any of the suits, No Last Two Tricks seems a reasonable bet. His worst suit, hearts, is short, and he has enough high cards in diamonds to mean that he needs to obtain the lead only twice, and he will be able to play hearts himself enough times to get the heart suit out of his hand and be safe enough.

Having high cards helps you get the lead to play on the suits that you want to get out of the way. A lack of high cards can be as bad as too many at No Last Two Tricks.

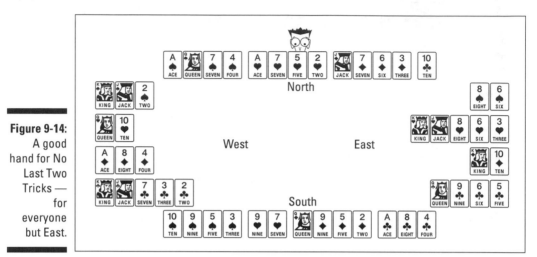

Figure 9-14: A good hand for No Last Two Tricks — for everyone but East.

North is first to speak, and she decides to double East and South because she has no obvious danger suits, but she does have aces to win the lead. East passes, with a terrible hand. She has poor clubs and a hand that suggests she won't have control of her own destiny. South decides simply to double East; he shouldn't be tempted to redouble North, although he may double West if South "owes" West a double and the game is winding down. The danger of South's heart and club suit is just too strong, but it wouldn't be wrong in certain circumstances to double the dealer.

The play unfurls as follows; the winning card in each trick is underlined.

West	North	East	South
♦8	♦7	♦<u>K</u>	♦9
♣<u>K</u>	♣10	♣9	♣8
♥10	♥7	♥<u>J</u>	♥9
♣J	♦6	♣6	♣<u>A</u>
♣2	♦J	♣<u>Q</u>	♣4
♣7	♠7	♣<u>5</u>	♠10
♥Q	♥<u>A</u>	♥K	♥7
♠<u>K</u>	♠Q	♠8	♠9
♦<u>A</u>	♦3	♦10	♦Q
♦<u>4</u>	♠A	♠6	♦2
♠<u>J</u>	♠4	♥8	♠5
♠2	♥5	♥6	♠<u>3</u>
♣3	♥2	♥3	♦<u>5</u>

It's a good thing that South took a cautious approach in the doubling! As it is, he loses 30 points, plus 30 to North and 30 to East for the doubles given and received. Those two players pick up 30 points each, and the total for the game comes back to –30.

 Counting all the cards is absolutely essential at No Last Two Tricks — and at all games except Fan Tan and possibly Trumps. By *counting,* I mean trying to remember how many cards — and which ones — are left in each suit. If that task sounds tough, perhaps I can console you by admitting that I'm pretty bad at it myself! The point is, though, that at No Last Two Tricks, you need to remember all the small cards. Ask yourself, "Is that ♠3 the smallest spade left in the game?" If not, discard it! If you're good at counting the cards, it gives you an edge and allows you to double the novices more often. They're not going to be as good as you at counting cards, and you should never miss an opportunity to double. You may think that you're a novice, too, but if you let people know that you've read this book, you should be safe enough; no one will double a *...For Dummies* reader!

It all adds up: the arithmetic at the end of the day

Throughout the preceding sections, I give you sample hands of each game in order to show you how the scoring works out in each game. Because Barbu is a conglomeration of games, it's important to see how the scores from these sample hands fit together. Notice that the totals of all the games comes to zero.

Trumps	65
Fan Tan	65
Barbu	–20
Hearts	–30
Nullo	–26
No Queens	–24
No Last Two Tricks	–30
	0

Scoring Barbu

In many ways, keeping an accurate score card is about the most difficult part of Barbu! The scorer has to keep track of the games each dealer chooses and who doubled whom. The scorer tracks all this information for two reasons:

- ✔ He needs to calculate the score on the hand.
- ✔ He needs to confirm that each player has doubled the other dealers twice during the cycle of the hands.

The dealer draws four columns on the score sheet, one column for each of the players, and makes note of all the pertinent details of the game as it progresses.

Table 9-1 shows you a sample score sheet after a few of the example hands shown in this chapter have been played. So far, the six hands scored up are West's Trumps, North's Barbu, East's Nullo, South's No Queens, West's No Last Two Tricks, and North's Hearts.

In Table 9-1, the doubles are marked on the score sheet for each player, against each one of the other players. Everyone must double the dealer twice, and the asterisks represent that. The hash-marks represent a redouble. MAX represents a double of all three players. (While different people have their own slightly different scoring systems, the fundamentals remain the same. If you avoid scoring penalty points and know when to double the other players, you're bound to do well!)

Table 9-1 shows the scoring for a game in progress. At the point of the game shown in Table 9-1, anyone could win or lose the game. One of the most exciting elements of Barbu is that the winner only emerges after the very last hand has been played. Due to the doubling required in Barbu, individual hands can shift large numbers of points.

If possible, don't save any doubles of the dealer for the last hand. If you do, you may find yourself redoubled by the dealer — an unsavory prospect that can mean the whole game going up in smoke around your ears.

After the 28th and final hand, the player with the highest-positive score (or the least-negative score) wins the game.

Game	(Dbls)	West	(Dbls)	North	(Dbls)	East	(Dbls)	South	Total
Table 9-1				**A Sample Score Sheet**					
West									
Trumps	—	40	—	0	—	10	N,E	15	65
Fan Tan									
Hearts									
Last Two Tricks	—	0	E,S	30	—	30	E	–90	–30
No Queens									
Barbu									
Nullo									
North									
Trumps									
Fan Tan									
Hearts MAX*	4	##W	–18	—	–2	—	–14	–30	
Last Two Tricks									
No Queens									
Barbu	—	–40	—	0	—	0	N,E	20	–20
Nullo									
East									
Trumps									
Fan Tan									
Hearts									
Last Two Tricks	—	–4	—	–8	—	–2	—	–12	–26
No Queens									
Barbu									
Nullo									
South									
Trumps									
Fan Tan									
Hearts									
Last Two Tricks									
No Queens MAX*	–6	E	–6	—	–6	—	–6	–24	
Barbu									
Nullo									

Part IV
Score As Many Points As You Can!

The 5th Wave   By Rich Tennant

"We needed this card to complete our deck, but you can have it back now."

In this part . . .

When playing the games in this part of the book, you try to capture high-scoring cards (each game has its own ranking list, where different cards become more or less valuable). Some of the games covered in this part, which include Pinochle, Piquet, Setback, and Clobyosh, also allow the players to get involved in a competitive auction.

Chapter 10
Pinochle

Most two-player versions of three-player games are only a pale imitation of the real thing. However, Pinochle for two players is actually a game that stands on its own. The game is especially satisfying because it allows a player with good memory and imagination to overcome the deficiencies of her cards, and Pinochle has enough variety in its possibilities to make it a challenging game at many levels.

All you need to play Pinochle is the following:

✔ **Two, three, or four players**

✔ **Two standard decks of 52 cards:** Actually, you only need the ace through 9 from the two decks, making two sets of 24 cards, or 48 in all. It's better, though not essential, if the two decks of cards have the same backs to them.

✔ **Pencil and paper for scoring**

Pinochle for Two

Pinochle is a game of scoring points. You score points in two phases in the game; first by having *melds* in your hand, which can be *runs* (AKQJ10), *marriages* (any king-queen or the special combination called the *pinochle*, the ♦J and ♠Q), or *sets* such as ♦Q ♥Q ♣Q ♠Q. You get to score these melds during the first phase of the play of the cards.

Pinochle on the Web

The Official Pinochle Player's Newsletter (members.aol.com/sharksinc/ pinochle/index.html) acts as a meeting place for Pinochle players on the Web. Besides offering Pinochle tournament news, the site also features a catalog of Pinochle clubs in the U.S., organized by state. Anyone interested in starting a local Pinochle club can contact the site's creator for more information on forming a club.

The players initially get 12 cards from the deck of 48, leaving a *stock* pile of 24 cards. They play out cards and then pick up new ones from the stock until no cards are left to pick up. They then go on to the second phase of the game, which involves playing out their cards until their hand is fully exhausted.

To begin, each player takes turns playing a card, and the higher card in the suit *led* (the suit of the first card played) takes both cards up; this is called a *trick*. Whoever wins the trick in this first phase picks up the trick and keeps it in front of him; he also gets the opportunity to put down one meld if he has one.

Pinochle is played with a *trump suit,* which means that one suit is the master suit. Any card in the trump suit beats any *side-suit* (any non-trump suit) card and wins the trick. The trump suit in Pinochle is selected at random at the start of the game. The tricks themselves aren't important, however; it's the point-scoring cards within those tricks that matter.

One issue to bear in mind is that you're playing with two identical decks, so players may play the same card on a trick. If two players play the same card, then the first one outranks the second one.

During the two phases of the play of the cards, 250 points are up for grabs. However, you need to keep in mind some odd points about the cards in Pinochle, which I describe in "Scoring the melds" in this chapter.

Ranking and valuing the cards

The cards rank the same way in all suits, whether the suit is a trump suit or a side-suit. The order, from highest to lowest, is ace, 10, king, queen, jack, 9. In other words, 10s are the second-highest cards, ranking below aces. And as you see in Table 10-1, the 10s are also valuable in the point-scoring.

When you play the cards, the tricks won or lost are *not* of key significance. What matters is the point value of the cards won in the tricks taken, so before you even start to play, you need to master the point values for each card. During the play, you aim to capture point-scoring cards rather than win tricks.

No less than three card-valuation scales currently exist: The Streamlined, Old-Time, and Revised valuation scales. Which scale of values you play is entirely up to you and your friends, but you need to agree on which scale to use before play begins.

Table 10-1 shows you how many points each card is worth in each of the three valuation scales.

Table 10-1	Pinochle Valuation Scales		
Card	*Streamlined*	*Old-Time*	*Revised*
Ace	11	10	10
10	10	10	10
King	4	5	10
Queen	3	5	0
Jack	2	0	0
9	0	0	0

Adding up the possible points

Because 30 points are at stake in each suit and because you play the game with a doubled deck, you have two sets of every suit, making 60 points in each suit. So you have 240 total points up for grabs in the play of the cards. Both players try to win as many points as they can, as well as make scoring melds (see the next section).

In addition, winning the last trick always wins you an extra 10 points, making 250 points in total in the first phase of the game. However, before the cards are played, you can claim your melds as a further way of scoring points.

In addition to the card points, a series of awards for melds also comes into play, which may or may not be claimed, depending on whether either player actually has any scoring sequences to claim. You don't always get to collect these meld awards, because the opportunity to score them depends on whether a player was actually dealt (or got to pick up) the right hand. These awards are called *melds,* and for the most part the scoring values associated with them are firmly agreed on.

Scoring the melds

You can score points for three different sorts of melds, called the *run,* the *pinochle,* and the *set.* You get to score your melds during the play of the hand, and you can use any cards in your hand more than once to make a second meld in a different category at a later turn. For example, you can put down the ♠Q in a pinochle and then reuse it to make four queens.

✔ **Run:** Runs are specific *holdings* (groupings of cards) in the trump suit (keep in mind that the trump suit is selected at random in the two-player game), and three holdings score you points. One equivalent holding in a side-suit gets you a minor award, too.

  • AKQJ10 of the trump suit (a *flush*) is worth 150 points

  • The 9 of the trump suit (called the *dix,* pronounced *deece*) is worth 10 points

  • King-queen of the trump suit (a *royal marriage*) is worth 40 points

  • King-queen in a nontrump suit (a *common marriage*) is worth 20 points

✔ **Pinochle:** The second meld is a combination of the ♦J and the ♠Q. One pair is good, two is even better.

  • Pinochle (the ♦J and ♠Q) is worth 40 points

  • Double Pinochle (both ♠Qs and both ♦Js) is worth 300 points

✔ **Set:** The third type of meld is a set of each of the four honor cards: Aces, kings, queens, or jacks.

  • Four aces (one of each suit), also known as *aces around* or *100 aces,* is worth 100 points

  • Four kings (one of each suit), also known as *80 kings,* is worth 80 points

  • Four queens (one of each suit), also known as *60 queens,* is worth 60 points

  • Four jacks (one of each suit), also known as *40 jacks,* is worth 40 points

  • Four 10s or 9s are worth 0 points

The deal

The players cut for the deal, and the player with the highest card deals the cards. The dealer shuffles the deck and then offers the cards to his opponent to cut. Each player gets 12 cards, with the dealer distributing the cards four at a time.

If the dealer exposes one of his cards, he must live with having given information away to his opponent. If he exposes one of his opponent's cards, the player has the option of accepting it or calling for a new deal. If you find a card face up in the stock, simply turn the card over and re-shuffle the stock.

The play

After each player has 12 cards, the dealer places the remainder of the deck (24 cards) in the middle of the table. The dealer then turns over the top card in the stock, which denotes the trump suit. He then sets that turned-over card beneath the stock, where it stays until all the cards have been used up.

Any card in the trump suit beats all the cards in the side-suits (non-trump suits).

The dix of the trump suit (the 9) is worth 10 points. If the top card of the stock at the first trick was the dix, the dealer scores 10 points immediately.

Phase One: Improving the hand and scoring melds

The players aim for two targets during this phase of the game. In the first endeavor, each player wants to leave herself with as many trump cards and high cards as she can for Phase Two, so that she can capture scoring cards and score points then.

But in addition, and perhaps more importantly, the players want to score points by putting down point-scoring melds from the cards remaining in their hands during Phase One. The snag is that the players are allowed to put down only a single point-scoring meld at a time, and only when they have won a trick. But after the player plays a card to win a trick, he can't use it in a meld, so he has to avoid throwing away the scoring (or potentially scoring) cards simply in order to obtain the lead.

During the first phase of the game, which lasts for 12 turns, the players exhaust the stock of 24 cards sitting in the middle of the table by playing out a card from their hand and then replacing it by picking up a card from the pile.

The non-dealer leads to the first trick, and he may select any card in his hand, as can the second player in reply — the second player doesn't have to play a card in the suit led (or *follow suit*) even if he has a card in the suit. Of course, if the second player doesn't follow suit or play a trump card, he loses the trick.

Whoever wins the trick (by playing the highest card in the suit led or in the trump suit) takes the face-down card from the top of the stock. The loser takes the next face-down card from the stock, whereupon the procedure repeats itself until no cards are left in the stock.

You have absolutely no obligation to follow suit in this phase of the game. You may well not want to follow suit if doing so involves using a card that you want to keep for a high-scoring trick later on.

On the last of the 12 tricks that make up this part of the game, the player who wins the trick gets the choice of the face-down card or the trump card, which is almost sure to be the dix because one player has usually claimed by now his 10 points by switching his dix with the initial trump card.

Some play that the winner of the last trick gets the face-down card and must expose it, while the loser gets the trump card. Either way, the winner of the trick has one final opportunity to score points by putting down a meld, or scoring combination.

When the stock is exhausted, the second phase of the game begins. The players play the 12 cards remaining in their hands and score points for all the scoring cards that they can capture. This is the second phase of the game; I cover it more fully later in this chapter.

A card used in a meld does double duty: It doesn't get removed from the game; it stays on the table as part of the player's hand. It can be used in the play to win or lose a trick, and at the end of the hand the remaining cards in the melds are picked up by the players and played out during the second phase of the game. While winning a trick in order to put down a meld may not be a problem in the early part of the game, getting the lead in an advantageous fashion toward the end of the first phase may be more difficult than it appears.

If you win a trick, put down any meld you want to score before picking up from the stock. After you pick up a card from the stock pile, your turn is over.

Whenever you put down a meld, you record the score for it; the points you get in the play from winning tricks are added up at the end of the hand.

Try to use 10s, if you can, to capture the lead; apart from being a high card, they serve little purpose in melding except for the trump 10 in the flush. However, winning tricks by playing a 10 scores you trick points in the process. Conversely, you want to get rid of your jacks or 9s if you're looking to lose a trick. The point is that you want to give up low-scoring cards, which are of little use in scoring melds, rather than queens and kings. Losing tricks that you could win is often better than winning them, if you preserve all your possible melding combinations in the process, especially in the early part of the game.

Bear in mind that if you lead a high card such as an ace early in the hand, you allow it to be trumped, or at best you pick up nothing of value from your opponent. The longer you wait to play an ace, the more likely you are to acquire something of value when you play it.

In addition, when you have a choice, you should lead from a long suit to make your opponent work harder at winning the trick. Your adversary is more likely to find that winning a trick in a suit that she is short of is difficult, and she may be forced to expend a trump card to do so.

Figure 10-1 lets you practice your strategy a little. The turned-up card is the ♣Q, making clubs the trump suit for the hand.

Figure 10-1:
A sample
hand.

As you look at this hand, you see that it has a marriage in spades (the king-queen), with the possibility — with a good pick-up — of four kings and a pinochle (the ♠Q and ♦J). If you can pick up the ♣Q (by getting the dix and switching it for the ♣Q or by picking up the other ♣Q directly), you may get a run in clubs.

Your strategy is to lead the ♠9, hoping to put down the marriage in spades quickly when you win a trick. Good cards to pick up from the stock are the ♣Q, the ♣9, or the ♥K.

Phase Two: Playing out the cards

The sole aim of this phase of the game is to score as many points as possible by winning tricks with point-scoring cards in them.

Phase Two of the game is much more straightforward and less strategically complex than the first phase. The players pick up any of their exposed cards on the table that have been used in melds and simply play out the 12 remaining cards in their hand or on the table. Each player (starting with the player who won the last trick) plays one card, as before, to a trick, and the player who plays the highest card in the suit led or the higher trump card takes the trick.

In this phase of the game, you must follow suit if you can (a difference from the first phase). If the second player has no cards in the suit led, she must put a trump on the trick and win it. The trump suit stays the same for both parts of the play, of course. If the trump suit is led, the player can discard anything she wants to get rid of, if she has no trump cards.

After both players play all their cards, each player looks through the tricks he has won and adds up the trick points he has taken (refer to Table 10-1 to assign values to each of the cards). These trick points are added to the scoring combinations from the first part of the game to make each player's total for the hand.

In the second phase of the game, a failure to follow suit or failure to try to win a trick by trumping the trick leads to the player scoring nothing for tricks in the entire hand — but he keeps the points he scores for melds. You can correct an error until you have played to the next trick.

In the sample hand I show you in "Phase One: Improving the hand and scoring melds," at the end of 12 tricks, you collect 170 points in the melds: When you pick up the dix of the trump suit and switch it for the ♣Q, you score 10 points; when you put down four kings, that scores another 80 points; you put down a royal marriage and subsequently two common (non-trump) marriages of kings and queens and score 40 + 20 + 20 for those marriages. That all totals 170 points.

You also collect points in the play in the first phase for winning tricks with scoring cards in them — maybe 50 points. Those points aren't totaled up yet; all the card points are added up at the end of the second phase.

Your adversary scores 100 points for four aces, a pinochle (the ♠Q and ♦J) for 40, and a common marriage for a further 20, making 160 points. He has 50 points in the play as well, also as yet unrecorded.

Pretend that you have the cards shown in Figure 10-2 at the end of the first phase of the game.

Figure 10-2:
Ready for
the second
part of
the play.

Your objective is to win as many tricks as possible in order to collect the scoring cards. Because you have been watching to keep track of the 12 trump cards and the six other aces, you know that your opponent holds five trump cards, including both aces, both the ♦As, and one ♠A. You're lucky to have the lead, because now you can lead your long suit and force your opponent to trump it. You should lead hearts at every opportunity and make your opponent trump them. In return, you will get to win tricks with your trump cards. If your adversary had the lead, he could take out some trump cards and neutralize your whole hand by leading diamonds, and maybe spades, too.

At the end of the second phase, each player adds up the points from the first and second phases; the player with the highest score wins. You lose the hand, though not by very much, which isn't surprising. With access to only a few aces, it's very difficult to do well in the play.

Getting the most from your melds

The key to the game is to put down as many combinations in the first phase of the game as you can; it's almost impossible to win unless you score decently in the melds. A player may use any card in more than one scoring combination, provided that it's used to score points with a combination from a different category of points. For example, you can put down four kings and then use the ♠K, which was already on the table, in a marriage by putting down the ♠Q. Then you could use the ♠Q with the ♦J for a pinochle and then use that jack with three other jacks to make a set.

You can't, however, use a king with one queen for a marriage and then reuse the king with another queen for a second marriage. No bigamy is permitted at Pinochle!

The timing of putting down sequences may be important, specifically if you're looking at a king-queen in the trump suit (a royal marriage), which you have in your hand as part of a flush, the ace-king-queen-jack-10 of the trump suit. If you put down the king-queen first, you can expand it by putting down the remaining cards in the flush later on for a further 150 points. But if you put down the flush first, you can't extract the king-queen from it as a further point-scoring move. As a rule, putting down marriages first gives you more flexibility in later play.

Having said that, make sure that you meld any aces you may have into a set of 100 aces as soon as possible — that way, you ensure that you can use them in the play to take tricks without worrying about losing the meld points.

As a general principle, you need to have the earlier scoring combination intact in order to embellish it. The 300-point award for double pinochle can only be attained if the first combination is still on the table in one piece.

While you want to put down a trump marriage and then the flush, doing so takes two turns. (You get to put down only one set at a time.) If the deck is running out of cards at the end of the first phase, you may have to settle for what you can get by putting down the flush and giving up on the secondary award. And if you're worried about your opponent having the right cards for a high-scoring combination such as a flush right at the end of the first phase, you should consider leading a high trump card — your adversary may not be able to win the trick except by playing a high trump card and thus he may disrupt his flush. Simply winning the last few tricks — especially if your opponent leads a high card in a tacit indication that he's keen to keep the lead — may be a good idea.

One way to save a turn in scoring melds is that in a single turn, you can put down four kings and queens at the same time, scoring 240 points in the process. You get 80 + 60 for the kings and queens around, together with the four marriages for 100 points (one for 40 and three for 20). The attraction of this play is not in getting bonus points but in economy of effort in claiming melds. The colloquial name for this play is a *roundhouse*, and it represents the only exception to the rule that you can only put down one meld at a time.

One other important thing to try to focus on is whether certain high cards still in your hand are ever going to be usable in a meld. As soon as your opponent puts down four aces, can your three aces ever make another set? Not if the eighth ace has already been played! In that case, use your aces to win tricks and take the lead.

If you hold two identical cards in your hand, one of which has been used in a meld and is thus on the table, visible to your opponent, make sure to play the one on the table first. No point in giving away information about your hand to your adversary!

On the right track (following the cards)

What separates the good player from the moderate one at Pinochle is his ability to remember which cards have been played during the first phase of the game. Initially, just keep track of the aces — all eight of them — and keep an approximate count of the trump cards. Even this task is a tall order if you aren't used to following the cards, and you're likely to find your count of the hand straying because you have other things to focus on during the hand. But the task in itself may be worthwhile; you get a better feel for the hand, and you may find that you get to understand more about the way the cards work because of the effort. The simple way to keep count is to track all the trump cards and aces as they're played. Don't include the cards in your hand in the count of the cards actually played.

Finishing the game

The object of the game is to be the first to score 1,000 points. If both players go past the winning post on the same hand, the player with the larger score wins.

If both players achieve the target on the same turn, you can break the tie in two additional ways. You can set the winning post at 1,250 (and if necessary, up to 1,500, and so on). Whoever reaches the new target first wins. Or you can allow a player who has passed 1,000 points during the play of the hand, or thinks he has, to announce it by *making a call.* If a player calls, the play of the hand stops, and the points scored thus far in the hand by the caller are totaled. If he's right, and he has passed the post, he wins the game; if he's wrong, he loses.

Pinochle for Three Players

Pinochle for three players (also called Auction Pinochle) brings in a whole different set of factors that you won't find in Pinochle for two — while perhaps reducing the need for careful study of the cards played, which is the characteristic of Pinochle for two. Instead, you have an additional bidding phase of the game, which gives the opportunity for daring and judgment — as well as the opportunity to lose heavily — through overbidding. During the bidding, the players compete for the right to name the trump suit and to become the *declarer.* The declarer takes on the other two players (the *defenders*) and is the only player permitted to score melds at all. As you can see, this change introduces a different feel to the game; with only one person scoring melds, obtaining the right to do so through the bidding is an important element of the game.

Two additional factors make Pinochle for three players intriguing:

✔ The first factor is the existence of the *widow,* some undealt cards that give the declarer the chance to improve his hand by an exchange of his cards. (See the next section for the mechanics of the widow.)

✔ The second factor, if you're playing for stakes, is the existence of the *kitty,* an extra pot of money, which adds an interesting gambling element to the game to further encourage optimistic bidding. If you score the game rather than playing for stakes, play that the first player to get 1,000 points wins the game. I suggest that you don't worry about the kitty until you have mastered the game, but if you really can't wait, see "How the kitty works" in this chapter for the details.

The deal and the widow

Pinochle for three players uses the same 48-card deck as in the two-player game. After the players cut for the deal and arrange their seating according to the cut, the dealer (the player who cut lowest) distributes 45 cards of the deck among the players, three at a time.

After dealing 8 cards to each player, the dealer sets aside three cards face-down as the *widow,* which the declarer takes up as part of his reward for taking the contract. (See "Making a bid for glory" for more information.) In some variations, a card of the widow is turned up at this point to let everyone in on part of the secret. Whoever gets to be declarer takes the widow, shows it to everyone before the bidding, and then throws away three cards face-down from his hand to reduce his hand to the same number of cards as everyone else.

The dealer must redeal if any card is exposed during the deal in any of the hands or in the widow. Similarly, if a player has too many or too few cards, the error can be corrected if it's spotted before the widow is picked up by the declarer. If the error comes to light after that point, the declarer is given his contract if the error is in the defenders' hands, and the declarer loses double the value of his contract if it's his hand that is wrong. (For whatever reason the declarer fails to make his contract, the failure is called *going bete.* Losing a double game is called *double bete.*)

Making a bid for glory

The bidding commences with the *Elder Hand,* the player to the dealer's left, being the first to *speak,* or make a bid. The bid represents the number of points he thinks he can make on the hand if he's allowed to choose the trump suit and then make his melds and score points in the play. (The players make their bids based on melds in their hands and on the high cards they have that will take tricks and score points.)

In some circles, the first player *must* make a bid; different people have their own ideas here, but 250 points is the normal minimum bid that you are allowed to make. The other players then have the option of passing or making a higher bid; every increase in the bidding must be in multiples of 10 points. After two players pass in succession, the bidding ends, with the highest bidder playing the hand against the other two players (the opponents), who play in tandem.

The other two players operate as a single unit. It's two against one — so winning tricks may not be easy for the declarer.

Some people only allow a single round of bidding; this restriction seems too limiting to me. The continuous bidding is more interesting and tactically demanding.

However, it's generally played that after a player passes in an auction, he can't reenter the bidding.

If you play that Elder Hand is permitted to pass, and subsequently all the other players pass, too, throw in the hand and have the next player deal a new hand.

A bid out of turn can be accepted or rejected at the discretion of the player whose turn it is to bid. An insufficient bid may be canceled, in which case no further penalty is incurred, or it may be accepted by the other players, at their discretion.

After the bidding ends, the declarer turns the widow face-up for all to see and takes the cards into his hand. After that, the declarer puts down any melds, using all the cards at his disposal. The declarer is the only player entitled to score melds, and if he doesn't have any melds, he is certainly going to be in trouble! The scoring table for melds is exactly the same as for the two-player version (see "Scoring the melds").

If the players are playing the rule whereby the Elder Hand must bid, then he may be forced to make a call with a wholly unsuitable hand. If this is the case, Elder Hand can concede failure of this contract without looking at the widow. Conceding is in his interest, because if he has a totally unpromising hand, he can limit his losses this way. As soon as the declarer looks at the widow, he loses a larger penalty if he fails to fulfill his contract than he would have lost had he conceded at the beginning. Even so, the declarer still has the option to limit his losses by conceding after viewing the widow.

Specifically, if you concede without looking at the widow and you're playing for money, you simply pay the kitty and not the other players. If you look at the widow and then concede, you pay a single stake to each of the players and to the kitty. Playing out the hand and losing costs you a double stake to everyone. Conversely, a successful bid leads to your being paid a single stake by all the players. And if the declarer makes his bid from his melds or is sufficiently close that he can claim with certainty that he will succeed, the hand doesn't have to be played out.

When bidding, you can classify your bids into three categories:

- ✔ **Safe bids:** Those for which you have the melds in your hand and a near certainty of the points in the play to make your bid.

- ✔ **Overbids:** Bids for which you need specific cards in the widow and a little bit of help from the other players in the play of the cards.

> ✔ **Psychic, or fake, bids:** These bids are designed to push up (or *run up*) the bidding, and you may have no practical chance of success if the second player pulls out of the auction — which may be referred to as *dropping the bidding*. You should limit this last category of bluff bids to the minimum — they become expensive if your bluff is called too often. But acquiring a reputation for experimenting in this way can be helpful; doing so may mean that you win the bidding more cheaply because nobody trusts you to have what you bid.

Melding by the declarer and planning the discards

All the melds that apply in the two-player game are equally available to the declarer in the three-player game. One big difference, however, is that he can put all his melds down at a single turn, rather than having to make the plays individually.

And one minor distinction arises in this form of the game because you can't first score points for a royal marriage and then for a flush (the marriage, which is worth fewer points, doesn't count).

After the declarer scores his melds, he discards (or *buries*) three cards from his hand. Those three discarded cards form part of his total points at the end of the hand, which gives the declarer a fair degree of flexibility to throw away the high-scoring vulnerable counting cards, such as kings and tens, that might be captured by someone else's aces. It may also give him the opportunity to throw away all his cards from a side-suit so as to allow him to trump his opponent's leads and thus generate additional chances to score points. You can't discard anything into the widow that you've already used in a meld.

After he takes the widow, the declarer nominates the trump suit.

Discarding the wrong number of cards from the widow or forgetting to discard costs the offending declarer twice his bid. Burying a card in the widow that you have used in a meld costs you a double game.

In selecting the cards to discard, you should always try to keep as many cards from your two longest suits as you can, while retaining aces in the other suits if necessary. Try to discard from short suits if you can. Throw away 10s, as the most vulnerable high-scoring honor card, if they're unprotected by an ace. All honor cards in short suits — if not utilized in melds —

are prime candidates for discarding. If you reduce your hand to an ace with no other cards in that suit, lead it as soon as you can. Otherwise, you may lose it to someone else leading the other identical ace first.

How the kitty works

The kitty represents an extra player when it comes to paying out or winning bets; it starts with no money in it, and players pay into it, either a single stake or a double stake, whichever is appropriate, whenever they fail in their contracts. They pay a single stake if they abandoned the hand without playing it out, a double stake if they play and fail. If the declarer fulfills a contract, he is paid by all the players, but *not* by the kitty unless the bid is for 350 points or more.

If you're playing for stakes, you should know that five different scoring tables are in use. You can use any of the five scales shown in Table 10-2 to pay off or be paid by others, in respect of your bids (and I have no doubt that many other such tables exist).

Table 10-2	Scoring Tables				
Bid in the range of	*A*	*B*	*C*	*D*	*E*
200-340	1	1	1	3	3
350-390	2	2	2	5	5
400-440	4	4	7	10	10
450-490	6	7	10	15	20
500-540	8	10	13	20	40
550-590	10	13	16	25	80

Look at how this scoring works in practice. A player who declares for 420 might abandon his bid before starting play, if he picks up a hopeless widow — in which case he would pay the value of his bid (somewhere between 4 and 10, depending on the scale in use) to the kitty and the same amount to all the players. Or he might play out the hand and succeed in his bid, collecting the same amount from everyone, including the kitty.

Playing out the hand and failing to score enough points leads to a double payout to everyone, including the kitty.

If the kitty runs out of money, everyone except the declarer contributes an equal amount to build it up again.

Winning — in spades

According to some, the scoring system rewards a declaration in all suits equally, but these folks are in the minority. The spades and hearts are generally accepted to be worth more than clubs and diamonds. In fact, the mainstream position is to value all contracts in spades as worth double the standard amounts; that means twice the payout and forfeit. For example, if you go for a bid of 300 and chose spades as the trump suit, you stand to lose twice as much as you would if you chose clubs as the trump suit.

Some people play that hearts are worth triple the norm; this change has to be specifically agreed to in advance. Even if the declarer had intended to bid in spades, he can make a concession after looking at the widow and just concede the single stake to the other hands and the kitty, because he can concede in clubs or diamonds.

This quirk of scoring gives the declarer the option to intend to contract in spades (and even more so in hearts, if you play the triple-score rule) on more marginal hands, because he can concede a single game on an unsuitable pick-up but play a double game with the right widow. The odds, therefore, move in the gambler's favor to win the bidding and hope for good news in the form of nice cards in the widow.

The play of the cards

Because all the cards in the deck are used and scored, 240 points are up for grabs during the play of the cards. And because the last trick scores an additional 10 points, 250 points are at stake on every hand in the play.

Keep in mind that the points in the widow count for the declarer, so they aren't taken out of play. Even though the cards that the declarer discarded don't feature in the play at all, they still count for him.

Just as in the two-player game, when two equal cards appear on the same trick, the first one put down outranks the second one.

Generally, the declarer leads to the first trick.

The rules of following suit are as follows:

- ✔ You can lead anything you like at any time.

- ✔ If you can follow suit, you must do so; if you're out of the suit led, you must play a trump if you can.

- ✔ If a trump is led, you must play a higher trump card to the trick if you can. This rule applies to both the second and third player. If the player doesn't have a higher trump card, she can play any trump card that she likes.

The rules about overtrumping, when the first hand leads a suit of which both the second and third hands have no cards, are conflicting. The second hand must trump, of course. Some play that the third hand must overtrump if he can, but the most standard position that I can ascertain is that the third hand must play a trump card but doesn't have to overtrump.

This particular rule about following in the trump suit is very useful to the declarer, who can, for example, hope to force someone into playing two high trump cards by leading a middle card in the trump suit.

The defense tries to look for chances to weaken the declarer's trump holding early if they can, if they can infer that he doesn't have many high trump cards. (They may be able to deduce this information from his decision whether or not to play on the trump suit early.)

One defender can try to throw high-scoring cards onto his defending partner's trick (or *smear* the trick). By doing so, he gives points to his partner and prevents the declarer from scoring the points.

Pretty much any error by the declarer (failing to follow suit or failing to trump a plain suit when able to do so) costs him a double game. A *revoke* (not playing a card in the suit led) by a defender costs a single game. You have the opportunity to correct a revoke until the start of the next trick.

A lead out of turn by the declarer can be accepted by the defenders if they want.

When playing out a hand as the declarer, bear in mind that you don't get any bonus awards for making more points than your bid. If you just concentrate on making good your bid whenever it's possible to do so, you will do very well. You need to focus on the cards from two angles:

- ✔ Try to remember how many trump cards and aces have gone, just as in the two-player game.

- ✔ Try to keep a rough count on how many points each side has scored. Keeping count tells you how much more you require for your bid and maybe indicates what you need to do to make the hand.

Preparing a bidding strategy

When you plan how much to bid, you can take a calculated risk on getting some help from the widow — but don't expect too much help.

With a hand such as the one in Figure 10-3, you have three useful cards that you could pick up: one in spades, one in hearts, and one in diamonds to complete a flush (AKQJ10). The ♠A would make four aces as well, but you can't count that possibility twice. In addition, either the ♣Q or ♣J would give you a set of queens or jacks. If you need one of three cards to improve your hand, you're a slight underdog to draw it from the widow.

Figure 10-3:
Hoping to
pick up the
right card.

The biggest mistake to make in bidding is to hope or assume that you will pick up a useful card from the widow. Keep in mind that an average of 20 to 30 points is what you should assume to be coming your way. You can hope to use the widow to improve your hand a little in the play, but not to make an additional meld.

As a general strategy in estimating how many points you will win, assume that for every losing card you have, the opponents are able to dispose of the two highest outstanding cards in the suit on that trick. So, for example, if you start the hand with the ♥10J9 and you throw the 10 into the widow, you should assume that the jack and 9 will attract four of the remaining five high cards (the aces, 10s, and kings) onto them.

The ability to win the last trick is similarly vital; because of the defenders' desire to save up their high-scoring cards for a trick won by their side, you can assume that the last trick (and, to a certain extent, the one before that) will be critical in most hands, containing quite a few high cards. If you win those tricks, you'll be in good shape to make your contract.

When to give up without a struggle

The question of whether to concede the hand when the widow hasn't proved especially useful is a very tough one. Keep in mind that concession involves giving up a single stake to all; playing and losing requires payment of a double stake. This principle applies whether you're playing for points or for money.

Generally speaking, when you're faced with a decision as to whether to play out the hand or concede, you need to have only one chance in three (or better) of succeeding to make it worthwhile to play out the hand. But if you're a better player than your opponent (and how could that not be the case after reading this book?), you might accept on slightly worse odds than that.

In the play, consider how you want the missing cards to be distributed so that you can make your bid good. Remember that if you're missing an even number of cards, the suit figures not to split for you (except for the 1-1 split, which is even money). If you're missing an odd number of cards, a suit will split as evenly as possible — 3-2 or 2-1 most of the time. You don't need higher mathematics at this point in your Pinochle career!

The game ends when one player wins 1,000 points. If you're playing for stakes, score after each hand and play until one player gets short on money or until you've played a predetermined number of hands.

Partnership Auction Pinochle

In the preceding two sections, I take you on a tour of variations of Pinochle where one player is pitted against the rest of the field. However, in Partnership Auction Pinochle, you get a chance to look at the final refinement. This version is a partnership game, one pair against another.

The game is played with the same 48-card deck used in the two- and three-player versions. Partners sit opposite each other, and you play the game either with set partnerships, in which case the players simply cut for the deal at the start of the session, or with changing partnerships, in which case you cut for the deal and positions at the start of each game. Everybody cuts the deck, with the two players drawing the highest cards taking on the players who draw the two lowest cards. The high-card team gets its choice of seats and deals the first hand.

The game is played to either 1,000 or 1,500 points; the first team to that score wins. *Counting down* is permitted — you can keep a running total of points scored during the hand and claim a victory as soon as your total goes over the limit. A false claim loses the game. If you aren't playing this rule and both teams go over the winning post on the same hand, some play that the declaring side wins; some play to a score 250 points beyond the winning post — 1,250 or 1,750, as the case may be.

The deal and the bidding

The dealer normally shuffles the deck and offers it to the opponent on his right to cut. Everyone receives a 12-card hand, dealt out in threes or fours.

When the deal is complete, the players, starting with the Elder Hand (the player to the dealer's left), have the option of bidding or passing until three players pass in a row; at that point, one player has bought the contract, and then he and his partner must make good the promise or pay the consequences.

Some people play that everyone is permitted only one bid — which, to my mind, destroys the competitive nature of the auction. This variation is known as Firehouse Pinochle.

When playing with a partner, the consequence of doing something wrong in the bidding is potentially more severe because of the fact that, in the process, you give your partner erroneous information about your hand. A bid made when it isn't your turn to speak is canceled, and it silences both members of the partnership for the whole bidding. Any bid that isn't as high as an earlier call must be increased until it's the highest call, and that, similarly, silences the bidder's partner for the whole auction.

Bids start at 200 or 250 points minimum and must increase in multiples of 10. After a player passes, he is barred from bidding again.

The mode of bidding described in the preceding paragraphs is relatively simplistic. The partner of a hand that passes has no idea whether his colleague is able to offer anything useful in the melding or play. To that end, an additional bid is permitted in some variations at the first turn of any player to speak. He may bid "Pass with help," which simply indicates that although he can't compete at the rarefied level that the bidding has already reached, he has some cards that may be helpful eventually.

The standard rules on misdeals apply concerning exposed cards or the wrong number of cards dealt out. In addition, some groups play the variation that a player with five or more 9s may call for a misdeal.

The melding phase of the hand

After the bidding ends, the players can claim their melds; each player claims points based on his own hand, which he then adds to his partner's points to form the partnership's total score. Obviously, this aspect of the game differs significantly from the three-player game, where only the declarer is allowed to meld and has the assistance of the widow.

The fact that all four players may score their sequences dramatically reduces the declarer's edge in the melding. He not only has no widow, but he also has to let the other players score up. However, the choice of the trump suit at least does preserve an edge for the declaring side — keep in mind that flushes only count in the trump suit. Of course, the declarer's partner is one of the three others involved, but he's outnumbered two to one.

You can use any card more than once, as long you use the card in a separate category of scoring. Each player can only use the cards in his own hand, of course, and can't co-opt his partner's cards.

Just as in the other versions of Pinochle in this chapter, after the melds are counted, the players pick up the cards and put them back in their hands before starting the play of the cards. Make sure that you remember what the declarer melded if you're a defender; track down his losing cards so that you can take full advantage of them by leading your high cards in suits where you know that he will have to follow suit.

Some people require that the declarer must make a minimum meld of at least a royal marriage, or 40 points.

If you're more than 250 points short of your bid before the play starts, you automatically *go set,* and you don't have to play out the hand. You lose the value of your bid, whatever that may be.

To determine how high you should bid, assume that you get no help from your partner and then compare that score with what might happen if you were facing a perfect hand. Bid somewhere closer to the lower level.

Playing the cards

The full 250 points are at stake in the play of the cards, as in all variations of Pinochle: 240 for the scoring cards and 10 points for the last trick.

Elder Hand, the player to the dealer's left, leads to the first trick, regardless of who the declarer is. The rules for following suit in three-handed Pinochle apply here, too — following suit is mandatory, and you must try to win the trick if the lead is a trump card. If you can't follow suit, you must play a trump card, and you must overtrump if you can.

The official sources can't come to an agreement as to what happens if you can't follow suit to a plain-card lead, but you can't overtrump a trump that's already played. My belief is that you must play a lower trump. These rules about trumping apply even if the trick is being won by your partner at the point you have to play. Whoever wins the trick leads to the next one, and so on.

Just as in the other variations of Pinochle, the first of two identical cards beats the second one.

The rules about wrongly played cards are quite in line with Auction Pinochle for three players. However, the fact that the game is a partnership one increases the penalties. For example, if you expose a card during the bidding, your partner is barred from bidding. In addition, the exposed card must be played at the offender's first turn. The nonoffenders may also be allowed to prohibit or demand the lead of that suit if the card isn't played on the first trick.

Prizes and penalties

By comparison to the three-player game, the scoring for Partnership Auction Pinochle is relatively sedate — no bonuses for spades, hearts, or the like; and no double penalties.

An unsuccessful declarer scores nothing on the hand for melds or tricks and simply loses the value of his bid. A successful declarer scores as many points as he took on the hand; in other words, scoring more points than you bid does count for something at this game. In turn, the policy of always ensuring your contract, which applies at the three-player game, has to be somewhat revised, because you may be sacrificing valuable additional points by a policy of caution in the play.

The defenders always score exactly what they win in tricks and melds on the hand *unless* they fail to win a single trick in the play — in which case they score nothing, nada, zip, and zilch. Take your pick — it all comes back to the same round zero.

The ability to win the lead is vital; the leader dictates the direction in which the hand must go. Always try to win the lead if you can see how you want the play to proceed. Similarly, the ability to lead your long suits and force out your opponents' trump cards is very important. Particularly if you don't have all that many trump cards, don't lead losing trump cards. Try to turn your side-suit cards into winners instead, so as to force out your rival's trump cards.

Chapter 11

Piquet

In This Chapter

▶ Understanding the basic concepts of Piquet

▶ Mastering the strategy of the discards and the play

*P*iquet is one of the most interesting and challenging games for two players. It combines a number of features that all the best games have — the luck of the cards, skill in improving your hand by the change of cards, and some subtle tactics in the play of the cards.

To play Piquet, all you require is the following:

✔ **Two players**

✔ **A standard deck of 52 cards:** You just need the aces through the 7s in each suit, making a 32-card deck.

✔ **A pencil and paper for scoring**

Piqueting Your Interest

Piquet consists of a fixed number of deals, six in all, also referred to as a *partie* (pronounced as in "Let's party!"). Whoever scores the most points in total during the partie wins.

You deal 12 cards to each player and try to improve the hand by a single change of some of the cards. You then score points in two phases: the declaration and the play.

All suits are of equivalent rank during the play. Within the suits, aces are high.

During the play, one player plays a card, and the other player must play a card in that suit if he can; he doesn't have to try beat his opponent's card if he doesn't want to. Whoever plays the higher card in the suit led collects both cards and wins the *trick*.

To score points, you make sequences in the declaration phase of the game, discussed in more detail later, and then win tricks in the play. The cards that make up the tricks are irrelevant in the play — it's the number of tricks you win that counts. One player writes down the scores for both players, but during the play, each player keeps a running score out loud of the points he has accumulated on the hand, and at the end of the hand the scorer simply writes down the total figure for that hand and updates the cumulative score.

During the declaration, you have three separate areas under which you can score points; during the play, winning tricks and simply leading to a trick scores you points. Additionally, taking more than half of the 12 tricks available — or better still, winning them all — adds to your score.

You need to keep precisely aware of how you and your opponent are doing, particularly if the match is close or if one of the players is approaching 100 points as the partie winds down. In addition to winning or losing the game, passing 100 is a very significant move and is known as *crossing the Rubicon* (see "Crossing the Rubicon" for more information).

The target is to win, naturally, by scoring more points than the other player, but if you can't do that, some defeats are more painful than others. A simple victory, if both players have scored more than 100 points, is worth 100 points plus the difference to the winner. So if I score 124 and my opponent scores 111, then I win 113 points, which is the difference plus 100 points.

However, if the loser of the game fails to score more than 100 points, the defeat becomes much more expensive. In that situation, the winner combines his score and the loser's score, plus an additional 100 points. The issue of whether you or your opponent can cross the Rubicon generates some of the more entertaining tactical battles in the game.

Playing the Game

Piquet involves many factors and two distinct phases. Have no fear — although Piquet seems a bit complicated on the surface, you can get comfortable with the game by reading this section.

Dealing the cards

The deal alternates between the players; before the first hand, the players cut the cards. Whoever cuts the highest card can choose whether or not he deals the first hand.

Piquet's rich roots

Piquet is an old, established game. It's a tribute to the subtlety of Piquet's rules of bidding and play that it has survived virtually unscathed for about 500 years.

Piquet most likely originated in either Spain or France, but no one can say for sure. The game has been played since the end of the 15th century, and it makes an appearance in literature in 1534 in a book by Rabelais, *Gargantua and Pantagruel*. In addition, Cardano's book on games of chance, a treatise on the mathematics of gambling games written in 1564, deals with Piquet at some length.

Piquet is a French word, but it's a faux pas to give it the French pronunciation — except in France. The game is pronounced *pick it*. It was originally known as *Cent* in England, because that's French for 100, a significant number in the original version of the game, which was pronounced *Saint*. Saint, in turn, became anglicized to *Sand*, another name for the game, but the name Piquet is absolutely standard now.

The game may have anglicized its name, but the French connection lives on happily enough. More than enough French vocabulary remains in the game to keep even the strongest Francophile happy.

 Deciding whether to deal or not is a no-brainer, because you don't want to end up dealing the final hand. Dealing a hand puts you on the defensive, and you want every advantage on the last hand. So whoever wins the cut automatically elects to deal the first hand, in order to not deal the final one.

The dealer shuffles the 32 cards and then deals 12 cards to each player, leaving the eight remaining cards face-down in the middle of the table. The cards in the middle of the table are called the *talon* (a fancy word for the stock). The dealer frequently splits the talon into piles of five and three cards to facilitate the play later in the game.

Traditionally, the hands are dealt out in packets of three and two, and sticklers for tradition will tell you to follow the same pattern in all your deals in the partie. As far as I'm concerned, if each player finishes up with 12 cards, that ought to be good enough for anyone.

The nondealer is referred to as *Elder Hand,* and the dealer is *Younger Hand.*

Claiming Carte Blanche

After the deal, the players pick up and sort their cards. If either player has a hand with no *court cards* (kings, queens, or jacks), she has a special hand called a *Carte Blanche.* She shows her hand briefly to her opponent (to prove that she has such a hand) while saying "Carte Blanche," and claims 10 points.

You should claim these 10 points, despite the inevitable giving away of information as you show your cards, because a hand with no court cards is likely to be so poor that getting 10 points quickly helps. Claiming Carte Blanche also prevents your opponent from getting a huge score on the hand. As you soon see, if your opponent can score more than 30 points without your registering anything, good things happen to him — and correspondingly bad things happen to you. By notching up 10 points quickly, you eliminate that possibility.

Only one hand can claim Carte Blanche, and it doesn't happen very often. The Elder Hand makes the claim before changing his cards. If it's Younger Hand who has the claim, she should wait until after Elder Hand has exchanged his cards before saying anything. (See "Exchanging Elder Hand's cards" and "Exchanging Younger Hand's cards" in this chapter for the details on that phase of the game.)

When you show your hand to your opponent, simply count out the cards face-up one by one. You don't have to give your opponent a chance to study and remember your hand.

Exchanging Elder Hand's cards

Elder Hand is first to take advantage of the opportunity to change his cards. His objective is to collect his cards into as many point-scoring combinations as he can. (See "Scoring the declaration phase" for more information about the point-scoring combinations.)

He puts a number of his cards face-down on the table and takes from the talon (stock) an equivalent number of cards. He must exchange at least one card from his hand with the talon and can exchange up to a maximum of five cards. The question of which and how many cards to throw is critical to the player's chances of success or failure.

You're trying to make a hand with long suits, long sequences in a suit, and also to have as many aces, kings, queens, and jacks as possible. It isn't easy to manage all those tasks! You should exchange the maximum of five cards unless you already have a hand that can beat your opponent for sure under most or all of these categories. While improving your hand, you want to prevent your opponent from improving his own collection by depriving him of as many cards as possible with which to do that, which means changing the maximum number of cards yourself. Nonetheless, don't throw away good holdings just to exchange more cards and prevent your rival from changing cards. The question of how many cards to change on a good hand can sometimes be a very awkward one, but when in doubt, change the maximum.

Elder Hand looks at his 12 cards and determines that he wants to go after certain suits or certain high cards in the pick-up. If he aims to pick up one of two cards (such as the ♦A or ♦10), the odds on his drawing one of the two cards that he needs are pretty favorable. Younger Hand has a much smaller chance of getting what she needs, because she usually has only three cards from which to draw, unlike Elder Hand's five cards.

Elder Hand must go flat out for the attack unless strategic considerations suggest that he's better advised to limit his opponent — to try to keep her under 100 points, for example. Normally Elder Hand discards his short suits completely unless he has sets of honor cards (which may be worth points) to preserve. So in the case of the cards in Figure 11-1, Elder Hand should keep his hearts intact and exchange the spades and diamonds.

Figure 11-1:
Keeping the long suits and exchanging the short suits.

The objective of the exchange is to try to get points for building up long suits and making sequences, as well as improving your tally of high cards for the play. In Figure 11-1, keeping the clubs is as likely to develop a long suit as keeping spades, and the chances of developing a sequence in clubs is much better because the ♣Q ♣J ♣10 is already a sequence.

With the cards in Figure 11-2, I would keep the four hearts and the three kings and hope that something nice happens. The hand has little obvious promise, but it would improve dramatically if you pick up some more hearts. More importantly, you have little else to try for!

Figure 11-2:
No long suits, but some nice sets.

Elder Hand tries to keep at least one long suit in his hand and hopes that the five cards he picks up are in the suits that he has kept. Keeping high honor cards with no long suit is rare, although some hands are so otherwise unpromising that this approach is reasonable. With the cards shown in Figure 11-3, keeping the aces, kings, and queens seems like the best option, because the chances of building anything out of the club suit look slim.

Figure 11-3:
Nothing but high cards — but plenty of them!

You decide to retain ♠A♠K, ♥A♥Q, ♦K♦Q, and ♣A and see what happens. But who's to say whether the pick-up includes ♦J ♦10 ♦9 or ♣K ♣Q ♣J? In one case, your selection is brilliant, because you end up with a five-card sequence in diamonds; in the other case, it's absurd — you could have had seven clubs, but you end up with only four. That's life!

Exchanging Younger Hand's cards

Younger Hand must also exchange at least one card, up to a maximum of five cards. However, the exchange is limited by the number of cards left in the talon, which is typically three after Elder Hand takes his five cards. Just as Elder Hand does, Younger Hand puts her cards face-down in the center of the table and then takes an equivalent number of cards from the talon.

Younger Hand should adopt a primarily defensive strategy unless her hand is clearly "good against the cards" — that is, she knows that she holds a winning hand because no matter what's in her opponent's hand, she has a better long suit, sequence, or even more high cards. In particular, she must try to ensure that even if she does lose the hand (and bear in mind that Elder Hand is favored to win because he gets to exchange more cards and also leads to the first trick), she doesn't lose too badly.

Younger Hand tries to prevent her opponent from taking all the tricks in the play, which may involve keeping some apparently unimportant cards in her own shorter suits. For example, with the cards in Figure 11-4, as Younger Hand you can justifiably be concerned that your opponent might get a decent pick-up and be in a position to take all the tricks by playing on hearts and clubs. (You know that your opponent is well-heeled in hearts and clubs because you don't hold any of those cards in your hand.) To prevent this scenario from happening, you may give up on the spades and trade in ♠Q ♠10 ♠7 to try to retain all your cards in hearts and clubs.

Figure 11-4:
Fighting a
defensive
campaign
by keeping
your short
suits.

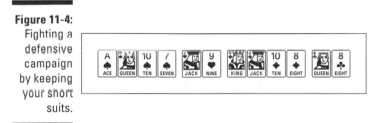

Elder Hand may turn out to have the cards in Figure 11-5. The question mark
represents an unknown card that doesn't become apparent until the very
end of the play. The unknown card may be in either of the two locations you
see in the figure.

Figure 11-5:
Eleven of
the cards
are soon
known, but
what is the
12th card?

If you throw your hearts away before picking up the ♥Q, you have a nasty
guess at the eleventh trick as to which card to keep for the last trick. Save
yourself the problem and keep the ♥J and ♥9 so that picking up either the
♥Q or ♥K leaves you well placed to take at least one trick in the suit.

Don't assume as Younger Hand that your opponent will get anything but the
best possible combination you can envision from the original 12 cards you
hold before the pick-up. Unless your hand is an automatic win, you should
follow a defensive approach and try to ensure that nothing too terrible
happens to you on the hand, even if, in doing so, you occasionally miss the
opportunity for putting together a good score as Younger Hand.

Announcing your intentions

If either player intends to exchange fewer cards than the permitted maximum (five cards for Elder Hand and three cards for Younger Hand), he
should make the announcement before starting to pick up from the talon.

You're permitted to keep your discards by your side, and you may consult them during the play of the hand to try to work out your opponent's hand.

If Elder Hand intends to take fewer than his maximum of five cards, he is permitted to look at the remainder of the five cards he could have taken, without showing those cards to his opponent. Younger Hand then has a larger number of cards that she can exchange, of course, but those cards that her opponent has seen are the first ones that she must pick up.

Elder Hand may elect to take fewer than five cards if his hand is really good to begin with. For example, if Elder Hand has the hand in Figure 11-6, he would keep his six hearts and two aces. He knows that his run of six is the longest suit and best sequence, and if he keeps his three aces, it will be the best three of a kind that either player can get. To preserve his hand, he should exchange only four cards.

Figure 11-6:
Knowing a good thing when you see one: exchanging fewer than five cards.

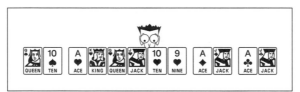

If Younger Hand doesn't want to take her maximum permitted number of cards, then she can turn over the balance of the cards face-up so that both players can see them, or she can leave them face-down so that neither player gets to see the cards.

Younger Hand should leave the cards face-down if she has thrown away all the cards from one suit; concealing such an unwanted suit is usually beneficial.

Scoring the declaration phase

After both sides exchange cards, the players must tally up their scores from the three areas of the declaration. In each of these categories, Elder Hand speaks first, and Younger Hand describes her hand only if she wants to contest the claim.

You may not wish to claim any of these bonuses if you feel that doing so may give your opponent too much information about your hand. After the declaration, you must compete for winning tricks, and claiming these bonuses may help your opponent form a good strategy for taking tricks away from you.

Claiming length (the Point)

Whoever has the longest suit scores as many points as the length of that suit. For example, a suit with four cards in it scores 4 points. The suit must have at least four cards in it; in practice, Elder Hand always has a suit of at least four cards. This suit-length award is called the *Point*.

If Elder Hand wants to claim this bonus — all such claims are optional — he says "Point of four," or "five," or whatever is appropriate.

Younger Hand can respond in one of three ways, depending on the nature of her hand. She can concede the points to her opponent by saying "Good," or she can indicate that she has a longer suit than Elder Hand by saying "Not good." Or she can say that she has a suit of equal length by saying "How many?" or "Making?"

If Younger Hand contests the claim with an equal length suit, both players add up the value of their cards. They count the face value of the card for a 7, 8, 9, and 10 and count 10 for a court card and 11 for an ace. Whoever has the higher value suit wins and gets the points.

For example, say that both players have a five-card suit. Elder Hand has ♠A ♠Q ♠J ♠10 ♠9 and Younger Hand has ♣K ♣Q ♣J ♣10 ♣7. Elder Hand adds up his cards; 11 + 10 + 10 + 10 + 9 = 50. He calls out that number, and Younger Hand, who only has 47, says "Good" without specifying her total. If the suits were the other way around, Elder Hand would call 47 (10 + 10 + 10 + 10 + 7) and Younger Hand would say "Not good; I have 50."

After the first category is out of the way, Elder Hand moves onto the second scoring opportunity, the Sequence.

Claiming runs (the Sequence)

You can also score points for the longest consecutive run of cards in a single suit, known as the *Sequence*. You can only count a sequence if it's three cards or more, such as ♦9 ♦8 ♦7. Therefore, unlike the Point, not every hand features a sequence, because you don't always have a run of three or more cards.

Elder Hand, if he wants to do so, says "Run (or Sequence) of three," or "six," or "seven" as appropriate.

Although the terminology in this game is elegant, calling things precisely by their proper names isn't essential. However, if you want to do so, the correct names for the sequences and their point values are as follows:

- ✔ Sequences of three are called *tierces* (sounds like *tears*) and are worth 3 points.

- ✔ Sequences of four are called *quarts* (rhymes with *sorts*) and are worth 4 points.

- ✔ Sequences of five are called *quints* (rhymes with *mints*) and are worth 15 points.

- ✔ Sequences of six are called *sixieme* (pronounced *sissy aim*) and are worth 16 points.

- ✔ Sequences of seven are called *septieme* (rhymes with *Betty name*) and are worth 17 points.

- ✔ Sequences of eight are called *huitieme* (sounds like *wheaty aim*) and are worth 18 points.

As you can see, the jump in value from the run of four to the run of five has a potentially significant impact on one's strategy in discarding and picking up. The need to improve a run of four to one of five is a pressing one.

In response to Elder Hand's call, Younger Hand has the identical three options as on the Point (refer to "Claiming length [the Point]" in this chapter). She can concede, claim victory, or compete as to the rank of the sequence by asking "How high?" or "Starting from which card?" (meaning "What is the highest card in the sequence?").

Of course, because Younger Hand can see enough of the picture from her own 12 cards (she is aware of which suit her opponent could possibly have a run in), she probably knows in advance exactly which sequence of five cards her opponent has, especially after Elder Hand's announcement of his point length. Therefore, unless Younger Hand expects to win the challenge, she doesn't need to give away information about her own hand by letting Elder Hand know that she has kept the cards that give her an equivalent length of sequence.

Whoever wins the battle of the sequences can claim any subsidiary runs (shorter sequences of at least three cards) that he has — if he wants to. Again, discretion can be the better part of valor here, and you should only claim these subsidiary runs if you believe that doing so will have no negative impact on your ability to win tricks in the play of the cards.

Holdings of three or four of a kind

After the Point and the Sequence are scored, Elder Hand looks to score points from holding three or four of a kind. Here, again, you have a minimum requirement, and this time you not only need to have a set of three, but it also has to be a set of honor cards — of 10s and higher. Nines, 8s, and 7s don't count.

The possible sets have the following names:

> ✔ Sets of three are called *Trios* (sounds like *tree-os*)and are worth 3 points.
>
> ✔ Sets of four are called *Quatorzes* (sounds like *quat-ors*) and are worth 14 points.

Your strategy for building a Quatorze may differ depending on your hand. If you have a sequence of five, it's clearly possible that your opponent has an equivalent sequence. However, a Trio of aces can't be matched by him; he may do *better,* with four kings, for example, but he can't equal it. You may not want to bother improving a Trio, for example, if you know that your opponent can't beat your Trio whatever he does, as happens if you have three aces and one of each of the other court cards.

Normally, you want to claim any other scoring Trios or Quatorzes you may have if you win the main battle. Very occasionally, you may hide a detail of your hand for devious ulterior motives — to give yourself an extra chance to take seven tricks, or maybe to take all 12 tricks.

If your opponent claims a Trio, some versions of the rules permit you to ask which honor card is missing from the set. As you can see, this issue is quite key, because whichever honor is missing is likely to be a suit that your opponent has discarded from, and that suit is thus a weak link in his hand. So finding out the answer can be very helpful in planning the best line of attack in the play. I think the better rule is not to permit such questions.

Repique and Pique: Piling on the agony

If either hand scores 30 points in the declaration phase of the game, that player achieves a *Repique* and scores an additional 60-point bonus.

If Elder Hand manages to reach 30 points in the play before Younger Hand scores at all, this is called a *Pique,* and it's worth 30 points to him.

In Figure 11-7, Elder Hand calls out his scores before Younger Hand, but the latter still manages a Repique.

Elder Hand calls "Point of five" by virtue of his spade suit. He is more hurt than surprised to hear Younger Hand ask how many his Point is worth (implying that she, too, has a Point of five). When Elder hand adds up his spades to 48, he hears Younger Hand say "Not good," because her heart suit adds up to 49. Elder Hand passes on the sequences, because he knows that Younger Hand has a run of five in hearts. Elder Hand instead says "Quatorze of aces and Trio of queens for 17."

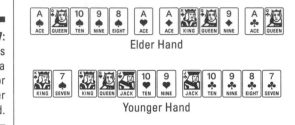

Figure 11-7:
Youth wins
out: a
triumph for
the Younger
Hand.

Elder Hand

Younger Hand

Elder Hand leads the ♦A to the first trick and keeps his running score at 18. He hopes that he has avoided a major tragedy, but Younger Hand has a nasty surprise for him. She calls out "Point of five for 5" (the heart suit), "Quint for 15 makes 20" (the heart sequence), "and a second Quint for 15" (the sequence in clubs) "makes 35 — 95 in total" (because of the 60-point bonus for scoring 30 points in the declaration phase).

The fact that Elder Hand called out his points first didn't prevent Younger Hand from obtaining a Repique, because the sequences are registered before the Trios, Quatorzes, and other sets.

If you're the Younger Hand and are concerned about the Pique because your opponent figures to score heavily in sets, preserving your low sequences, even a 789, in the hope that your opponent has no runs at all sometimes proves wise.

Note that the Pique and Repique are relatively rare. The average score off a hand is about 25 for Elder Hand and 15 for Younger Hand.

Playing and scoring the cards

After scoring the declaration phase, the play of the cards begins. The object here is simply to win as many tricks as possible.

In Piquet, whoever plays the higher card in the suit led (the suit of the first card played) wins the trick. Players must *follow suit* (play a card in the suit led) if they can; otherwise, they can *discard* (or throw away) whatever they want. The winner of each trick leads to the next one. When a trick is finished, it's turned face-down and kept in front of the player who won the trick.

Some play that the tricks are kept face-up and may be consulted during the play. A good player should be able to remember all the relevant cards, but you may need to consult your cards from time to time to jog your memory.

During the play, Elder Hand is usually on the offensive, for a few reasons. He gets to lead to the first trick and thus can register a point. After he has done that, Younger Hand can't register the Pique (Elder Hand scores a Pique when he gets to 30 points before his opponent scores at all). The first lead is also a vital advantage in the play of the cards because he can lead his long suit and create winners for himself in the suit. Because he could also exchange five cards (while his opponent could only exchange three), he usually has the better hand. Younger Hand frequently sacrifices her long suits in the exchange in order to set up a better defense for herself, which also means that Elder Hand is likely to have control in the play.

When in doubt, play the card you're known to hold. If you can follow suit with the ♣K or ♣Q but have claimed three kings in the declaration, let go of the king first, because your opponent knows that you hold it. Conversely, remember what your opponent claimed for sequences and Trios in the declaration phase, too, and try to reconstruct his hand from that.

Each player has 12 cards, so 12 tricks are up for grabs. The play of the hand comes to one of three endings, depending on how many tricks go to each player:

- ✔ **A draw:** Each side takes its trick score — keep reading for more information on trick scores.

- ✔ **A win for one side:** That player gets an additional 10 points added to the trick score.

- ✔ **A *capot* (sounds like *cap-o*) or *blitz* (sounds like *blits*):** One side takes all the tricks, which is worth 40 points (instead of the 10 points for the win), plus the trick score.

After the cards are played, the reckoning of the trick score begins:

- ✔ You get 1 point for leading to each trick.

- ✔ If the second player wins that trick, he gets a point, too. Each side, therefore, gets one point on the trick if the player who plays second to the trick wins it.

- ✔ You get an additional 1-point bonus for winning the last trick. Occasionally, you may aim to keep a good card to the very end to win the last trick.

    Some people make the last trick worth 10 points, which certainly has a significant impact on the play of the cards.

At the end of each hand, each player records his score for the hand, adding the scores for each hand as play progresses.

Crossing the Rubicon

When the players reach the last pair of hands (you play six hands in all), during which each player is Elder Hand once and Younger Hand once, some of the most interesting tactical concerns come up. Some issues arise when one hand is trying to reach a total of 100 points, or to *cross the Rubicon* — or, alternatively, is trying to prevent his opponent from doing so. (Refer to "Piqueting your Interests" for the details on how crossing the Rubicon can impact the final score of the game.)

Sometimes you have to accept the fact that you aren't going to manage to cross the Rubicon and reach 100 points, and you realize that any points you do earn go to your opponent — hardly a recipe for wanting to work hard to collect scores. In such a case, you should avoid registering unnecessary points in the declaration phase by calling combinations equal to your opponent's claims for the Point and Sequence (but not for the sets, of course), which you can do even if your combination is better than his.

In Figure 11-8, you see the first of the last two hands of a partie, with both players going into the pair of hands on a score of 70 points. The first hand is likely to be played without any special tactical issues arising; the second may be influenced by the precise score in the match and who is closer to 100 points.

Figure 11-8: West wants to improve his hand by going for spades and aces.	A♠ Q♠ 10♠ 8♠ K♥ 9♥ 7♥ K♦ Q♦ 9♦ J♣ 10♣ West Elder Hand East Younger Hand K♠ 9♠ A♥ Q♥ 8♥ J♦ 10♦ 7♦ A♣ Q♣ 9♣ 8♣

In the exchange, Elder Hand discards his low hearts and diamonds and his two clubs and picks up a little help. East throws his diamonds away and gets very little. The new hands are shown in Figure 11-9.

West claims a Point of six, for his six-card spade suit. East says "Good." West also has a run of three, and East, with her ♥Q ♥J ♥10 asks, "How high?" West says "From the ace," and East concedes. West then claims a second run of three, making his total 12 points. Three kings give West 15 points, and he starts by leading the ♦A, calling out his total of 16 as he does.

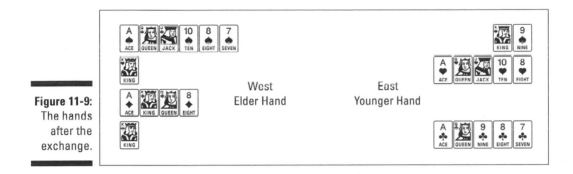

Figure 11-9:
The hands
after the
exchange.

West
Elder Hand

East
Younger Hand

When East throws a club away, West plays three more diamonds and collects another three clubs from East, making his total 19. West has taken the first four tricks and wants to get seven, or at the very least six tricks, to avoid giving his opponent 10 points for taking most of the cards.

At this point, you might think that West has few options other than leading the ♠A and hoping for the best, followed by leading a second spade, but that isn't the right play. East's discard of clubs at the first trick indicates for certain that she threw three diamonds away in the card exchange; with only three discards, how else could she have discarded so as to leave herself with no diamonds at the first trick? She must have thrown her three diamonds away, and thus West knows every card in his opponent's hand.

East started the play with five hearts, five clubs, and two spades, and now she's down to the bare ♣A. Thus West plays a club now, at which point he has a score of 20, and East plays her ace to take the trick, her first point. She leads her five winning hearts to get to 6 points and then leads a spade at the end. West takes the last two tricks for a final score of 23-7, West. Because the tricks were split six-all, no one gets the 10 points for taking the majority of the cards.

So West leads 93-77 going into the final hand. West is only slightly concerned about his own ability to cross the Rubicon and is more concerned about winning. At the same time, he wants to try to prevent East from crossing the Rubicon if he can. East is equally worried about all the issues, but winning the game comes first.

The final deal is shown in Figure 11-10. East has an awkward and rather uninspiring hand. It seems right to keep the spades and one top card in each of the suits. The chance of the sequence in spades is her most promising prospect of collecting a decent hand. It also looks right to keep the ♣Q, not the ♣K, because she might get four queens that way.

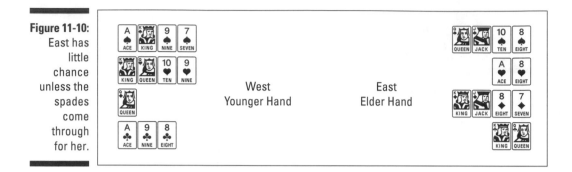

Figure 11-10: East has little chance unless the spades come through for her.

West wants to win and hold East back in equal doses. Therefore, it seems logical to throw the low clubs and the ♠7. The alternative is to change only the clubs, but a third chance at drawing the ♥J seems a very fair investment.

After the exchange, the new positions are shown in Figure 11-11 — bad news in a way for both players, but especially East, who needed something nice to happen and didn't get it.

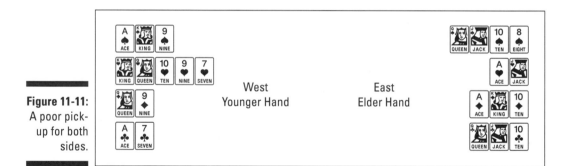

Figure 11-11: A poor pick-up for both sides.

Going into the scoring, the score is 93-77 in favor of West. East claims a Point of four, but it's no good because West has five hearts. The loss of the Point is really bad news from East's perspective, because she now knows that her opponent has five good hearts. East can collect 3 points for her sequence in spades and 3 more points for three 10s if she wants to. However, she would still be 15 points behind, with no realistic chance of crossing the Rubicon by getting to 100 points or of winning the game by overtaking her opponent. Because she knows that she has no way to win seven tricks on the play of the cards (because her opponent will take four tricks in hearts and the aces and kings), she claims nothing. Claiming nothing may look like a very defeatist policy, but because East knows that West has the ♠A♠K, ♣A, and five hearts, she can do nothing. The score is thus 0-5 after the declaration, because West has no runs or Trios.

East leads the ♦K and follows up with two more rounds of diamonds, on the third of which West discards the ♣7. Now East's ♣10 loses to her opponent's ♣ A (which makes the score 4-6 in favor of West), and West leads the ♥K. East plays her two club winners (bringing the score to 7-7), on which West throws two hearts. At this point, East has six tricks, and now she leads the ♣Q. West could win and take the rest of the tricks by leading his cards from the top, but that would lead to the tricks being split and no one getting the 10-point award. Instead, West, who really wants to rub it in, plays his ♣A and ♣K (to take the lead at 8-9), and leads the ♥10. This lead allows East to take the last two tricks for a score of 21-10 after winning the 10 points for the majority of the tricks.

West wins the game with 103 points to East's 98 points. Because East failed to cross the Rubicon, West gets to add East's score, plus an additional 100 points. After the final tallying, West finishes with 301 points (103 + 98 + 100 = 301). (Refer to "Piqueting Your Interest" for more on how crossing the Rubicon can impact the final scoring.)

Chapter 12

Setback

In This Chapter

▶ Understanding how to play Setback

▶ Discovering the variations of Setback for different numbers of players

Setback combines a relatively simple bidding phase with a moderately thought-provoking phase of cardplay. It is, therefore, ideal as a game for folks unfamiliar with the bidding techniques of the more complex pursuits such as Bridge (see Chapter 7). Setback can serve as a useful stepping stone to such games.

Setback packs more variations to the square inch than most of the games set out in this book, but don't let this fact worry you; just concentrate on the main game initially. Most people play only a couple of the variations indicated in this chapter, and I acquaint you with the most popular variations.

To play Setback, you require only the following:

- ✔ **Between two and eight players:** The ideal number of players is probably four, so that everyone has a chance of winning the hand, but three players also poses an interesting series of problems.

- ✔ **A standard deck of 52 cards:** In some varieties of the game, you may also require a joker or two.

- ✔ **Pencil and paper for scoring**

What's It All About?

Setback is a point-scoring game. All the players get six cards, and then a single round of bidding determines who picks the *trump suit*. The trump suit is the boss suit, meaning that a card in the trump suit beats any card in any other suit.

Whoever guarantees during the bidding to take the most points is called the *pitcher* and gets to choose the trump suit. The pitcher has to fulfill his guarantee or he loses the number of points he bid.

Players score points by taking tricks that contain certain cards. A *trick* involves each player putting down one card from his hand, and the player who plays the highest card (or trump card) in the suit that's led wins.

After a series of hands, the game is won by the first person to reach 11 points, or any other number that the players decide on in advance.

In Setback, you can play a trump card at any time, if you have one, and take the trick. However, trump cards prove an exception. When a trump card is led, you *must* play one if you have one.

All the suits are equivalent in the bidding in Setback. No suit outranks any other suit until the pitcher selects the trump suit.

Divvying up the deck

Setback uses the standard deck of 52 cards, with aces high and 2s low. At the beginning of the contest, everyone cuts for the right to deal, and whoever draws the highest card deals the first hand.

Dealing is a distinct advantage at Setback because the dealer may sometimes win the bidding war and get to choose the trump suit more easily than the other players. (Find out more about the dealer's advantage in "Dealer's choice?")

Setback information on the Web

For more information about Setback, visit Umesh Shankar's (a Setback fanatic) Web page. Shankar's The Official Setback Page, at www.fas.harvard.edu/~shankar/ setback/index.htm, delivers a set of rules and a very interesting list of possible variations to the game. The site also promises a Setback newsletter in the near future.

That's a fact, Jack

Setback has the distinction of being responsible for retitling one of the playing cards whose name is taken for granted these days. Until the advent of Setback, the youngest monarch was known as the *Knave,* and in England, he is still sometimes referred to by that name. But Setback gave him the name *Jack,* and he has come to be known by that title as a result.

The dealer shuffles the cards and then offers them to the opponent on his right to cut, if she wants to do so, prior to the deal. The dealer deals out the cards face-down, clockwise, but not one at a time. Instead, he distributes six cards to each player, parceling out the cards three at a time to each player in turn. The remainder of the deck isn't used at all during the hand, and the dealer can safely place these extra cards off to one side. At the end of each hand, the deal rotates one place clockwise.

If the dealer forgets to offer the cards to the opponent on his right to cut or if he exposes an ace, 2, or jack during the deal (which, as you see later, are potentially significant cards for the play because points may be awarded for possession of these cards), then he loses the right to deal, and the deal passes one place to his left. If any other accident occurs during the deal, no punishment is handed out; the dealer simply gathers in the cards and deals the hand again.

Mastering the bidding

The bidding begins with the player to the left of the dealer; the player to the left of the dealer is also referred to as *Elder Hand.* She has the option of passing or selecting a number between one and four, which represents the minimum number of points she intends to win if she has the choice of the trump suit. See "Knowing the score" to find out how much your hand may be worth. Bear in mind that the bid relates to *points,* not *tricks.*

After the Elder Hand has *bid* or *passed,* the bidding progresses around the table, ending with the dealer. Each player has one chance, and one only, to make a bid or pass.

For a bid to be legal, it must outrank the previous bid, or *call* — with one exception, which is detailed shortly. The suits themselves have no ranks, so a call of three from a player intending to use clubs as the trump suit, for example, isn't outranked by a call of three from a player who intends to use any other suit as the trump suit. Suits are simply never mentioned in the bidding. A player's bid is based on how many of the scoring points he thinks he can get; you see in the section "Knowing the score" what wins you points.

Each bid must outrank the previous call; any bid of four wins the bidding outright.

One variation to bidding four is simply to lead a card on your turn to bid. This move implies that you have made a call for four, the maximum, and are setting the trump suit. It's just tough luck if you were about to make a call of four and someone gets there first — that's just the luck of the draw.

At the end of the round of bidding, one player, the highest bidder, wins the bidding and thus has the right to nominate the trump suit and try to make the number of points she says she can take. This player is known as the *bidder* or *pitcher*. The pitcher *leads*, or plays, to the first trick, and the card that she leads determines the trump suit for the hand.

If anyone commits the error of making a bid out of turn or making an insufficient bid (one that doesn't beat a previous bid) the call is canceled, and the bidder doesn't get a second chance to make a correct bid.

The points that the pitcher has undertaken to score have very little to do with tricks — she is trying to collect certain cards that score points. However, at this point in the game, neither she nor anyone else necessarily knows what all those cards are.

Quite a few people play that the bid of one is simply too easy to achieve, and thus the smallest legal call is two. This variation isn't especially significant because a call of one is unlikely to win the bidding in any event, but keep this interpretation in mind.

Dealer's choice?

If the bidding comes back to the dealer without reaching the four-level, the dealer can take (or *steal*) the contract by equaling the previous highest bid; so if the last bid was two or three, the dealer can repeat the bid and steal the contract. However, in most circles — not everywhere — he can't outbid anyone who has gone for the maximum.

Some people consider that the dealer's privilege is outdated and no longer play this rule. Personally, I like the rule, and I feel that it doesn't prejudice anyone unfairly because everyone gets to be dealer an equal amount of the time.

If everybody passes and doesn't bid, the hand is considered dead, and the same dealer reshuffles the cards and redeals the hand.

Some people play that if everyone passes to the dealer, he must bid the minimum amount. If you play this rule, you may also play that the minimum call is one rather than two, because scoring two points is quite a difficult undertaking. However, I know people who do make the dealer bid with a minimum of two; the combination of forcing the dealer to bid and making him bid two works together as a good strategic device to pull the dealer down when he is ahead. Everyone passes, hoping to force the dealer to bid and then make him lose points when he fails in his attempt. Of course, nothing is guaranteed — he may make the bid, and the plan may backfire badly.

Playing your cards right

The objective of this phase of the game is capturing the tricks with the key cards (see "Knowing the score") in them. The high bidder has the lead for the first trick and must lead whatever suit is to be the trump suit at the first trick. Normally, the pitcher leads his highest trump card, unless it's the jack, which is a card you try to retain for later, as you see in "Knowing the score."

After the high bidder pitches the trump suit, the other players must play a card in the suit *(follow suit)* if they can. In fact, if the trump suit is led at any point in the play, you must play a card in the trump suit. You don't have to try to win the trick — any trump card will do. If you have no cards in the trump suit, you can play whatever card you want.

After the first play, if any suit other than the trump suit is led, the options are more generous. You can follow suit, or you can play a trump card even if you aren't out of cards in the suit that's been led. If you're out of the suit led, you can either trump the trick or *discard* (throw away) anything you want.

This rule about trumping while you still have a card in the suit led has a big impact on the strategy of play, so always keep it in mind. The pitcher naturally wants to take care of everyone else's trump cards as quickly as possible, so that they don't do any mischief with them; see the section "Planning a Strategy in the Play" for more information.

You can play Setback with the rule that you must always follow suit if you can, but doing so robs the game of one of its distinctive charms, I believe. On the other hand, using the standard rules about following suit makes Setback easier to play, which may be helpful if you're playing the game with children.

Whoever wins the trick leads to the next trick.

If the pitcher is caught *revoking* (not following with a trump card to the lead of one or discarding on a plain-suit lead when he could follow), then he loses the value of his bid; the hand is played out in full, and the other players score whatever points they make. If a *defender* (any player other than the pitcher) revokes, she loses the value of the bid, and all the other players get to add the amount of that bid to their scores — including the pitcher, whether or not he would have made his bid.

Knowing the score

The tricks themselves at Setback are almost irrelevant. What *is* important is the location of three key cards. Whoever wins the tricks that contain those cards scores points in the process, so you may find that winning one trick can give you a series of points, whereas winning all the tricks but one may mean nothing — or less than nothing.

Scoring occurs at the end of the hand, when all the players inspect their tricks. Four points are awarded in the play; 3 of the 4 points are easy to work out, but the fourth point is less straightforward:

- **High:** Whoever has the highest trump card (and therefore, by definition, wins the trick including that card) scores 1 point for doing so. The highest trump card may not be the ace, of course, because the ace may not have been dealt.

- **Low:** Whoever wins the trick that includes the lowest trump card scores a point for accomplishing that feat.

- **Jack:** Whoever takes the trick that includes the jack of the trump suit also scores 1 point. This point may or may not be awarded — it all depends on whether the card is dealt or not. If the jack is also the highest trump card, whoever has it gets 2 points for his good fortune.

- **Game (also known as the *most*):** Whoever has the most *scoring cards* in the hand wins a point. Each player goes through his tricks one by one and awards the following number of scoring points: aces are worth 4 points, kings 3, queens 2, jacks 1, and 10s 10 points each. Whoever scores the most wins the game point. If two players tie for the game point, no point is awarded at all.

Some people play that the low-trump award goes to the player who is *dealt* the lowest trump. My personal view is that you always want to give the award to the trick winner, because the other approach introduces too much luck into the equation. Check out this matter with your opponents in advance in a new game. The presence of jokers makes a difference to the interpretation of this rule — see the sidebar, "Playing around with jokers" in this chapter for more details on playing with jokers.

After all players complete the reckoning, the first chore is to check whether the pitcher made his contract. If so, he scores whatever points he collected, including any *overtricks* (points taken in excess of his bid). If he makes 3 points and only contracted for 2, he still scores all 3 points.

If the pitcher fails in his contract, he is *set back* by the number of points equivalent to his bid — hence the name of the game. If the pitcher bids 3 and doesn't succeed, he loses 3 points, whether he finishes up with 0,1, or 2. If the pitcher fails in his contract and loses more points than he has, his score is circled on the scoresheet, and he is described as being *in the hole*.

The defenders individually register their points, too, whether or not the pitcher succeeds in his bid.

Passing the winning post

Setback is normally played to a fixed score, agreed on in advance, and whoever gets to that score first wins the *rubber,* meaning the whole contest. However, you won't find much agreement as to what score you normally play to. Playing to 7 yields a short game; playing to 21 can produce a marathon. In between those extremes, you can play to 11, 15, or to any other number the players agree on.

You don't have to pass the target as the pitcher to win; you can manage the task as the defender, too.

If two players pass the mark on the same round, follow these rules to break the tie:

- ✔ If one of the players involved is the pitcher, then the pitcher wins.

- ✔ If neither player is the pitcher, then the 4 points are awarded in the following sequence: first the High, then Low, then Jack, then Joker (if it's in use), and, finally, Game point. Whoever reaches the target first, using that order of allocating the points, wins.

Playing around with jokers

In some parts of the United States, a joker in the deck introduces a fifth point into the game. The joker usually counts as the lowest trump card, ranking below the 2. (In some versions of the game, the joker is treated as ranking above the highest trump card, which is clearly a bad idea because it can lead to a normal bid being beaten by the presence of an unpredictable factor.) The Joker point goes to whoever wins the trick with the joker in it.

The existence of the joker doesn't affect the status of the point for the low trump card, but playing with the joker provides an argument for saying that the low point goes to whoever is *dealt* the low trump card rather than whoever wins the trick with the low trump card in it. Otherwise, the point for the joker and the point for the low trump card are awarded in identical fashion.

If the pitcher leads the joker at the first trick, he can name whatever trump suit he wants. However, leading the joker is unlikely to be a sound tactic; you want to save the joker to win a trick with it.

Shooting the moon

Bidding and making all 4 points is a pretty rare feat. Anyone who bids 4 points successfully — which is also known as *Smudge, Slam,* or *Shoot the Moon* — wins the game outright in most circles. However, in most circles, this rule only applies if the player involved isn't *minus* (or *in the hole*) at the time. If that is the case, the player involved has to be content with simply scoring her 4 points.

If the joker is in play, then a call of Smudge requires all 5 points, making it even more difficult to achieve.

With four players, the chance of a particular card being dealt out to one of the other three players is only just better than one in three. So if you're trying for a Smudge without having the jack of the trump suit in your hand, you have only a moderate chance of finding someone else with that card.

Conversely, the chance that your king of the trump suit is the boss (or that your 3 is the smallest trump) should be about a two in three shot. Then you're hoping that a card is *not* dealt out; with the jack, you're hoping that it is out there. So this bet represents decent odds, if you like a gamble.

Planning a Strategy in the Play

You can easily go about the play of the hand without giving much thought to how you play your cards. But if you play this way, don't expect to end up in the winner's circle too often.

To win at Setback, keep the following points of strategy in mind as the play progresses:

- ✔ The ace of the trump suit is always good for 1 point. The king of the trump suit is a favorite to be worth a point as well. However, strategy and tactics are relevant to the issue of whether to play the odds on a suit headed by the king. You have a good chance to win the high point with the king (see "Knowing the score" for more information on the high point), and still a fair one with the queen of the trump suit. If you're desperate, possession of the jack of the trump suit as your high trump card still gives you a one in four chance to have 2 points for the jack of the trump suit and the high trump card.

- ✔ With three trump cards, you can generally assume that you can win at least one trick with your trump cards. Other players are unlikely to have three trump cards.

✔ Don't play your aces in the side-suits until you have gotten as many trump cards out of your opponents' hands as possible. If you have trump cards to spare, lead the high trump cards and don't save them for a rainy day. Otherwise, you stand a fair chance that your high cards in other suits may be trumped by an opponent.

Losing an ace can affect your chances on the game point — and perhaps on the low trump card, because another player may use his 2 of the trump suit to take your winner and simultaneously score some points toward the game point.

✔ Don't lead your 10s as the first play in a suit unless you're absolutely desperate and think that doing so is the only way to get the game point. Bear in mind that 10s can be trumped — or simply beaten by a higher card, and other players will fasten onto your 10 because it scores so highly for the game point. Also, because, on average, no more than two 10s are out on any hand, the difference between winning a 10 and losing it to a rival may make all the difference on your chances of scoring the game point. At the very least, try to lose your high cards to the right opponent (one who isn't a threat to take the game point).

✔ As a defender, keep in mind that you still score the points you make whether the pitcher succeeds or not. But when a player other than the pitcher is close to winning, you want to avoid letting him pick up points in the play. Letting the pitcher score her low trump, the jack in the trump suit, or even the game point may be to your advantage, rather than seeing those points fall into the wrong hands. Bear in mind that so long as no one has passed the post, the next hand may see you win outright, however bad your cumulative total is. The saying "While there is life, there is hope" is never truer than at Setback.

✔ Try to avoid leading the jack of the trump suit on the first trick. If someone else takes the trick, you virtually write off your chances of winning the contract on the hand. If you have a trump suit without the ace, king, or queen, start with a middle card to try to get all the opponents' trump cards out of their hands

✔ If you're the pitcher, be sure to lead more than one round of trump cards to try to ensure that you collect the point for the low trump — unless you already acquired it on the first trick or you hold the card yourself. The point is that if you don't have the low trump, someone else can score up the point for the low trump by playing the card on a *side-suit* (a suit other than trumps).

✔ Conversely, of course, as a defender you can infer that a pitcher who leads one round of the trump suit and then switches to another suit has the low trump himself. In such a case, playing trump cards yourself to try to prevent him from scoring up the low trump may be to your advantage.

✔ When bidding, be more aggressive when you're the first, or possibly second, to speak. Players with genuinely good hands are unhappy about selling out, and you may be able to tempt them into overbidding.

Partnership Setback

The partnership version of Setback is played with two teams (usually of two players each) sitting opposite each other.

The bidding proceeds as in the solo game (see "Mastering the bidding") with the dealer being able to steal the bid at his turn with a call equal to the previous highest call. If the first three players pass, the dealer must bid two, the minimum amount.

In the partnership game, you're working with your partner. You and she want to pick your joint best trump suit, of course, and although you have the option of outbidding her by making a bid after your partner has done so, that is a fairly unusual thing to do. You can imagine that a long, strong trump suit of your own, which may be valueless for your partner, may tempt you to overcall her — use discretion, but you'll know the right hand to overcall your partner when it comes along!

Smudge, or *shooting the moon,* requires that all six tricks be won by the pitching side in addition to the 4 regular points. Smudge is worth 5 points, the fifth point being for winning all the tricks. As usual, overtricks made by the pitching side count, with the exception of the additional fifth point for taking all the tricks. Therefore, on a non-Smudge bid, the maximum number of points for the pitching side is 4; you don't get the point for taking all the tricks except when bidding Smudge.

One relatively common variation is for all four players to have a chance to improve their hands after the bidding is over. After the trump suit is declared by the pitcher, each player takes a turn to discard face-down all his unwanted cards (which generally means all non-trump cards) and to pick up an equivalent number from the deck. This procedure is called the *draw.* Of course, the effect of this draw is to randomize everyone's hand, and I can't say that I'm in favor of this rule, but it does at least make the game more exciting — in a way.

Scoring points is easier to achieve in the partnership game because it isn't one person against the rest, so playing to 21 points doesn't produce an epic game. However, one of the requirements of Partnership Setback is that to win the game, you must pass the target by making your contract on a hand where your side is the pitcher. (This rule doesn't apply to the solo game.) If you accumulate enough points as a defender to reach the winning post, you must still wait to pitch a hand to win — which can lead to a position where you win the game but have fewer points than your opponents. If, for example, your opponents have 23 points but you have 18 points, and then you pitch for 3 points successfully, you win, despite being behind at the end of the game!

In one variation, the pitcher is permitted to lead a suit other than the trump suit on the first trick while announcing the trump suit at the same moment. When she does so, no one is permitted to trump this trick, even if they genuinely have no cards in the suit, in which case they throw away from another suit. Normally, the pitcher takes the opportunity to lead a high card such as an ace or 10 that might otherwise get trumped, hoping to collect another high-scoring card from her partner to boost her chances of getting the game point.

Setback for Smaller and Larger Numbers of Players

With two players, the game drags unless you beef up the hands by using the draw described as a variation in the preceding section. The suggested number of cards is eight.

With three players, eight cards is again the best number, though some perfectly good variations use six cards only. Both the defenders gang up on the one pitcher. Three-handed Setback tends to be a game favoring a conservative approach in the auction, because the odds tilt against the pitcher.

With six players, deal eight cards to everyone. After the trump suit is announced by the standard auction process, discard two cards from your hand. This route works as a substitute for the draw after the bidding.

Nine-Card Setback

Nine-Card Setback features two partners facing one another in a four-player game. The rules are pretty much the same as for the six-card variety, with a few obvious differences:

- The first difference is that 6 points are at stake on each hand — although, as usual, not all the points are necessarily awarded. The additional 2 points are given to whoever wins the trick with the 5 of the trump suit each hand and to whoever wins the highest spade in circulation.

- Because of the greater number of tricks available, the minimum bid goes up to three tricks.

- After the pitcher declares the trump suit, all players can discard up to four of their cards and get replacements from the undealt stock.

✔ The pitcher isn't required to lead the trump suit to the first trick but announces it as he makes the first lead.

✔ One quirk of the scoring is that although you need to obtain 21 points to win, the scoring is done in reverse fashion. Each team starts with 21 points, and for every point you register, the total is reduced by 1. Accordingly, if you fail in your contract, you're said to "go up," because that's what happens to your cumulative score.

✔ To win the rubber, you must reach 0 by making a contract. If you accumulate points in defense to bring you to zero, you're deemed to come down to 1. You can only advance to the winning post on a bid.

It is clearly an advantage for the more powerful hand in any partnership to be the fourth person to play to a trick, if he can. That gives them the opportunity to make their play based on the cards played to the trick; a weak hand may not be able to gain from that flexibility. To compensate for that fact as a defender, try to trap the pitcher by ensuring (even at the cost of overtaking your partner's winner) that the pitcher plays second, not fourth, to the trick if you can.

Chapter 13

Clobyosh

Clobyosh is an entertaining game that requires accurate judgment in both the bidding and the play. It offers the opportunity for sharp pleasures and disappointments, and it's definitely the sort of game where a skillful player has a distinct advantage — maybe not enough to overcome consistently bad cards, but an edge nonetheless.

To play Clobyosh, you need the following:

- **Two players**

- **A standard deck of 52 cards:** Take the deck and remove the 2s through the 6s, leaving a 32-card deck.

- **Pencil and paper for scoring**

Understanding Clobyosh

Clobyosh is a game with *tricks*. A trick involves one player putting down a card. The other player must play a card in that suit if he has one. The player who plays the higher card takes the two cards and sets them aside, face-down — that's a trick.

If the second player has no cards in the suit led, he must play a card from the *trump suit* to win the trick, if he can. Even a small trump card beats any card in a *side-suit*, a suit that isn't the trump suit. If a trump card is led, the second player must win the trick if he can by playing a higher trump card.

Clobyosh features a series of relatively short hands. The hand falls into three stages: bidding, scoring points, and playing.

By winning the bidding, one player obtains the right to determine the trump suit; to win, that player must outscore his opponent by taking the majority of the tricks. If he does so, he is rewarded, and if he fails, he is heavily punished.

To win, you need to score more points than your opponent and reach the winning post of 500 (or, in some variations, 300) first. Getting to 500 scores you one *rubber;* Clobyosh is normally played as the best of three rubbers.

Ranking and Naming the Cards

Clobyosh has a particularly interesting hierarchy of the cards — in fact, at various times, you have to keep three different ranking orders in mind simultaneously!

The cards rank differently depending on whether you're making sequences (such as KQJ or 1098) before the play starts or playing the cards out in the "play" phase of the game. In addition, the ranking order of the cards changes in the play, depending on whether the suit in question is the trump suit or just a regular suit.

The good news is that in the part of the game where you're making and claiming sequences, the cards rank in the regular order, from ace (high) down to 7.

However, in the play of the cards, regular (nontrump) suits rank in the following order, from highest to lowest: A, 10, K, Q, J, 9, 8, and 7.

And if that isn't confusing enough, the trump suit has the following order from highest to lowest: J, 9, A, 10, K, Q, 8, and 7.

This ranking order is also relevant for the scoring, because Clobyosh is all about accumulating points by capturing tricks with scoring cards in them, rather than simply winning tricks.

You also should be aware that some of the trump cards have special names:

- ✔ The jack of the trump suit (the highest trump card) is known as *jass.* He is also known as the *boss* or *jazz,* pronounced *yass.*

- ✔ The 9 of the trump suit, the second-highest trump card, is known as *menel,* pronounced *muh-nill.*

- ✔ The 7 of the trump suit (which plays only an insignificant role, as the lowest trump card) is known as the *dix,* pronounced *deece.*

Mastering the Scoring System

Knowing about the scoring system lets you appreciate which cards are important when it comes to the play of the cards.

In the nontrump suits, the cards have the following values:

- ✔ **Ace:** 11 points
- ✔ **Ten:** 10 points
- ✔ **King:** 4 points
- ✔ **Queen:** 3 points
- ✔ **Jack:** 2 points

In the trump suit, most of these cards retain their values, but the high trump cards are promoted, as befits their augmented status:

- ✔ **Jack:** 20 points
- ✔ **Nine:** 14 points
- ✔ **Ace:** 11 points
- ✔ **Ten:** 10 points
- ✔ **King:** 4 points
- ✔ **Queen:** 3 points

The aces, 10s, kings, and queens retain their point-scoring values, whatever the trump suit.

Playing the Hand

The game starts off quite normally: The cards are dealt, and then the players pick up their hands and determine whether or not they want to try to choose the trump suit or pass. First comes the deal.

Dealing the cards

Proceedings start before the first hand, with a cut for deal for the first hand; the person drawing the lower card gets the dealing duty. If you draw equal cards, cut the deck again. For the purposes of the cut, the cards retain their regular ranking order, with the aces as the highest cards.

For subsequent deals, the responsibility of passing out the cards goes to the winner of the last hand, because not dealing is an advantage, and the winner of the last hand of a rubber deals the first hand of the new rubber.

Initially, the dealer shuffles the deck and offers the cards to his opponent to cut the cards if she wants. After the cut, the dealer distributes three cards in one parcel to each player and then does the same again, leaving each player with an initial hand of six cards.

The dealer next turns over the top card of the remaining cards, to determine what the initial trump suit is. If neither player wants the turned-over card as the trump suit, a new suit may be chosen (see "Making your bid for the choice of the trump suit"). The top card is put under the *talon* or *stock* (the remainder of the deck), perpendicular to the deck so that the card is at least partially visible.

The deal may go wrong in several ways:

- If the dealer exposes one of his opponent's cards, the deal is *void,* and the same player deals again. But if he exposes one of his own cards, the other player has the option to abandon the deal or play on. The second player should abandon the deal if the card is a high-scoring one (a jack, ace, or 10) but otherwise should play on.

- The dealer may deal out too many cards and the hands may get picked up. If the error is discovered before play begins, the other player may pick out a card from his opponent's hand and then look at it before putting it back in the deck. Any hand short of a card may add additional cards from the top of the deck to make up the shortage.

  However, a player who doesn't discover that he has the wrong number of cards until after the play has started is heavily punished. Whoever has the wrong number of cards concedes all the points he scores on the hand to his opponent.

Making your bid for the choice of the trump suit

After the deal, the first stage of Clobyosh is the *bidding,* in which the players determine the trump suit for the hand, if the trump suit suggested during the bidding proves unacceptable to both players.

During the dealing, the dealer turns up the top card of the stock, which represents the initial possible trump suit. The players can accept the suit of the upturned card as the trump suit or decline it.

The nondealer gets the first chance to speak, and she has three possible choices:

- ✔ With a good hand for the initial trump suit (one with at least three cards, including the jass, menel, or dix), she can decide to play in the suit. If she wants to do that, she says "I take" or "Take it."

- ✔ With an unsuitable hand for that trump suit (any hand that doesn't look promising for the suit of the turned-up card), she can decline, saying "I pass."

- ✔ The third and most complicated (and also rarest) option only arises when she has a moderate hand for the trump suit (some length, if not great strength) and a bad hand for everything else. In that case, she may say "Schmeiss," (pronounced *shmice*), which is an offer to abandon the hand. The dealer can accept, in which case the hand is abandoned, or refuse, in which case the nondealer must play the hand in the suggested trump suit in just the same way as if she had accepted.

The bid of schmeiss accomplishes one important thing — it prevents the dealer from picking his own trump suit. He can only abandon the hand or let the nondealer choose the trump suit. On the other hand, this bid passes the final responsibility of whether to play out the hand at all from the nondealer to the dealer, and there's significant strategic advantage to that choice. Because you would bid yourself on any really promising hand, the conclusion has to be that you make a bid of schmeiss partly as a spoiling tactic; if you call it on the first round, it should be with a hand that has no potential for any suit but the trump suit.

If the nondealer accepts the choice of the trump suit, the dealer has no options, and the bidding ends. If the nondealer bids schmeiss, the dealer can abandon the hand or refuse to abandon, which sets the trump suit in the turned-over suit. But if she passes, the dealer has the straightforward choice of taking the trump suit or passing.

If both players pass, then the bidding reverts to the nondealer, who has the same set of options (accepting, passing, or schmeiss), but also she can pick the trump suit of her choice. If she decides to try her luck, she picks the trump suit, saying "I take in . . ." the suit of her choice. The one restriction is that she can't take the original trump suit; she must pick a new suit.

If the nondealer passes a second time, she leaves it up to the dealer to name a suit of his choice or pass. But again, the nondealer has the option on a marginal hand of trying schmeiss, this time without naming the trump suit until the dealer confirms that he wants him to play out the hand.

As before, the call of schmeiss prevents the dealer from picking his own trump suit, but may force the nondealer to make a bid on what, by definition, isn't a cast-iron hand; if it were, she would already have taken the trump suit! On the second round, the ideal hand on which to make a call of schmeiss is a hand with only one moderately good suit in it and a marginal decision whether to bid or pass.

If the nondealer passes a second time, then the dealer has the final option: He can select the trump suit of his choice, if he wants, or pass for a second time, whereupon the hand is abandoned. The dealer abandons the hand whenever he has no clear-cut call.

Similarly, if the nondealer bids schmeiss on the second round, the dealer has the option to accept and abandon the hand, or he can insist that the nondealer play out the hand in his preferred trump suit. He normally only insists on playing out with a good hand, one with which he thinks he can defeat the bid.

Whoever wins the bidding and gets to pick the trump suit isn't competing on a level playing field thereafter, because bidding and failing to make your bid good — called *going bait* — carries a very heavy penalty. The player who picks the trump suit becomes the *maker* and must outscore his opponent, the *defender*. Although the defender's points always count for his side, the maker's points may backfire on him if he doesn't win. In a loss, the maker's points are scored for the defender — which can prove very expensive. See "The Day of Reckoning" for more information on scoring a hand.

In choosing the trump suit, you alter the ranking order in one suit. Because the jack and 9 are the highest cards in the trump suit, you should consider choosing the trump suit that improves your hand the most. You need to select a trump suit that ensures that you finish up with at least some of the high trump cards.

If no one makes a positive bid, the hand is abandoned, and the deal passes to the other player. But if someone chooses a trump suit, then the dealer deals three more cards, taking both players' hands up to nine cards. Then the bottom card of the deck is turned face-up on top of the deck. This card plays absolutely no part in the game except to give the players a little more information about the missing cards — 12 cards are still face-down in the talon (stock).

If either player chooses the original trump suit, each player may change the dix (the 7 of the trump suit) with the original turned-up card on the first round of bidding.

Don't bother to change the dix with the 8 of the trump suit, because you gain no points and simply give away information about the cards you have in your hand. Less obvious, but equally clear, is the advice not to exchange the dix for the face-up card if you have a trump suit of only one or two cards and the upcard is not the jack or 9. If you exchange it, you probably just give points away to your opponent. You allow your adversary to lead his top trump cards and thus capture something of value, rather than acquire an irrelevant trump card.

Silence is golden? What to bid and when to bid it

You should almost always make a bid in a trump suit when you have both the jass and the menel (the jack and 9 of the trump suit) unless the rest of your hand is completely without promise. Conversely, you're relatively unlikely to succeed if you make a bid without both of them.

Bidding for the trump suit on a holding of J9 is certainly better than bidding simply on length in the trump suit alone; without the top trump cards, you're unlikely to win the hand because high trump cards have such an impact on the play. Of course, having one of those cards and a sequence in the trump suit (such as JQK or 10JQ) is also very good news for scoring points.

You should consider selecting the trump suit with 40 guaranteed points in your hand, and because 10s aren't a sure thing to win the trick, counting them as worth 5, unless you have the ace as well, is a reasonable estimate. (See "Mastering the Scoring System" for more information on assigning points to your cards.)

Normally, a score of 60 points is enough to win the hand.

Combining and harvesting: scoring your points for sequences

Before the cards are played out (or, more specifically, as the first card is played), both players have the opportunity to score points for the sequences that they hold. Only one of the two players can score points during this phase of the game. Three sequences are possible:

- ✔ A run of four or more consecutive cards in the same suit is worth 50 points.

- ✔ A run of three cards in the same suit is worth 20 points.

- ✔ *Bella* or *bela* (also known as *ballot*), the king and queen of the trump suit, is worth 20 points. (Actually, you claim bella as you play the second card of the KQ combination.)

Remember that for this phase of the game only, the cards rank in their regular order (AKQJ10987) rather than the standard Clobyosh order! For example, the J9A of the trump suit isn't a sequence, nor is A10K a sequence in a side-suit. However, J109 of the trump suit and AKQJ in the trump suit are legitimate sequences.

The timing of the claim for the points is important. When the nondealer leads to the first trick, he claims whatever points from sequences he may have. However, that isn't the moment to claim bella, if you have it. Say "Bella" when making the second play of your king or queen.

If you have no sequences as the nondealer, call out "No sequences" at the first trick, leaving it up to the dealer to claim whatever sequences he has.

The dealer, in turn, plays her first card, saying "Good" if she can't beat the sequence; "No good" if she has a better one herself; or "Equal" if appropriate.

If the combinations are equal, then the nondealer says "Mine is *x* high," naming the highest card in the sequence. Now the dealer says "Good," "Not good, mine is *x* high," or "I have one also," if there is still a tie. At this point, the tie is broken by two rules: If one of the sequences is in the trump suit, then that one wins. Otherwise, the nondealer's sequence wins.

Whoever has won the battle of the sequences and has made the initial scoring run can now claim any further sequences of 50 or 20, after his high sequence has been established. But no matter who wins the battle of the sequences, a player with bella can score it up at the appropriate time, if he wants.

You don't have to show your sequence at the time you claim it, but an improperly called sequence turns out to be expensive. In such a case, the full hand's score of both the offender and nonoffender goes to the nonoffender. Some people actually show the sequences when the claim is conceded by the other player, but this policy seems to be the exception rather than the rule.

If you don't claim the sequences at the first trick, you lose the opportunity to claim them at all. Normally, you claim any sequence that you have. The only reason not to claim a sequence is if you're the maker, and you haven't had a chance on the hand and don't wish to give points to your opponent. However, giving up all hope before the play of the cards is surely premature; unless you really have no hope at all, claim your points.

Far more likely is that as the dealer, you don't respond to the nondealer's claim of a sequence when you have an equal-length sequence of low cards, such as a sequence of 789 or 910J. By saying "Equal," you allow the nondealer to start reconstructing your hand, but you may be able to judge that you have no chance of success in the claim because you can tell from your own hand that your opponent's sequence must be higher than yours.

For example, say that you hold the cards shown in Figure 13-1.

Figure 13-1:
Getting a
picture of
the hand.

The nondealer chooses hearts as the trump suit and leads the ♦A, saying, "Sequence of 20." Whether his sequence is in clubs, hearts, or spades, it can't be lower than queen-high and may be higher than that. Thus you can't win, because your sequence's highest card is the jack. So why tip the nondealer off to the fact that you have a sequence yourself? If he can work out that you have a low sequence including the ♠10, he may avoid playing spades and force you to lead the suit yourself, in which case you may lose the opportunity to score your 10.

Unlike the case of claiming sequences, you may, as maker, be able to work out later on in the play that claiming bella won't enable you to win the hand. In that case, scoring bella simply gives points to your opponent, so don't make the claim. If you think you have a chance of losing as maker and you have a bella, delay playing the second card of the sequence until matters have been clarified — one way or the other!

Playing out the cards

You must *follow suit* by playing a card in the suit led if you can; however, you must trump the lead if you can't follow suit. You must also beat a trump card that has been led, if you can. You can, of course, throw away whatever you like if you have no trump cards.

If you *revoke* by failing to follow suit when you can do so, by failing to trump when out of a suit, or by failing to play a higher trump card when one was led, the penalties are severe. Again, the nonoffender takes all the score of the offender on the hand in question.

After the opening lead, when the players claim sequences, play progresses just like any normal trick-taking game; whoever wins the trick takes it and turns it face-down and then leads to the next trick.

If, for some reason, the wrong hand leads to the trick, the card may be picked up if the mistake is noticed, but no other penalty is assessed. However, if the second player follows to the trick, the cards stand.

No scoring is done until the end of the hand (see "The Day of Reckoning" for the details on scoring), and the tricks themselves are worth nothing. Only the point-scoring cards within the tricks matter.

One exception to this guideline exists: Winning the last trick actually carries a bonus of 10 points, and as such it's worth fighting for. Keep a high card or a trump card for the last trick, if you can.

During the play, you may inspect the last trick played — but *only* the last trick. However, if a revoke (a failure to follow suit) is suspected, you may go back to check for that if necessary.

Try to avoid leading from *tenaces* (broken sequences of cards, such as 107 or K7); you're more likely to score points by waiting for your opponent to lead the suit so that your honor cards win the trick. The logic behind this advice is that you can determine which of your high or low cards to play if your opponent leads the suit, but you have to commit yourself in advance if you lead the suit.

Frequently, you can lead your long suits to set up winning cards in the suit for yourself. When you do that, you force your opponent to use up his trump cards (because he must trump if he can't follow suit), often on low-value cards of yours. In fact, the third or fourth round of a suit is an excellent card with which to lose the lead. Doing so forces your opponent to trump if he can, and you hope that, as a result, he has to lead a suit for you, and maybe let you capture one of his honor cards in the process.

If you just have insignificant, nonscoring cards in the trump suit, leading that suit is a good idea, particularly if you're strong in the side-suits. By making this play, you avoid sacrificing your high cards to your opponent's trump cards, and you make him do the work of leading the other suits. You force him to make the first move — to which you hope to have an effective counter.

However, try to avoid leading trump cards if you have cards in the trump suit that might score points, such as the ace, 10, king, and queen, particularly if you don't have the jass. On the other hand, leading the jass, if you've got it, is generally sound, although you may weaken your chances of collecting the last trick by doing so.

Play comes to an end when everyone has played out all nine of their cards. Whoever wins the last trick gets the 10-point bonus. Then it's time for each side to add up the points scored from the sequences and from the scoring cards taken in the tricks captured.

The Day of Reckoning

After the play ends, the pleasurable or painful moment of scoring is upon you. The defender (who is always, at the very least, able to score his own points) counts first. He records any sequences he made at the first trick, scores bella (if he had it), and then adds the point value of all the cards he has won.

The maker then does the same. If the maker wins, as he usually does at least two out of three times, then both players write their scores on the score sheet. However, if the maker loses (which is called *going bait* or *bete*), then the defender gets the combined scores of both players.

As you can see, the impact of this scoring is highly significant. If the maker gets into a close game, he may be looking at a game of 65-55, where he stands to win 10 points if he comes out on top or loses 120 if he fails. Not surprisingly, this uneven scoring means that you have to be fairly confident of your ground before making a bid.

The deal alternates to the other player after the scoring.

Winning the Game

At the end of each hand, the scores are tallied, and if either player has gone over 500, he wins. If both players have achieved the feat simultaneously, the higher score wins.

A complex variation is more challenging and more fun. When one or both players get close to the winning post, each player keeps a running total of the points, including combinations that he has scored, and that running tally allows either player to claim in midhand that he has won. The penalty for failure is death, so to speak — a false claim loses the game.

If the game is close and you're playing this variation, you want to bid for a trump suit that lets you lead a jack. You want to retain the lead, claim any sequence, and play your high cards early.

Part V
Matching Cards

The 5th Wave   By Rich Tennant

"Sure I'll play Fan Tan with you. If you match cards like you match shirts with ties, this should be an easy win."

In this part . . .

You've come to the right part of the book if you're looking for information on Eights, Fan Tan, and related games, which are all games in which you strive to go out as fast as possible by matching cards. Each game has its own definition of what it means to "match a card," and I explain the rules of each game in depth in this part.

Chapter 14

Eights

In This Chapter

▶ Discovering how to play Eights

▶ Working through the play for Mau Mau, Neuner, and Switch

*U*ntil I started writing this chapter, I had no idea that so many varieties of games came from such a simple start. This chapter takes you on a tour of several games in the Eights family.

Eights: Simple Is As Simple Does

What could be more simple than Eights? Until you add a few complexities, Eights is not a challenging game.

To play Eights, you require the following:

✔ **Two or more players**

✔ **At least one standard 52-card deck of cards:** No jokers are used in most versions of Eights, but you may well need at least one more deck of cards, because the game can be adapted to large numbers of players.

✔ **Paper and pencil for scoring**

The object of the game is to be the first to dispose of all your cards. Everyone plays for himself, rather than in partnership, no matter how many players participate.

The first player to go out scores points according to the cards left in his opponents' hands. The first player to reach 250 points wins.

Dealing the cards

The players cut for the deal, and the person who draws the lowest card deals the cards, one card at a time, clockwise and face-down. Thereafter, the deal progresses one place to the dealer's left.

Each player starts with the same number of cards:

- ✔ With two to four players, each player gets seven cards.
- ✔ With more than four players, each player gets five cards. When the number of players climbs above six, add a second deck.

Playing your cards right

After all the cards are dealt, the dealer puts the remainder of the stock face-down in the middle of the table and turns over the top card to start the discard pile. The player to the dealer's left has the first opportunity to play a card. He has three distinct choices about which card to play:

- ✔ He may play a card that coincides with the *suit* (clubs, spades, diamonds, or hearts) or the *rank* (2s, jacks, and so on) of the top card.
- ✔ He may play an 8: All 8s are *wild* — meaning that you can play an 8 at any time, no matter what the previously-played card was. Moreover, when you play an 8, you can nominate any suit (but not a rank), and the next player must play a card of that suit or put down another 8 in order to earn the right to name a new (or the same) suit. If he can do neither, he must pick up a card from the stock. (If the first card turned over is an 8, then the first player can play whatever he likes.)
- ✔ He may pick up the top card from the stock and add it to his hand if he is unable or unwilling to play a card.

If the first player plays a card, he places his card on top of the discard pile, and his play now dictates what the next player, to his left, can do. That player has the same three choices: He can follow suit or match the rank of the card just played; play an 8; or pick up a card from the stock.

And so the play goes on. For example, if the card turned over is the ♠7, the first player can play the ♦7. That card allows the second player to play the ♦Q. The third player must next play a diamond, a queen, or an 8 — or he can pick up.

In Eights, it isn't necessarily *right* to play just because you *can*. For example, you may not want to let go of an 8 at an early moment in the game; you may want to keep the 8 to dictate what suit is played at the end of the hand. Also, you may sometimes find that building up a supply of cards in one suit (or *cornering a suit*) early in the game is an advantage — doing so may allow you to make a series of moves at the end of the game when no one else can play and has to pick up cards. However, life isn't that simple. The last thing in the world you want to do is to be left with a bunch of cards as the game winds down (see "Paying the price when your opponent goes out" for the details).

Paying the price when your opponent goes out

The game concludes when one player gets rid of all his cards. At that point, the damage is assessed on the other players:

- ✔ Each *court card* (the ace, king, queen, and jack) is worth 10 points.
- ✔ All other cards, except the 8, are charged at their face value. For example, a 2 counts for 2 points.
- ✔ The 8s come in at a painful 50 points each.

The winner collects points from everyone else. Folks usually play that the first player to 250 points wins and that the winner receives an additional 100 points.

When the game is apparently reaching the finale, make sure to unload your 8s as fast as you can, because the penalty for still having an 8 at the end of the game outweighs the tactical advantage in keeping an 8 to play later.

Mau Mau

Mau Mau, which rhymes with *pow pow,* offers the simplicity of Eights, with a few twists thrown in to make things interesting.

To play Mau Mau, you need the following:

- ✔ **Three to five players**
- ✔ **A standard deck of 52 cards:** Remove the 2s through 6s and set them aside.
- ✔ **Pencil and paper for scoring**

After you select a dealer for the first hand (everyone cuts the deck, and the person who draws the lowest card deals), each player receives five cards, and the rest of the cards are put face down in the middle of the table as the stock.

The dealer turns up the top card of the stock, and then the first player must play a card that matches the turned-up card either in rank or suit. Alternatively, he may play a jack, which acts as a wild card, allowing the player to name the suit that the next player must follow. The suit that he chooses doesn't need to be the suit of the jack that he plays. (If the first card turned over is a jack, the first player can play any card he wants to play.)

The play then moves clockwise to the next player, who must play a card that matches, either in rank or suit, the card that the first player put down, or play a card in the suit that the first player named when he played a jack.

A player who is unable to *follow suit* (play a card in the correct suit) may draw one card from the stock, as long as any cards remain in the stock. After picking up, she may play that card if she can or wants to. Whether she plays a card or not, the turn moves clockwise, and the next player has the same options.

In Mau Mau, you can also draw even if you can play one of the cards in your hand. The only reason I can think of to do this is if you want to hold on to a jack.

The first person to get rid of all his cards says "Mau Mau" as he does so. At that point, everyone is penalized by the value of their cards according to the following scale:

- ✔ **7s and 8s** = 0 points
- ✔ **9s** = 9 points
- ✔ **10s** = 10 points
- ✔ **Jacks** = 20 points
- ✔ **Queens** = 2 points
- ✔ **Kings** = 4 points
- ✔ **Aces** = 11 points

As an alternate scoring scale, you can make jacks worth 2 points each and 8s and 7s worth their face value. I prefer this alternative, because I don't like getting rid of all my cards and catching my opponent with no points at all, even though he has cards left in his hand.

The first to accumulate 100 penalty points loses and buys the drinks.

Neuner

As with the game of Eights, Neuner, which sounds like *newn-er,* involves matching cards, with the ultimate goal of getting rid of all your cards. However, in Neuner, your hand can grow to unspeakable proportions as you wait for luck to come your way.

To play Neuner, you need the following:

- **Three to five players**

- **A standard deck of 52 cards:** Remove the 2s through 6s and set them aside. Also include a joker, making a total of 33 cards in play (use the ♣2 if your deck doesn't have a joker).

- **Paper and pencil for scoring**

After you select a dealer for the first hand (everyone cuts the deck, and the person who draws the lowest card deals), the dealer gives five cards to each player.

The dealer then places the rest of the deck in the middle of the table and turns over the top card to create the stock. The player to the dealer's left starts, with play progressing in a clockwise direction.

The first player must play a card that matches the turned-up card either in rank or suit. Alternatively, he may play a joker or a 9, which act as wild cards, allowing the player to name the suit that the next player must follow. If you play one of these cards, you can name the suit to be played next.

If the upcard is a joker, the first player may play any card first. If the upcard is a 9, you must follow the suit of the 9 or play a wild card.

If a player is unable (or possibly unwilling) to play any of the cards in his hand, he draws cards from the stock until he has a legal card that he is prepared to play. He must play that card on that turn, rather than waiting until his next turn. This rule can lead to a rapid buildup of cards.

When the stock is exhausted and a player has no legal move, the turn passes to his left. If no player has a legal card to play, the player who put down the last card can then play whatever he wants.

When someone goes out by playing the last of his cards, play stops, and the winner scores the total of the points left in all the players' hands according to the following scale:

- **7s and 8s** = 7 and 8 points, respectively

- **9s** = 15 points

- **10s** = 10 points

- **Jacks** = 2 points

- **Queens** = 3 points

✔ **Kings** = 4 points

✔ **Aces** = 11 points

✔ **Jokers** = 20 points

The first player to reach 150 points wins the game.

You can draw cards even when you have a card you can play. Doing so permits you to build up a supply of cards — and thus reduce your opponent's options by leaving him with a card that he can't play as you tackle other suits. This tactic may allow you to go out more quickly in the long run. Beware, however, because this strategy may backfire catastrophically if your opponent goes out when you have such a big hand.

Switch

Switch is also known as Two Four Jack or Black Jack (not to be confused with Blackjack). Switch resembles Uno, a commercial game played with a special deck of cards.

The object is to get rid of all your cards first. However, a series of obstacles can make that simple endeavor slightly complicated.

To play Switch, you need the following:

✔ **At least two players:** You can play Switch with any number of players, from two upward, but a group of five to eight is probably ideal.

✔ **A standard deck of 52 cards:** With four or more players, add a second deck, and with eight players, bring in a third deck.

✔ **Pencil and paper for scoring**

The proprieties of Switch

The players cut for the deal, with the player drawing the lowest card doing the dealing. The dealer doles out the cards one by one, face-down, in a clockwise direction. With two players, the dealer gives 12 cards to each player; otherwise, each player gets ten cards. After dealing the cards, the dealer turns over the top card of the stock.

The player to the dealer's left starts the game by playing a card of the same suit or rank as the upcard, unless the upcard is a jack; see "Identifying some key cards" for more information.

However, a number of cards change their identities in Switch. Instead of being part of the "extras," they become stars, with a mind — and role — of their own.

Play goes clockwise around the table, at least initially, but that order can certainly change, depending on which cards are played. See "Identifying some key cards" for the details on how the sequence of play can change.

Identifying some key cards

In Switch, some cards can influence the play in special ways:

- **Aces:** Aces are wild and can be played at any time, allowing you to nominate the suit to be played thereafter.

- **2:** In Switch, 2s are bad guys. When you play a 2 on a card of the appropriate suit, you offer the next player a choice of alternatives. If he has no 2 (or if he has one but chooses not to play it), he must draw two cards from the stock and miss his turn. If he has a 2, he can play it and avoid picking up additional cards.

  If the second player puts a 2 on the first 2, the next player gets even more unpalatable alternatives; he must play a third 2 or draw *four* cards. And the fourth player must play a 2 or pick up six cards, and so on. As soon as a player picks up some cards, the spell is broken, and the count goes back to zero.

  After the 2s stop being played, the next player to go must follow the suit of the last 2 played.

- **4:** If you think that 2s are painful, then 4s are much, much worse. The 4s start a count beginning at four cards. The first player must play a 4 or pick up four cards from the stock; the second player has the choice of playing a 4 or picking up eight cards, and so on. Again, after the 4s are played, the next player must follow the suit of the 4.

- **Jacks:** Jacks give the game its name. A jack reverses, or *switches,* the direction of play. After someone plays a jack, the next turn goes to the player to the right of the person who played it. If the upcard at the start of the game is a jack, the dealer goes first. The next jack played reverses the direction again, back to normal.

Going out and scoring

When you reduce your hand to one card, you must announce "One card" as you play your next-to-the-last card.

If you forget to say "One card," and someone else notices (they will!), you lose your next turn and must pick up a card from the stock.

The player to run out of cards first wins. The winner scores the value of the cards left in everybody's hand. Most cards are scored at face value, with the following exceptions:

- **Aces** = 20 points
- **2s, 4s, and jacks** = 15 points
- **Kings and queens** = 10 points

The first player to reach 150 points wins the game.

The secret society of Crates players

Crates stands for Chicago Cutthroat Crazy Eights. The game was invented at the end of the 1960s on Chicago Circle Campus by a group of otherwise respectable citizens. The two main proponents of the game are now a professor of psychology at an Illinois university and a Zen master in Albuquerque. What started as a local fad, played mainly by the Bridge players at the college, spread into a craze among Bridge players nationally, and you still occasionally find tables of Crates players at national Bridge tournaments in the United States.

Crates differs from most card games in that it is cloaked in secrecy. The game of Crates has a constitution, and the official secretary and scorekeeper of the Crates association insists that the first and most critical rule of the game is that you can't tell anyone the rules of Crates.

Traditionally, players discover how to play Crates the hard way. A group of experts invites one novice to a game of Crates and lets the novice work out what is going on — that's exactly how I figured out the game.

I don't intend to breach the cardinal rule of the game, but I do want you to know a few things about Crates, should you ever get an invitation to play. I can tell you that a *rubber* of Crates is 15 hands long. Each player gets eight cards in the first hand. The next hand has seven cards, and the sequence goes down to one card and they come back to eight cards again.

I don't think that I would be giving away too much about the game to say that, like Eights, Crates involves matching cards.

I'm sworn to secrecy about further details of the game. If you're interested in playing Crates, hang around Bridge players.

Chapter 15

Fan Tan

*Y*ou can get along just fine playing Fan Tan with remarkably little grasp of the underlying strategy. However, to be really good at Fan Tan, you can't rely solely upon the luck of the hand you are originally dealt. To play Fan Tan well requires a fair degree of skill and an understanding of the mechanics of the game; I tell you everything you need to know about this exciting game in this chapter.

Fan Tan also works very well as a gambling game, and I tell you how to bring the monetary element into the game, too.

To play Fan Tan, you need the following:

- ✔ **Four players:** You can also play Fan Tan with three, five, or six players, but four is ideal.

- ✔ **A standard deck of 52 cards without jokers**

- ✔ **A pencil and paper for scoring**

Your Fan Tan Mission

The objective of Fan Tan is relatively uncomplicated. You deal out the entire deck of cards among the players. You then spend the game trying to get rid of all your cards before the other players can manage the same feat.

You get rid of your cards by adding them to an already existing *run,* or sequence of cards in each suit, which build up during the play. You can play a single card at a time whenever it's your turn. You have to build the cards up and down in consecutive order, starting from the 7 in each suit. After someone plays the 7 of a suit, the next player can legally put on the 6 or 8 of the suit. If the 6 is played, the next player has the choice of adding the 5 or 8. If the 8 is played on the 7, the next player can put down the 6 or the 9, and so on.

Whoever gets rid of all her cards first wins.

Wheeling and dealing

To determine who gets to deal first, deal the cards face-up until someone receives a jack; the lucky person to get the jack deals the first hand. For subsequent hands, the deal passes one place clockwise.

If you play the game for money, everyone puts in his initial *ante,* a fixed unit, before the start of the hand. (You can make the stakes whatever you like; it only takes a small stake to get the blood racing. Because additional bets may well be made, a nickel may be quite enough for the ante!)

The dealer shuffles the cards and offers them to the player on his right to cut. He then deals out all the cards, face-down and clockwise. If you're playing with four people, everyone gets the same number of cards. If you're playing with three, five, or six players, some players get more cards than others (you just can't divide 52 evenly by 3, 5, or 6). This imbalance gets corrected over the course of a round of hands, because everyone gets extra cards on some hands during play.

If you play the game for stakes, the players with fewer cards each put in an extra unit to compensate for starting the game with such an advantage. These stakes are put into a central receptacle, or *kitty,* which can just be the middle of the table.

Getting down to the play

The player to the left of the dealer has the first opportunity to play. If she has a 7 in any suit, she must play it, putting it face-up in the center of the table. If she doesn't have a 7, she passes.

If the game is played for money, any player who passes must put an additional unit into the kitty. As you can see, Fan Tan's original name, Play or Pay, was very much to the point.

In England, the player with the ♦7 starts with that card. If you're playing the gambling variety of the game, you may not want to play this variation because it prevents one or more players from passing and contributing additional stake money to the kitty.

The next player can make one of the following plays:

✔ She can play a 7 in another suit if she has one. If she wants to play another 7, she places it directly above or below the other 7.

You don't have to play another 7 if you have another legal move that you would prefer to make.

✔ She can build either up or down on any 7 that's already been played. If she has an 8 or a 6 in the appropriate suit, she puts it down to the right or left of the 7.

✔ If she can't make any other move, she passes.

Similarly, the next player can either build up or down from the existing structures or pass.

In Fan Tan, aces are only low, rather than high. You can only play an ace after a 2, not after a king.

If you can play, you must do so, however tactically unwelcome it may be to release a card that you would rather keep in your hand. Often, you find that you don't want to play a card that simply makes other people's lives easier — but that's life, I'm afraid. If you fail to play when you could have done so, the penalty is either social ostracism or, as the Mikado said, "Something with a little boiling oil in it." A player who is caught holding back in a stakes game can't win the hand on which the offense occurred.

After a few turns around the table, the cards form into piles on both sides of the 7s that may look like the ones shown in Figure 15-1. In the spade suit, for example, the ♠8, ♠9, and ♠10 are nestled beneath the ♠J, and the ♠6 and ♠5 are invisible below the ♠4.

In Figure 15-1, the next legal cards to play would be the ♠Q or ♠3, the ♥9 or ♥2, the ♦10 or ♦4, and the ♣9 or ♣6. The next player to go can play any one of those cards — or must pass if he can't make any of those moves.

When a pile comes to the end of its natural life (when an ace or king has been played and the sequence can advance no further), turn over the pile to indicate that fact.

The first person to get rid of all his cards wins, and play stops. He takes the kitty, if the game is being played with stakes, but before he does that, all the other players put in one unit for every card left in their hands.

Figure 15-1:
Going high
and low in
all the suits.

Expanding your Fan Tan smarts

To play Fan Tan well, you need to familiarize yourself with a few essential elements of strategy.

If you only have one card that you can play, you don't have much choice but to play it. Your Fan Tan strategy starts when you have more than one card you could play.

If you have more than one playable card, look first at the suits in which you hold *end cards,* which are the aces and kings in each suit. End cards pose all kinds of problems because you can't get rid of them until every other card in the suit has been played, usually close to the end of the game.

You will have some end cards in almost every game of Fan Tan you play. Your strategy revolves around persuading people to play cards in the suit in which you hold end cards.

Choosing between 7s

Starting at the very beginning, your first idea is to play as quickly as possible any 7 in a suit where you have an end card. Similarly, if you have a 2 or a queen, think about playing the 7 in that suit right away, if you have it. If you play in a four-player game and you hold back a 7 in a suit where you have cards that are close to the end, you may increase your chances of not finishing last, but you reduce your chances of winning.

For example, pretend that you get the cards shown in Figure 15-2.

Figure 15-2:
Letting go
of the hot
potato.

You want to play the ♠7 as soon as possible to encourage others to play on the suit. You have both a high (♠K) and a low (♠3) card in spades — time to get cracking on the suit at once! But with your mid-range cards in hearts, you may keep the ♥7 back for as long as possible, because it seems to be to your advantage to have players unable to play hearts for the time being. If hearts are the last suit played, you're more likely to win the game.

Given the choice, you should play on suits in which you have end cards (the ace, 2, king, and queen) rather than suits in which you're comfortably placed with middle cards (between the 3 and the jack).

Playing your end cards

In general, you want to minimize other people's opportunities to play — and thus to restrict their freedom of action, so that they have to release cards that they want to retain in their hands. Following that logic, playing an end card (an ace or a king) whenever you can is a good idea. The end card gives no new opportunity to play to anyone. Make the other players release cards they are reluctant to let go, which in turn allows you to play your other cards.

Playing a sequence

Similarly, for the same reason that end cards are potentially attractive plays, you often find that you can use a run in your hand to force others to play. A run occurs when you hold something like the ♠Q ♠J ♠10 ♠9; the play of the 9, 10, or jack gives no other player an additional opportunity and thus can force your opponents to make moves which they would rather not do. With any luck, those moves help you get your end cards out.

Think carefully about whether you want to release a single card rather than play your end card or work on a sequence or run. The answer depends on whether you want your opponents to play on the suit in which you have the single card, or whether you want to hold that card back to inconvenience them and make their lives more difficult.

Use your sequences after you've made all your plays in the suits where you have end cards, and not until then.

Double-Deck Fan Tan

All your friends will want to join in when you play Fan Tan. That's where Double-Deck Fan Tan comes in — it's a great game for large groups, when a single deck leaves you with too small a hand to start with.

To play Double-Deck Fan Tan, you need the following:

- **Seven or more players**
- **Two standard decks of 52 cards without jokers**
- **A pencil and paper for scoring**

You play Double-Deck Fan Tan just as you play Fan Tan — see "Your Fan Tan Mission (Should You Choose to Accept It)" for the details. You will obviously have eight rows of cards in Double-Deck Fan Tan, instead of the four rows in traditional Fan Tan.

With two of each card circulating in the deck, you have no assurance that you'll be able to put down your cards when a space arises, because someone may fill in the vacancy first. More 7s may be around, but you still don't know exactly when you can get your cards out; when the player on your left puts down the ♦J, will you be able to get your ♦Q out, or will someone with the other ♦Q beat you to it?

Double-Deck Fan Tan is more random than standard Fan Tan, and thus less strategic, which you may view as a disadvantage. At the same time, Double-Deck Fan Tan equals out skill levels, so it's appropriate for adults and children playing together.

Trump Fan Tan

Are you getting bored of regular Fan Tan? Well, try spicing it up by the introduction of a *trump suit* (a wild suit).

You play Trump Fan Tan exactly as you play traditional Fan Tan — see "Your Fan Tan Mission (Should You Choose to Accept It)" for the details — with one important difference. In Trump Fan Tan, the spade suit becomes wild, meaning that you can play every spade as the equivalent number in any other suit. Take the cards in Figure 15-3 as an example.

Figure 15-3:
Spades can have multiple identities in other suits.

You can use the ♠10 as the ♥10, ♦10, or ♣10. This card can get you out of a jam in any of those suits.

What happens to the ♦10 if you displace it with the ♠10? Logically enough, cards displaced from their suits by spades go into the spade suit and can only be played there.

WARNING!

The rules of the trump suit don't apply to the ♠7, which specifically retains its identity as a spade. You can't put down the ♠7 to represent any other 7. But all other spade cards can represent themselves to be the equivalent number in any other suit.

TIP

Play your spades as early as you can in the place of cards in other suits, unless you have good reasons to keep your wild cards for play in another suit — one in which you have end cards, perhaps. But all things being equal, you want to mess up other people's strategy by playing your spades as soon as possible.

Getting left with a usurped king or ace is very bad news, because the spade suit always seems to get built right at the very end. Because players put their spades down as quickly as possible as wild cards, you have to wait for some time before the spades themselves are advanced with all the leftover cards.

Crazy Tan

Folks with a tenuous grasp on reality really seem to enjoy Crazy Tan. Proceed with Crazy Tan at your own mental risk.

The basic idea is similar to Fan Tan, in that the object of the game is simply to get rid of all your cards — see "Your Fan Tan Mission (Should You Choose to Accept It)" for the details. You need all the same equipment for Crazy Tan, too.

However, you give seven cards to each player, thus leaving a stock of undealt cards. The player to the dealer's left leads, if he has a 7. If he can't play a 7, then he picks up a card from the stock pile. If he picks up a 7, he must then play it.

If the first player can't put a card down and has to pick up a card that isn't a 7, the next player is under slightly greater pressure. If the second player can't play, she must pick up *two* cards. And if the third player can't put a card down, he picks up *three* cards. As soon as anyone picks up a card that she can play, the count goes back to zero. Of course, the more cards you pick up, the more likely it is that you pick up something that you can play.

To speed up the game, you can introduce *runs* into the game. Instead of playing only one card at a time, whenever you have a sequence or run in the same suit, such as the ♥9 ♥10 ♥J, you can put them all down at the same time.

If I introduce one variation, I can introduce a second; how about *multiples?* Multiples allow you to play two or more of the same card at the same time. In other words, when you have two 10s (from different suits) that can be legally played at the same moment, you may put them down on the same go.

If multiples aren't enough for you, you can go to the well again. How about *multiple parallel runs?* If you play the concept of both multiples and runs, then multiple parallel runs won't faze you. If you can put down two 4s at the same time or 432 at the same time, you can try to put down 432 in two suits at the same time! A multiple parallel run may not happen very often, but you will look back on it with great pleasure when it does.

Part VI
Adding and Climbing Games

The 5th Wave   By Rich Tennant

"Well, the first thing old Lucky's gonna do is try to sucker someone into a game of Cribbage, and then he's gonna skunk him. And you don't want to be skunked by old Lucky."

In this part . . .

Adding and climbing? That sounds like a lot of work, doesn't it? Well, I can promise you that the two main games I discuss in this section, Cribbage and President, are more fun (and less work) than those two words may imply.

One of the features that renders President and Palace unique is the idea that a successful performance at one hand entitles you to a higher status than those who have performed less well. As such, for the next hand, the poor performers have to subsidize the more elevated players by giving up some of the more precious cards in their hand, thereby creating a vicious circle that makes it difficult for the lowlier players to break out from their low status.

Chapter 16

Cribbage

C ribbage is a game of experience and intuition rather than strict mathematical calculation. In a given situation, one card may be the right one to play and another the wrong card, and you may have no way to calculate which card is best. Sometimes you just have to take a chance and sniff out the right thing to do. It's also a fast game, where experienced players can complete a game in 10 or 15 minutes — slow play is not encouraged. You may want to start playing Cribbage with other relatively inexperienced players.

Cribbage is a finicky game — it features many rules and regulations, and it may seem that a rule of etiquette governs almost every aspect of the game. Cribbage also has a vocabulary all its own, which means that you need to know a few specialized words in order to play.

That's where this chapter comes in. I tell you everything you need to know to get started.

To play Cribbage, all you require is the following:

✔ **Two players**

✔ **A standard deck of 52 cards, without any jokers**

✔ **A pencil and paper for scoring:** Cribbage is frequently played with a Cribbage board, and some people think that using the board is an integral part of playing the game. However, the pencil and paper version of scoring does equally well in a pinch.

Cribbage on the Web

The American Cribbage Congress (ACC) Web site (www.cribbage.org/) is the place to go for online Cribbage news and information. You get it all here — Master Rankings, a list of tournaments in the United States organized by date or location (with telephone numbers to contact organizers for more information), and details about joining the offline version of the ACC. In addition, you find lists of clubs in the U.S. by region, a library of playing tips, and a set of links to other Cribbage and gaming sites. Don't leave this Web site without visiting the gallery that features pictures of Cribbage boards!

Starting Off on the Right Foot with Cribbage

Cribbage is a game of scoring points. You start out with six cards, from which you discard a couple of cards, leaving yourself with four cards. You get opportunities to record points during two phases of the game — in the play of the cards and then from totaling up your hand.

Dealing the cards and getting started

To start the game, both players cut the deck, and whoever draws the lowest card is the first dealer. The other player becomes the *pone,* which is just a crazy Cribbage term for *non-dealer.* The deal alternates for each hand in the game thereafter.

Don't fret if you're the first to deal. You're actually in luck — it's a distinct advantage to deal.

For every hand, the entire deck is shuffled by the dealer, who offers the cards to the pone to cut. The dealer then deals six cards face-down, one at a time, to both players, and puts the rest of the deck, the *stock,* in the middle of the table.

Some play that the pone doesn't get the chance to cut the cards before the deal, and if the dealer makes the mistake of offering the cards to the pone, the pone can go right ahead and deal the cards, usurping the right to deal the hand. The logic behind this approach may be that Cribbage is considered a gentleman's game and that no one can be suspected of doctoring the cards, so the cut is irrelevant. This trusting attitude seems to me to assume too much. In the words of a Russian proverb, "Trust — but verify." Check which rules your opponent plays by before you start the game.

Each player picks up his six cards and discards, or *lays away,* two cards face-down from the six he was dealt. Those pairs of cards go into the *crib* to form a third hand of four cards that gets scored for the benefit of the dealer — which explains the benefit from dealing. The dealer gets two hands with which to score points, as opposed to the pone's one hand. Please see "Choosing the right cards to lay away" for tips on choosing which cards to put into the crib.

If a misdeal of any kind occurs, either because the dealer deals the wrong number of cards or because a card is exposed in the deal, the cards are automatically redealt, so long as the error is caught before both players make their discards. If the mistake comes to light after the players have made their discards, the player with the correct number of cards can take 2 points and demand a redeal. Alternatively, he can ask the player with the wrong number of cards to take an additional card from the top of the deck or, if appropriate, to put her excess cards back into the deck.

If you intend to play a *rubber* of three games, the players swap the right to deal the first hand on the second game. If, at the end of two games, each player has won once, then the players cut again for the right to deal the first hand of the third game.

Cutting the deck

After both players decide which of their four cards to keep, the pone cuts the rest of the deck, and the dealer turns over the top card of the cut deck to reveal the upcard or *starter.* This card essentially becomes part of all three hands — the dealer's and the pone's hands and the crib; see "Phase 2: Scoring the hand" for more information. The starter doesn't register in the playing of the hand.

At this time, you can score the first points of the hand. If the upcard is a jack, the dealer scores 2 points; these 2 points are known as *two for his heels.* These points must be claimed and recorded by the dealer before any cards are played (see "Recording the score").

Phase 1: Playing the cards

The play of the cards gives players their first serious chance to score points. During the play, the players take turns playing one card from their hand. Their goal is to form certain combinations of cards and thus to score points.

During the play of the hand, the players must keep track of the cumulative value of the cards that have been played. The cards have the following values:

- ✔ Aces are low; they represent 1 point.

- ✔ All *court cards* — kings, queens, and jacks — count 10 points each in the play.

- ✔ The numeric cards get their face value. For example, a 3 is worth 3 points.

How it all happens

The pone leads by putting one card face-up in front of herself and announcing the cumulative total of the value of the cards — in this case, the value of her card.

The dealer then plays a card and calls out the combined total of the value of the two cards, marking up any points that he may have scored in the process (see "Spelling out the types of combinations" for more information on which combinations score points).

Play continues by the pone playing another card and calling out the cumulative total, and so on. Each player keeps his played cards face-up in front of him rather than mixing the two hands, and all the cards remain visible during the hand. Although the played cards can form combinations with the other player's hand, each player keeps his cards in a separate pile.

You can play any card at any time, with the following exception: During the play of the cards, the cumulative total of the value of the cards can't exceed 31 points. Sooner or later (usually sooner), one player finds herself unable to play a card without taking the total over 31. When that happens, she passes, saying "Go" to the other player, who must play any further legal cards if he can. He scores 1 point for being the last to play, which is called *1 point for go*. However, if either player can take the total to *exactly* 31 points, he gets 2 points for doing so; if you score 1 point for go, you only get 1 further point for bringing the total to 31.

When the total value of the cards reaches 31, or when neither player has a legal card to play, both players turn over their played cards and start off anew with their unplayed cards. The hand that had to pass and conceded

1 point for go is the first to play, and both players take turns again to play their remaining cards. Again, the last to play scores 1 point — or 2, if he takes the total to exactly 31 points.

As you can see, the dealer must score at least 1 point in the play, whatever else happens; because he plays second, he is bound to score the 1 point for playing the last card at some phase of the play.

Some people play that the dealer can't win the game by scoring 1 point for go. This rule ensures that the pone gets the chance to score her hand at the end. However, because life is generally unfair to the pone anyway, I don't see why you should make her life any easier artificially.

Spelling out the types of combinations

The idea of this phase of the game is to score points by achieving any of the following combinations of cards:

- ✔ If you bring the cumulative total of your cards and your opponent's cards to 15, you score 2 points.

- ✔ If you match, or *pair,* the card played most recently by your opponent, you score 2 points. For example, if the first player puts down a 10, you score 2 points by playing a 10 in another suit.

- ✔ If you make a *pair royale* (play a third card of the same value), you score 6 points for the achievement.

- ✔ If you play a fourth card of the same value, you achieve the rare feat of a *double pair royale,* which scores you 12 points. I don't remember the last time I saw a double pair royale.

- ✔ If you and your opponent play cards that form sequences, you score points for the length of the sequence. A *sequence* means, for example, 789 or 423 or QJK. For example, if three cards are played consecutively (two by one player, one by the other) that can make up a sequence, it scores 3 points for the player who puts down the third card.

Be careful with this one! The cards don't necessarily have to be played in sequential order for the sequence to register, and the suits of the cards are irrelevant. If player one plays a 7, player two plays a 6, and then player one plays a 5, that counts as a valid sequence; so do the cards played in the order 576 or 756.

A sequence of three scores 3 points, a sequence of four scores 4 points, and so on. The player who put down the fourth card scores the points for the sequence of four, of course.

Determining a strategy to score points in the play

You can maximize your opportunities to score points during the play by keeping the following tips and hints in mind.

Choosing the right cards to lay away

The first time you can affect your chances in the play comes when you select your cards to lay away in the crib. The points scored in the crib go to the dealer. You score points for making pairs, combinations of 15, and sequences in the crib (see "Phase 2: Scoring the hand" for the details).

You can't reduce Cribbage to a series of mathematical rules, but a number of guidelines can help you maximize your opportunities when it comes to discarding cards into the crib.

Your first consideration is to try to keep the best combination for your hand. But at the back of your mind, remember that you want to help yourself in the crib if you're the dealer and not help your opponent if it's his crib.

If you're the dealer, try to throw into the crib *touching cards* (a 6 and 7 or 9 and 10), a pair of cards totaling 5 or 15, or a plain-old pair of cards. Especially promising nonpairs to throw into the crib are a combination such as a 7 and 8 or a 2 and 3, because they offer possibilities in at least two directions.

The single most promising card to lay away is a 5, because it combines so well to 15 with court cards. Lay the 5 away if you have no more than one total of 15, unless the 5 fits into a sequence in your hand. If, as the dealer, you have ♠5 ♥K ♥8 ♥6 ♦A ♣2, you may discard the king and 5 and hope that your opponent lets go of some high cards, too. The 5 is wasted if you keep it in your hand because you can't make any combinations of 15 if you keep the 5, and that's the best use for a 5.

As dealer, throw cards totalling 15 into the crib. For example, if you have the ♠2 ♥Q ♥3 ♦10 ♣9 ♣6 and you're the dealer, discard the 9 and 6; the combinations of 15 that you have left in your hand offer you some good chances in the play of the cards, and the cards you discard give you some promise in the crib.

As the pone, your first thought must be to keep a good hand together if you can. If you have a choice of actions, try to discard extreme cards — that is, a high and a low one.

If you can possibly avoid it, don't discard a pair or cards that add up to 15 — although sometimes you can't avoid it. For example, what if you have a hand such as ♠7 ♥Q ♥8 ♦9 ♦7 ♣5? You want to keep the 9877 combination, worth 12 points, but that requires you to let go of the queen and the 5, a highly volatile combination of 15. But what else can you do? If you keep 8775, it scores only six points, and while you may improve the hand on many starters, the 9877 has so much potential that you should damn the torpedoes and throw the queen and the 5.

Keep in mind that you can utilize your opponent's cards when you're playing the cards, but in scoring the hand, you use only your own cards.

When you have a choice between breaking up a pair of sequences and doing something else, you should generally keep the sequences. But sometimes disrupting the hand a little, to ensure that you don't pass your adversary something on a plate, is worthwhile. For example, if you are the pone with ♠3 ♠2 ♥K ♥7 ♣A ♣8, you can keep K32A for 5 points, but letting go of the 8 and 7 is too much. Keep 832A for 3 points and discard the king and 7, which don't hold out much promise together.

Leading to the first play

When you're the pone and you need to lead the very first play, you can choose from two strategies:

- ✔ **You can restrict your opponent's opportunities to score points.** Try to lead a card with a value less than 5. If you lead a card with a face value of 5 or higher, your opponent can pair it off or make a total of 15. At the same time, you want to retain at least one low card for later on in the play, so that you keep the possibility of playing a card as the score moves toward 31. For example, with ♠8 ♠2 ♥2 ♦5, the lead of either 2 makes a good start. But with ♠7 ♥7 ♥2 ♦6, you should keep the 2 for later use in the play and lead a 7.

- ✔ **You can lead one card from a pair.** You invite your opponent to score 2 points by pairing up your card, whereupon you can play the third card and collect 6 points of your own. So if you start with the ♠7 ♥7 ♥2 ♦6, lead a 7.

If you don't have either of these options, lead your highest card and take it from there.

Thinking about the whole hand

Planning for the worst in the play is normally the right approach. Consider what play you can make to ensure that if your opponent matches the card you play or makes the cumulative total up to 15, you can retaliate. Try to have a point-scoring reply available to you in such a situation.

For example, if you hold ♥7 ♦9 ♦7 ♣2, you lead a 7, hoping to play your 9 if the dealer makes 15 with an 8 to form a sequence or to play your other 7 if the dealer plays a 7 to make a pair royale.

If you're the dealer, bear in mind that pairing up the lead for 2 points is fraught with danger. You run the risk that your opponent has a third card of the same value and can make a pair royale for 6 points. However, you have a little insurance if you can reply to such a move with a further score. It's also sound to pair up if you've already seen a third card of that number either as a card you put in the crib or through your opponent's earlier play.

So if the pone opened by leading the ♠Q, and you, the dealer, had ♦K ♥Q ♥J ♦6, you'd play the 6 — not the king or jack, because of the risk of your opponent making a sequence; and you would not want to play the queen because of the chance of a pair royale coming up.

However, on a lead of the ♦9, when you have ♠9 ♥2 ♦4 ♣3, you should pair up the 9, because you can play the 4 to make 31 for 2 points if a third 9 appears from your opponent.

Always avoid taking the total to 21 if you can do so, unless you have scored points in the process by making a pair or sequence. Say that you hold ♥4 ♦9 ♦2 ♣4. When you lead the ♥4, your opponent plays an 8. Don't play the 9 to bring the total to 21, because doing so allows your adversary to peg 2 points easily if he has a 10 or court card in his hand. Instead, play your second 4, which takes the total past 15 and gives nothing away.

Try to avoid leaving your opponent the chance to make a three-card sequence — unless you can respond to it by scoring points yourself or unless you actually have scored points in creating the opportunity for your adversary. If you have ♦Q ♦J ♦9 ♣10 and your opponent leads a king, play the 10 or 9 rather than the queen or jack to prevent him from being able to make a sequence.

If you have ♠8 ♦A ♣7 ♣6, you leap at the chance to play an 8 for 15 and 2 points on your opponent's lead of the ♥7. (Note that you don't play the ♣7 because you have no reply to a third 7.) However, if you play your 8 and your opponent replies with a 6 for 3 points, you can pair it up for a further 2 points. If he plays a 9 for 3 points at his second turn, you can play your 6 to make 30 for a sequence of four cards, and with any luck, you can then play the ace to make 31 for 2 more points.

Phase 2: Scoring the hand

After you finish playing, you pick up your hand (the cards you've been placing on the table in front of you) and go on to the main phase of point-scoring. For this scoring phase, both players get to treat the *starter,* or turned-up card, as a fifth card to supplement their hands for pairs, sequences, and combinations of 15, but you can't use your opponent's cards, as you could before.

First, you score up the pone's hand, then the dealer's. After both hands have been scored, the dealer scores up his crib.

The significance of this order of scoring is that toward the end of the game, each player scores three hands in a row (two as the dealer, and then one as the pone) — which can have a significant impact on the strategy of the game.

The points that you score up in your hand and in the dealer's crib by and large come from the same categories as those for which you scored points in the play, but a couple of modifications complicate matters. Cards, including the starter, can be used in more than one combination. You score points according to the following criteria:

- ✔ Each combination that adds up to 15 is worth 2 points (however many cards are involved).

- ✔ Each pair is worth 2 points.

- ✔ The value of a sequence of three, four, or five cards is equal to the number of cards in the run. (Keep in mind that AKQ doesn't count as a run, because aces are low.)

- ✔ If all four cards in your hand are of the same suit, you have a *four-card flush* worth 4 points. (Be careful; the rules about the four-card flush don't apply to the crib, where you need the five-card flush detailed next.) No points are awarded for a flush in the play of the cards.

- ✔ A *five-card flush* (five cards in the same suit), using the starter as well, scores 5 points, in either player's hand. (This flush can also apply to the crib but is really quite rare.)

- ✔ If you have the jack of the suit of the upcard, it's worth 1 point and is always referred to as *one for his nobs*.

- ✔ The crib hand is scored in exactly the same way as your own hand, except for the restriction on four-card flushes.

Prime Cribbage numbers

Some numbers at Cribbage are impossible to score — 19, 25, 26, and 27. Because you can't score 19, referring to a hand as being worth 19 points is the humorous way of referring to a hand worth nothing.

Flushes, or sets of cards in the same suit, tend to be the poor relations when it comes to Cribbage hands. Consider them to be the last resort, and unless you can't do anything else, let them go. With all the cards in the same suit, you have no possibility of sequences and pairs. Flushes don't count in the play, just in the scoring, which takes place after the play.

Recording the score

Although it isn't essential for scoring, a Cribbage board can be useful. The board is a relatively simple device, with four rows of 30 holes in each of them. If you don't have a Cribbage board, you need to draw some holes on a piece of paper, as shown in Figure 16-1. You can then keep score by using coins or other small objects as markers.

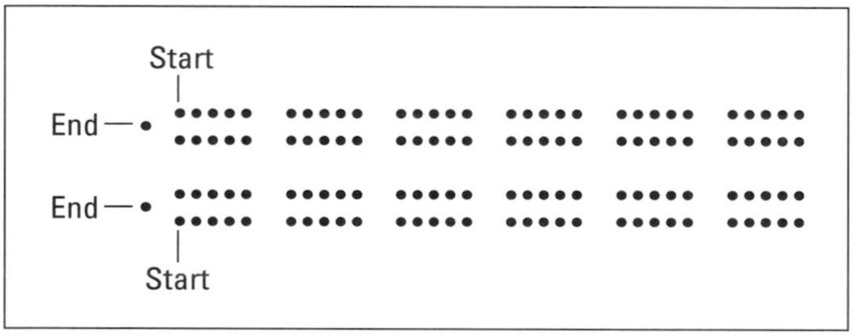

Figure 16-1:
The Cribbage board in all its glory.

Start

End —

End —

Start

Each player uses only one side of the board, either the top or the bottom. The object of the game is to go around the two tracks the same way a horse goes around a racecourse, and, just as in a horse race, the idea is to complete the circuits before your opponent does so. Beginning from the start point, the race involves going twice around your half of the entire circuit and then scoring 1 more point. Because each point you score advances you one more space, you can see that you need 121 points to complete your journey and win the game.

Players each get two pegs (or coins or other markers if you're keeping score on paper) to record their points. When you score your first points of the game, you put one peg on the board and then hop over the *leading peg* with the *trailing peg* as you score subsequent points, so that the board always shows how many points you recorded on your last score. Beginning from the start, you move up the outside part of the track and then back down the inside track.

For a short game, just go once around the course — in other words, to 61 points. The first player to reach or exceed the winning score takes the game, and play stops right there, even if the other player is panting to peg a high score.

In some versions of Cribbage (especially in the five-card variation described later in the chapter), the pone gets a head start of 3 points to compensate her for the loss of the deal.

Reaching the finishing post

When you're reaching the end of the game, you often find that a general strategy of preventing your opponent from *pegging out,* or winning, can override what may otherwise be the optimum strategy. If you're in the lead, you must play cautiously; if you're behind, you need to go all out for the win.

Say that both players have 100 points, and you're the dealer with ♥Q ♥8 ♥7 ♥2 ♦5 ♣8. You keep 8872 and throw the queen and 5 into your crib for 15 points. When a 6 is turned up, you realize immediately that you have 14 points in your hand and a promising crib. You're the favorite to win, because you only need to scrape up a few points from the play. What's more, as pone on the next deal, you have the first hand of the next game to count as well if you don't make it to 121 on this hand. So you must avoid giving away points, and you tackle the play as cautiously as possible. On the lead of an 8, you play your 2, rather than risking that your adversary has another 8. If he could play an 8 to make a pair royale, the 6 points would be worth much more to him than the 2 points for the pair are worth to you.

Conversely, if you're in the pone's shoes at 100 points each, you have to plan your discards on the expectation that your opponent will reach 121 over the course of this and the next hand. Therefore, you must go all out for the big win, come what may.

For example, if you pick up ♠K ♣4 ♥A ♦6 ♦4 ♣6, the best combination may be to keep K44A — cards that may improve to a decent hand on the turn-up of an ace, king, or 4 as the starter. But even turning up those cards isn't enough to give you a reasonable chance to win. Keep 6644 instead, which, on the turn-up of a 5, becomes a game-winner.

Don't get left in the lurch!

If you're playing Cribbage for stakes (and it's easy to do so, by playing for a penny a point — or a dollar, if you're a big spender!), additional gambles can be introduced into the game, rather than just playing a simple win/loss score. One such gamble is the ominously named *lurch* (or the even less-attractive *skunk*).

Lurching involves beating your opponent before he scores 60 points, an almost impossible feat in practice. If you're lurched, or *left in the lurch,* you lose a double stake.

Alternatively, some play that you can be *skunked* if you fail to reach 91 points or *double skunked* (the same as being lurched) for failing to reach 61 points. Being skunked costs a double game (the margin of victory is doubled for the winner), and a double skunk costs a quadruple game (the margin of victory is multiplied by four).

If you're gambling, you can also play a special scoring system for *dozens,* where you win a small additional stake for each hand in which you score more than 12 points during the play of the hand. You get a similar amount for any *nineteens* (0-point hands) that you manage to obtain in the crib. If you play these additional options, you need to keep a separate record of these elements on the scoresheet.

Don't fall foul of Muggin's rule!

If you play in a tough school, you may occasionally fall foul of (or benefit from) *Muggin's rule,* which entitles one player to point out a failure by the other player to score all the points to which he is entitled. The player who spots the forgotten points gets to claim those points for herself. Particularly if you're playing in a fast game, the occasional combination may get away from you, but the pain associated with Muggin's rule is enough to encourage you not to do it again! Not everyone plays this rule, and in games where one player is better than the other, handicapping the weaker player seems even more inappropriate to me.

You can correct any error in your score during the play if you spot the error before any more cards are played. If you play with a board, putting up the wrong pegging allows your opponent to call Muggin's rule at once.

Similarly, a failure to score your hand correctly can be corrected up to the moment of the cut for the deal of the next hand, if you aren't playing Muggin's rule.

However, if you claim too many points for yourself, your score is corrected and your opponent gets points equal to the number you overscored yourself.

Five-Card Cribbage

Five-Card Cribbage is another, earlier form of the game that I outline in the preceding portion of the chapter. The two games are the same structurally, and the main difference is that both players are dealt only five cards each and throw two cards away to leave themselves with only three cards. The crib still has four cards in it. The deal is more important, relatively speaking, in Five-Card Cribbage than in the six-card variety, which may explain why it's standard practice in this game for the nondealer to get 3 points right away in recognition of his handicap.

The play of the cards

In Six-Card Cribbage, each player plays out all his cards, and when the cumulative total reaches 31, the play starts again. In the five-card game, you get only one run-through of the cards; when the total gets to 31 or neither player can legally play a card, the play stops. Consequently, it's very unlikely that all the cards are played, and so the scoring is likely to be lower than in the six-card variety. All the types of scoring combinations are the same as those in the six-card variety. See "Spelling out the types of combinations" for more information.

Scoring the hand

All scoring is the same except that a flush in the hand only scores 3 points — logically enough, because it involves only three cards. See "Phase 2: Scoring the hand" for more information.

Reaching the finishing post

Because scoring is so much more difficult with fewer cards in each hand, the game only goes to 61 points.

Cribbage for Three Players

The game of Cribbage for three players resembles the six-card variety for two players (see "Starting Off on the Right Foot with Cribbage" for more information). The dealer deals out five cards to all the players and then puts one card into the crib directly. Each player throws only one card away, getting everyone back to a hand of four cards, with four cards in the crib also.

The player to the dealer's left cuts the cards to produce the starter. He then leads, and the players take turns to play, with one player scoring 1 or 2 points when neither of the other two can play. Each player plays strictly on his own, although you can imagine that it is in the interests of the trailing players to gang up against the leader if they can.

The player on the left of the dealer is the first to score, then the other nondealer, and finally the dealer.

Scoring for three on a regular Cribbage board is close to impossible, so you probably have to resort to pencil and paper or use a specially designed board.

Chapter 17

President

The game of President may come as an interesting surprise; it has very little in common with any of the other games discussed in this book and has a distinct feel of its own. Unlike almost every other game you may have come across, the results of a game of President extend beyond the scoring — the winner of the previous deal is entitled to improve his hand for the next game at the expense of the loser. Much good-humored abuse of privilege can take place in President.

The other peculiarity of the game is that it isn't obvious whether you should play at all on your turn, and if so, what card you should put down. President is a *climbing* game; your plays are determined by whether you can beat the previous player's card. Each play must equal or outrank the previous one.

You need the following to play President:

▶ **Four or more players**

▶ **A standard deck of 52 cards:** Jokers aren't essential but come up in some variations. If you have more than seven players, add a second deck.

▶ **Pencil and paper for scoring**

Mastering the Basics of President

You succeed at President by getting rid of all your cards before everybody else — or at least by not being the last player to get rid of them all. Everyone is dealt approximately the same number of cards. At each of your turns, you have the option of *following* the cards that have been played by playing cards of your own or of *passing,* or not playing a card. If you play first, you can make any legal play you want. Sounds easy, doesn't it? Well, it is — up to a point.

The rank of the cards is straightforward enough, with 2s the highest card, and then the regular sequence applies from the ace down to the lowly 3.

Dealing and playing the cards

The dealer for the first round, selected at random, deals out all the cards, face-down and clockwise, one at a time. For subsequent rounds, the dealer is based on the results of the previous round.

Due to the number of players at the table, some people may get an extra card, but that fact doesn't really present a problem; because those players are the first to play, this inequality evens out — supposedly.

The player to the dealer's left plays first, putting face-up on the table one, two, three, or four cards of the same value.

One fairly common variation for the initial play is to have whoever has the ♣3 to put it down, either on its own or in a set of 3s. Whichever rule you play, the hand continues in the same fashion.

After the initial card is played, the opportunity to play progresses in a clockwise direction. However, for any other player to put down cards, she must put down a set of the same number of cards — that is, if the first player put down three cards, all subsequent players must put down three cards. In addition, those cards must have a higher rank than the cards already played. At each turn, the next player can follow with the same number of cards of a higher rank, or he can pass.

President has many names

Many people know President by a different name. Among other names by which you may recognize it are Rich Man Poor Man, Landlord and Scum, just plain Scum, or Warlord and Scumbags. The game is also popular in Hungary, where it's known as Huberes (meaning *vassal*). However, it's most commonly known by a seven-letter expletive that I can't print here; think of it as a "fundamental" problem. So President it has to be, at least for the time being.

For example, say that you have six players, and C puts down the first card. The play may take this form:

A	B	C	D	E	F
		3, 3	Pass	5, 5	Pass
6, 6	Pass	J, J	All Pass		

"All pass" means that everyone passed after this point — no one had a play that she was willing or able to make.

In some variations, a single card played by itself is only beatable by a higher card of the same *suit* (clubs, diamonds, hearts, or spades). This rule makes the game considerably harder — probably too hard.

When you play a card (or cards) that everyone is unable or unwilling to top, the trick is over. The cards are swept away, and whoever played last on the previous trick starts the sequence of plays again, playing whatever card or cards he wants to play.

Some folks play that only one time around the table is permitted per trick. In the preceding example, then, play would have stopped when B passed. Because A was last to play, she would lead to the next trick. This option seems inferior to me, because it leaves the last person to play on a trick in too favorable a position — she knows that if she plays on this trick, she gets to lead the next trick, which is a huge advantage. In the mainstream variety of the game, a player doesn't know whether his play will win the trick — a difference that has a big impact on strategy.

You can pass even if you have a legal move — and you may well want to. For example, say that someone leads a single card, and you're left with a high pair and a low card. If you would have to split up the pair to play, you should pass. The logic behind this decision is that if you get to play your high pair later on, you may force everyone else to pass. Then you can win the trick, and you can get rid of your awkward low card by leading it on the next trick. Playing just one of your high cards reduces your chance of winning a trick.

When you're the player leading the trick, letting go of your lowest cards first is almost always right. The problem with keeping a low card, such as a 3, is that you can never play it *on* anything. You have to wait to get the lead, and you can't do that if you have nothing left with which to get the lead, can you?

Some people play that *triplets* (three of a kind) outrank *doubles* (two of a kind), which outrank *singles* (cards on their own). These people maintain that a higher-ranking card is still necessary, so a pair of 5s can be played on a 4 but not on a 6. Some even play that a triplet of a lower number can be played on a pair, so, for example, you can play a pair of 7s on a queen. Both of these versions take some of the fun out of the game because they give you too much flexibility with your doubles and triplets.

Ending a hand

Everybody takes turns playing cards, if they're willing and able to do so, until one player runs out of cards. (If a player goes out when he is the last to play on a trick, he obviously can't lead the next trick, so the player to his left starts up the next trick.) Whoever is first out wins and becomes the *president* on the next hand. But play doesn't end at the first person out; play continues until only one player is left holding cards; that person becomes the *scum*. The finishing order determines who plays first, second, third, and so on for the next hand.

After the scum has surfaced, the scoring kicks in. The winner, and president for the next hand, gets 2 points, and the runner-up, or *vice-president,* gets 1 point. The scum, or *beggar,* loses 2 points, and the second-to-last player, the *worker,* loses 1 point. Everyone in between (the *congressman* and the *citizen*) scores nothing.

When nearing the end of a hand, you need to plan your strategy and, if possible, try to recall how many high cards are still out. Keep track of the aces and 2s if you can. When players are down to only a few cards each, you may have difficulty deciding whether to split up a pair in order to try to get the lead. Say, for example, that you're left with ♠K ♦K ♣4, and the last play was a single jack. Most of the other players have two to five cards left. You may not want to split up your kings if plenty of aces and 2s are still out. Your pair of kings are very powerful if played together, because no one is likely to have a higher pair. However, if you can tell that your king is likely to win the trick, play it. Then you can lead your 4 and have a good chance to get rid of the other king at one of your next turns.

Starting over: Who can do what to whom

All players acquire a social status, as well as points, as a result of the first hand. After the scorer does the arithmetic, the players title themselves according to their finishing position. The titles allocated are the *president,* the *vice-president,* the *congressman,* the *citizen* (which applies to all players in the middle of the pack), the *worker,* and the *scum* or *beggar.*

Before the next hand starts, everybody switches seats. The president gets to seat himself in the most comfortable chair, and the other seats are then arranged in clockwise order so that the vice-president gets the next best chair (to the left of the president), and so on. The scum is left to kneel on the floor or sit on a box or something equally uncomfortable. At this point, the next hand is dealt, and the scum has to follow a ritual here, too.

Only the scum is allowed to handle the cards; he shuffles and deals the cards and also clears away the cards at the end of every trick. No one else is permitted to interfere in the scum's duties, and the penalty for forgetting is to become the scum for the next hand, regardless of the finishing order on the hand. (Some play that the president deals the cards for the new hand after the scum prepares them, but that rule doesn't seem right to me, because the scum is supposed to do all the work.)

Before the new hand starts, the scum's humiliation is increased. The scum must give the president his two highest cards and receive the lowest cards in the president's hand in return. (Some people play that the president can give the scum any two cards he likes, but most people play that he must throw his lowest cards.) Similarly, the worker must give the vice-president his highest card and receive one in return. No one else exchanges cards. These exchanges obviously weight the odds heavily in favor of the status quo.

Just as the lower players must give up their best cards, so the top dogs must give up their lowest cards — even if it means splitting a pair to do so. The consequence of being caught infringing the rule is becoming the scum on the next hand.

In this game, it's considered right and proper for the president to seek to abuse his power over the lower players. Although the day of reckoning is always potentially just around the corner, you must make the most of your role as president while you can. Even if you get unseated as president later, you can look back happily on your day in the sun.

After the appropriate cards have been exchanged, the play of the hand begins, as I describe in "Dealing and playing the cards." The player to reach 11 points first wins.

Following with an Equal Card

The rules that I set out in the preceding section require that each card played be higher than the previous one. However, one school of thought allows you to play an equal card or pair of cards. Obviously, this variation only works if you're playing with more than one deck.

If you play the equal-card rule, it allows an additional twist: When you play an equal card, the next player has to miss a turn. In fact, the number of equal cards — whether one card, a pair, or a triple — played represents the number of players who have to skip a turn.

Some people restrict the play of equal cards by allowing the play of an equal card only if it is of the opposite color. So you can follow the ♥7 with the ♣7 or ♠7 but not the ♦7.

Conversely, some people introduce the idea of *suit ranks,* taking the Bridge valuation of spades as the top suit, followed by hearts, diamonds, and clubs. In that case, the ♥7 can only be followed by the ♠7, rather than the ♦7 or ♣7. If you play this rule, then any pair of cards that contains the spade ranks above the pair of the same number that doesn't.

Two variations are associated with the play of four of a kind:

✔ Four jacks can appear consecutively on the table in any of three different ways, and playing the cards in two pairs produces no excitement. However, playing four jacks at one time turns the game upside down — it inverts the ranking of all the cards for the rest of the hand. When you follow suit, you must do so with a *lower* card or set of cards, rather than a higher one.

When the suits are reversed, if you play that you can follow a card with its equal, the rank of the suits reverses to clubs, diamonds, hearts, and spades (in that order), and the superior pair is the one containing the club. A reversal almost certainly unseats the president and makes him finish last, not first; he generally has the best hand in terms of high cards, so when the "best" is reversed, he suddenly has a poor hand. The reversal lasts just for the one hand. If another four of a kind is played on the same hand, it restores the ranking order of the cards to normal.

✔ If four players play four single cards of the same rank consecutively, it produces an even more active revolution: The ranks of the cards are turned upside down, so that you have to follow with lower rather than higher cards. What's more, the order of play is reversed to playing counterclockwise, not clockwise. This reversal also applies only for the single hand. (Playing the four single cards is uncommon but not impossible, particularly if you don't follow the suit-ranking rule.)

Running Wild: Jokers and 2s in President

If you play with jokers, they can be used in two ways:

✔ **As the highest card (above the 2):** If more than one joker is included as a high card, mark them up to distinguish which ranks above the other one.

✔ **As a wild card:** A joker can be used in a set to make two 3s into a set of three 3s, for example. If you play the rule about allowing equal combinations (see "Following with an equal card"), a pure combination of two 9s beats a joker-9 combination.

The 2 can also be treated as having extra powers. In the mainstream version of the game, 2s simply rank as the highest cards, so to beat two aces, you need to play two 2s. However, if you aren't using jokers, you can play that a single 2 beats a combination of two, three, or even four of a kind. (Other people use other cards, such as the ♣3 or ♦J, as a wild card in this way, but these groups are in a distinct minority.)

In the Hungarian variety of President, all jokers, 2s, and 3s are wild.

Palace

Palace is also known as Karma, but it's far better known by a name which makes it onto George Carlin's list of words that are unacceptable on television.

Palace goes back to the standard theme of trying to get rid of all your cards as quickly as possible, but it introduces a number of elements that complicate the strategy, making the game both delightful and infuriating.

To play Palace, you need the following:

- **Three to six players**
- **A standard deck of 52 cards:** Jokers are necessary for the six-player game and are recommended, but not compulsory, for smaller groups.
- **Pencil and paper for scoring**

The target of the game is to get rid of all nine of the cards you are dealt. You get three sets of three cards — three in your hand, three on the table face-up, and three face-down. You have to get rid of them in that order — and yes, you have to get rid of your face-down cards without knowing what they are!

Unlike President, the regular order of cards, from ace to 2, applies here. Jokers are wild and can be played at any time, but they also have a special significance in this game that's unlike any other game that I have come across; see "Using the special cards" for more details.

Dealing and setting up

A dealer is selected at random for the first hand, and then the deal rotates clockwise thereafter.

The dealer gives each player nine cards. He starts by giving each player a parcel of three cards face-down.

The players then spread out the cards into a horizontal row without looking at them. Next, the dealer deals another three cards, which are turned face-up, one on top of each of the face-down cards. Finally, he deals three cards that the players pick up as their hands.

The balance of the deck (no cards remain when you have six players — all 54 cards are dealt out) is put face-down in the middle of the table as the *draw pile,* or *stock.* Players can pick up these cards during the course of the hand.

Before play starts, each player has the option of exchanging cards from her own three face-up piles into her hand. Players can make this exchange in any order they like; they don't have to take turns. Making your face-up cards as high as possible is a good practice.

Playing the cards

The player to the left of the dealer is first to play, and he starts the ball rolling by leading from the three cards in his hand. Players can use only the cards in their hands at this point in the game. The leader can play any number of cards of the same rank, putting the cards face-up to form the discard pile. Throughout this game, the *number* of cards led is irrelevant — all that matters is the *rank* of the card. The leader ends his turn by refilling his hand to three cards from the draw pile in the middle of the table, and the turn moves clockwise.

The next player must either play one or more cards of the same or higher rank, or he must pass. If he passes, he must pick up the whole discard pile, and his turn is over. If he makes a legal play, he picks up a card or cards from the draw pile to replenish his hand, and the next player has the same options. If a player passes and picks up the discard pile, then the player to his left starts the ball rolling again by leading.

This phase of the game takes some time, as players play, pick up from the stock, or pick up the discard pile. But eventually, all the stock is used up, and the game reaches a position at which a player has used up all the cards in his hand and has no cards left to play. At that point, and only then, a player may play from the face-up cards.

If the player wants to play one of her three face-up cards, she does so, and play continues. If she is unable or unwilling to play one of those cards, she puts one of her three face-up cards onto the discard pile and then picks up the whole pile as her hand. By transferring one face-up card to her hand, she has reduced the number of her face-up cards and has perhaps made it easier to make a play the next time around. Of course, before she can play a face-up card, she has to get rid of her new hand — which may take a while.

Eventually, a player works his way through his three face-up cards. On his next turn, he turns over, at random, one of his three face-down cards. This card may be one that he can play, in which case play continues, or it may be one that he can't play legally, in which case he picks up the discard pile and the newly-turned-up card as his new hand. Again, he has to work his way through the process, but at least he has disposed of one of his face-up cards.

When a player reaches his last face-down card and plays it legally, he wins the game. Alternatively, if his last face-down card is an illegal play, he simply picks up the discard pile and uses it up before he wins.

If you're playing the variation of the rules that allows you to rearrange your hand at the start of the game (see "Dealing and setting up"), pick up the low cards from your face-up cards and put them into your hand, and put down high cards as your face-up cards instead. Doing so gives you more flexibility in the later stages of the game and is a particularly good idea if you have a draw pile in the game.

Using the special cards

Some cards have special roles to play:

- ✔ The 2 is both high and low. You can play a 2 on any card legally, but the 2 then reverts to its role as the low card. So the next player can play anything he wants on top of the 2, because any card outranks a 2.

- ✔ When someone plays a 10, it removes the whole discard pile from play. The cards in the pile are set aside for the duration of the game, and the same player who played the 10 gets another turn. Now, of course, he can play any card he wants.

  The 10 can be a lifesaver, but it can save your opponent's bacon, too. If you have a choice of plays, you may want to keep the 10 if you can see that you're less likely to be in trouble over the next few turns than your opponents. Conversely, if the 10 is the highest card in your hand, you may well want to play it and clear the decks rather than pick up the discard pile. You can't play a 10 if the discard pile is at jacks or higher. (In some variations, however, 10s act as a wild card and can be played at any time.)

- ✔ Jokers can be played at any time and are *transparent* — that is, they have no value as a card; the pile keeps the value of the card played just before the joker.

Jokers, however, reverse the direction of the game, from clockwise to counterclockwise or vice versa. Playing a joker makes the last player have to beat his own card, an opportunity for sadistic merriment, which is only out-rivaled when the tormented one plays a second joker and returns the favor.

✔ When a set of four cards of the same rank is played (either singly or as a combination of plays), the whole discard pile is removed as if a 10 had been played, and the player who completed the set of four gets to play again.

✔ In some variations, a 7 must be followed by a lower card rather than a higher card. Sevens aren't wild; they can only be played if the previous card was a 7 or lower. And they don't cause a permanent revolution — after the next player plays a card lower than 7, the player after that must beat the low card, and the natural order of things resumes.

Who wins — and who loses?

You can play Palace until one player wins by getting rid of all his cards, whereupon the hand stops. But it is more in keeping with the spirit of the game for the hand to continue until a loser is determined, too. This player (because I can't call him by his real name, I'll just call him the *scum*) takes on the role of the scum in the game of President, and he must handle the cards, buy the drinks, and generally abase himself (see "Starting over: Who can do what to whom" for the humiliating details).

Part VII
Banking Games

The 5th Wave   By Rich Tennant

"It looks like you've been playing cards instead of practicing your counting again."

In this part . . .

*I*f you are tired with taking on all the other players, it can be pleasant to have a feeling of solidarity by playing against the bank, a single entity, frequently in the shape of the casino, where banking games are normally played. In return for a few percentage points in their favor, the casino will allow you to play Baccarat and Blackjack, and to spend as much or as little money as you want. Aren't they nice?

Conversely, some gambling games are not played against the casino; instead, it is every man for himself. That's the case with Poker, which I also discuss in this part of the book.

Chapter 18

Blackjack

In This Chapter

▶ Picking up some Blackjack basics

▶ Looking at the differences between Social Blackjack and Casino Blackjack

*B*lackjack is played in two similar ways, depending on whether you're playing a social game at home or playing in a casino. I deal with the friendly, at-home variety of Blackjack first and then tell you about the more formal casino version of the game.

To play Blackjack, all you need is the following:

✔ **At least two players**

✔ **At least one standard deck of 52 cards, without the jokers:** The standard game of Blackjack requires only a single deck of cards, but if you have more than seven players, add a second deck.

✔ **At least 20 chips:** You can use matchsticks or anything else you want to keep score, just as long as you can count with them.

Social Blackjack

In this form of Blackjack, the dealer gives you two cards to start, and you have the option to acquire as many more cards as you want. The object of the game is to make your cards total as close to a score of 21 as possible without going over that total. If you do go over 21, you lose the hand automatically.

You compete solely against the banker in Blackjack. Although other players are at the table, their performances are irrelevant to you. Each of the players takes on only the banker.

The first thing to keep in mind is that the suits of the cards mean nothing. You're only interested in the numerical values of the cards. Fortunately, this area of the game has no complexities — well, virtually none:

- Each card takes its face value from 2 to 10.
- The ace is worth either 1 or 11; each player has the option, depending on his hand, of choosing either value.
- The court cards — the jack, queen, and king — are all worth 10.

Getting started

After everyone organizes her starting chips (or matches, or peanuts, or whatever you use to keep score), the group needs to agree on minimum and maximum bets. If everyone wants to play a friendly game, a minimum of one and a maximum of three units — thus allowing bets of one, two, or three chips — makes sense.

Next, you need to select the initial banker, who deals the cards and plays against all the other players. To select the dealer, deal out cards face-up to each player in turn. Whoever gets the first jack is the banker.

Dealing the cards

The banker cuts the deck (by splitting the cards into roughly equal portions and putting the bottom half above the top half) and then takes the top card and turns it face-up. Next, he transfers this face-up card to the bottom of the deck, a procedure called *burning the card*. The purpose of this exercise is to alert everyone when the deck is fully used up and when the banker must shuffle the deck.

Some people play that if the card turned over is an ace, the banker puts the card back in the deck and cuts again to find a new card.

Louis XV liked Jack

Blackjack derives from Vingt-un (French for 21), a French game popular at the court of Louis XV in the eighteenth century and also favored by Napoleon in his exile at Saint Helena.

Blackjack may have acquired its modern name from a casino promotion that offered special odds on an ace plus a black jack.

Blackjack also goes by the names Vingt-et-un and Pontoon, especially in the United Kingdom.

The banker now deals one card face-down to all the players, starting from the player on his left and going clockwise. When everyone, including the banker, has a face-down card, the betting commences.

If the banker omits a player and accidentally doesn't deal him a first card, that player can demand a card at any time until the second round of dealing begins. After that point, the player is out for the duration of the hand. If the banker deals a player two cards instead of one at the first round, the fortunate player gets some options. She can either discard one of the cards and carry on as normal, or she can play both cards as the first card of two separate hands — in which case she must put up an extra unit. Any other time that a player gets an extra card, the player has his choice of which card to take but must discard the unwanted extra card.

Placing bets

The players look at their cards and can then bet any amount from the minimum *stake* (bet) up to a maximum stake, both of which should be agreed upon in advance by the players.

How players bet

Clearly, all the players want to bet as much as they can on their first card if they have a suitable one or bet the minimum if they don't have a good prospect. So what kind of card makes for a good bet? The best card is an ace, followed by court cards and 10s, and so on, down to the 7. Next best after the 7 is the 2, then the 3, and on up to the 6, the worst card.

A high card, coupled with another high card, gets you close to 21. A low card may give you more options in the play, but a middle card can leave you stuck in the middle with nowhere to go — if you draw a high card, you're left with a hand that is neither close to 21 nor small enough to allow you to draw another card safely.

This system suggests that you put the maximum stake on an ace or court card and a moderate stake on a 9 or an 8 — and perhaps on a 2, 3, or 7. Put the minimum on a 4, 5, or 6.

As the banker, you can draw some inferences from other people's bets, which may prove useful to you later on.

After the players have had a moment to consider their cards, the player to the left of the banker gets the first chance to bet. He simply places the units he wants to bet in the middle of the table, and then the next player gets her chance to bet, and so on, until it's the dealer's turn to bet.

How the banker bets

After the players make their initial bets, the banker looks at his card. If he likes his chances, he may double the stakes for everyone, by simply saying "Double!" If the banker doubles, everyone who stays in the game plays to win or lose twice the amount of money.

Doubling the stakes is probably the right strategy if he has an 8 or higher, although he may vary his strategy depending on whether the players have generally been betting high or low on this hand. The higher they bet, the more cautious the banker bets.

If the banker doesn't like his cards enough to double, he says nothing, and the players play for their initial stakes.

Choosing to withdraw or double

If the banker doubles, the other players can do any of the following things:

- They may withdraw — which is probably the right move on a 5 or 6, but players must know the banker's temperament to make this decision. If players withdraw, they lose their initial stake.
- They can accept and play for double stakes.
- They can accept and say "Redouble!" to quadruple the stakes — in which case someone gets taught a sharp lesson!

As a player, you should probably only redouble if you have an ace, unless you can see that the banker's judgment may be temporarily impaired by previous losses.

Moving on to the second round

After the first round of betting, the dealer gives everyone a second card face-down.

In some games, the banker turns his second card face-up, a huge advantage to the players; and in some circles, the players' second cards are dealt face-up, too. These variations have a huge bearing on strategy (see "Deciding on a strategy of drawing cards").

Should I stay or should I go?

After the initial hand of two face-down cards is dealt out, play proceeds clockwise starting with the player at the banker's left. That player looks at his hand; he hopes to see a *natural,* which is an ace and a 10 or court card, totaling 21.

If the player doesn't have a natural (and one rarely does), the player has two options, depending on how close the total of his two cards comes to 21:

- ✔ If the player is happy with his score (which usually means that he has 17 or more), he doesn't want any more cards. The player *stands* or *stands pat.* (Standing is also known as *sticking,* especially in England.) He can say "I'm good" or put his chips on top of the cards to indicate that he is standing pat. After indicating his choice, the player's turn is over, and the banker switches his attention to the next player.

- ✔ If the player decides that he wants another card, which he certainly does when his total is 14 or less, he can express it in a couple of ways. He can say, "Hit me" or "Again" (or "Twist" in England). The banker gives him another card — face-up this time. After that, the player has the option of receiving further face-up cards until he is satisfied with the total he has achieved.

The player keeps his first two cards face-down, so the banker knows some but not all the story at this point. The player turns over his hand only when the banker completes play.

Each player has the same options offered to her until everyone has her turn. The banker then turns over his cards and has the same options as the players had — to take more cards or to stick where he is.

Finishing the hand

If the player accepts another card and thereby takes his cumulative total over 21, he *goes bust* and loses. He must give up his stake, no matter what the banker does subsequently.

Anyone caught not surrendering her hand when she has gone bust must pay a forfeit of an additional stake.

Paying the players

If the banker busts, he must pay everyone who is left in (he has already collected the stakes of the players who have gone out either by choice or by busting). When the banker decides, at some point in the hand, to stick, every player turns over his hand. The dealer pays off all the players closer to 21 than he is while collecting the bets from everyone further away from 21 than he is.

If a player ties with the banker, the banker wins. All the players who go bust automatically lose their stakes, no matter what the banker does.

Natural consequences

If the banker gets a natural, he collects twice the stake bet by everyone — except from a player who has a natural himself, who has to pay only a single stake.

If a player gets a natural and the banker doesn't, that player gets twice his stake in return and, more importantly, takes over the deal for the next hand. The new banker reshuffles the entire deck before dealing the new hand.

If the banker gets really unlucky and two players pick up a natural on the same hand, the player who was dealt his cards first takes precedence and acquires the deal. The banker has to pay both players the double stakes, of course.

Two other treatments for the transfer of the deal are common. The first is that the deal passes after a certain number of hands, rather than when a player gets a natural. The other option for the banker is that he may *sell the bank* to the highest bidder if he calculates that he can't afford to pay out the field. Whoever bids the most takes over the deal. Because the bank generally has a big edge, selling the bank is something you do only in the case of a dire emergency.

Special payoff hands

If a player has a hand of five cards that total less than or equal to 21, it's called a *five-card trick,* or *five-and-under.* A five-card trick is an automatic winning hand, whatever the banker's cards total (unless the banker has the same or a natural, in which case he wins), and it pays double stakes. A *six-card trick* pays out four times your stake. The unlikely event of getting seven cards that total below 21 pays eight times your stake.

The possibility of a five-, six-, or seven-card trick is what makes a starting card of a 2 or 3 a reasonable beginning at Social Blackjack.

Social Blackjack has two other special hands:

- ✔ If you get to 21 with a hand consisting of a 6, 7, and 8, that hand pays you a double bet.
- ✔ If you get 21 via three 7s, you get a triple payment.

All these bonus awards apply only to the player, not the banker. The banker wins the hand with these two combinations, of course, because each means that he has 21, but they don't score anything special for him.

Getting ready to start over

At the end of the hand, the banker puts all the used cards face-up below the burnt card and then deals the next hand. When he comes to the burnt card in the middle of the deal, he shuffles the remaining portion of the deck, burns another card, and then completes the deal. The cards aren't shuffled at the end of each hand, only when the burnt card is reached.

Planning your play: basic strategy

Of course, much of your success at Blackjack has to do with the cards you're dealt. However, you can influence you chances of success by knowing how to respond to the cards you're dealt.

Splitting pairs: what to do with identical cards

If a player's first two cards are the same denomination, she has the option of *splitting* her cards.

After the banker declares her bet, the player who wants to split her cards turns them face-up and makes them into two separate hands, putting out one additional stake so that each hand has an amount equal to the original bet on it. The banker deals one face-down card for each hand, and the player plays each hand separately. The player now has two hands with a stake in each one. She can win both hands, lose both hands, or win one hand and lose the other.

If you have either a pair of aces or a pair of 8s, you should always split, whether the banker doubled you or not. The question as to whether to split is different in Social Blackjack (where the banker's cards aren't known) from that of Casino Blackjack, where a card of the banker's hand is known; (see "Splitting cards: When to stay together, when to break it up"). Don't split 2s, 3s, 4s, 5s, 6s, 9s, or 10s under any circumstances. Split 7s only if the banker hasn't doubled you.

If you split a pair of aces and subsequently turn one into a natural, you are *not* entitled to take over the bank. And you only get paid a single stake, not twice the stake.

If you're playing the variation where the banker turns up one of his cards, you know much more about his hand, but you should still **never** split a pair of 4s, 5s, 6s, 9s, or 10s. You should still always split aces, and split 8s unless the banker has a 9 or 10 showing. Split 2s, 3s, and 7s whenever the banker has a 5, 6, or 7 up.

Doubling down: when to up the stakes

If a player wants an extra card, he doesn't have to receive it face-up; he has a more risky option if he likes his hand, called *buying a card.* If a player's cards total 10 or 11, the player can double his bet and receive precisely one more card face-down. If you want to partake of this option, just say "Double down," and the dealer gives you an additional card.

You only want to buy a card when your cards total 10 or 11 because then your chance of drawing an honor card and getting a good total is pretty reasonable.

The downside to this approach is that a player isn't allowed to draw or buy an additional card thereafter, and by increasing the stakes, you leave yourself more exposed to loss. So you need a good hand to buy a card.

Casino Blackjack

Blackjack in a casino closely resembles the social form of the game (see "Social Blackjack" in this chapter) — except that Casino Blackjack is always played for money, of course. Additionally, Casino Blackjack has a degree of formality that doesn't apply to the social game.

When you arrive at the casino, the dealer will be there waiting for you and your money. At the casino, the following items will be at hand:

- ✔ **At least one deck of cards:** Most casinos play with at least four decks.

- ✔ **A casino table:** Blackjack is played at a semicircular green baize table with space for at least six or seven people to sit down.

The professional banker, known as a *croupier* (pronounced *crew P.A.*), has a *shoe* (a device from which to deal out the cards that avoids the risk of the cards getting turned over or accidentally seen) of four or more decks of cards. (A few casinos still play with single or double decks, but these places are now the exception rather than the rule.) The banker plays on behalf of the *bank* (the casino itself), who naturally wants to see him win. In the background, to the rear of the table, the *pit boss* (or supervisor) stands behind the banker, and the *croupiers* at other tables cast a watchful eye over the proceedings.

Betting at the casino

Most casinos have a minimum and a maximum bet. Most casinos have a table with only a $5 minimum, and you can play for less at many places, particularly in Reno, Nevada. As to upper limits . . . well, after you finish this book, your confidence may be high, but I'm not sure that you'll ever have to worry about breaching the bank's maximum bet rules.

The critical distinction between the casino game and the social one is that all bets are made in advance of the first card — you don't see the first card before you bet.

In Europe, the betting on a hand isn't limited to the player who picks up the cards: Any spectator (also known as a *kibitzer*) may also bet in advance on the hand. This variation is also played in some casinos in the United States.

How good a bet is Blackjack at the casino? The answer is not too bad. The banker's edge comes from the fact that the players have to commit themselves to drawing a card — and possibly going bust (going over 21) — before the banker plays out his hand. Even assuming good play by the gambler, this factor converts to about a 2 percent edge for the banker. Furthermore, the payouts for the players' really good hands aren't so generous at the casino — no bonus hands exist, and a natural for the player pays three to two odds, not double odds.

On the other hand, several factors weigh in on the side of the gambler at the casino:

- The player gets to see the banker's first card.
- The banker doesn't get to double the table, like at Social Blackjack.
- The banker's natural only pays him single odds — to even things out, I suppose.
- The banker doesn't win ties; they're a stand-off. This factor is the biggest one affecting the gambler's chances.

Overall, the player is better off than the bank. A good Blackjack player can hope to at least break even in the long run.

Casino formalities: dealing up and getting started

At the start of a game, the banker shuffles all the decks together and asks a player to put a marker into the bottom half of the decks somewhere. Only 75 percent or so of the deck is normally used before the cards get shuffled again at most casinos. The banker reshuffles the deck early because some expert players take advantage of their mathematical skills and can figure out when the deck is more suitable for the player than for the bank.

Before the deal, each player puts her bet down on the table. She can't reduce her bet thereafter, but the banker doesn't have the option to double the bet, either, as he does in Social Blackjack.

After all the bets are placed, the banker doles out a face-up card to each player and to himself. No further betting is permitted. A second card is dealt face-up to the players but face-down to the banker.

At this point, only one further action can take place before the player plays out her hand. If the banker deals himself an ace, he can offer insurance to everyone against his having been dealt a natural on this hand. This insurance allows the player to make an additional bet that pays off if the dealer has a natural but loses otherwise, a gamble paying odds of two to one if the dealer gets his natural. This is a bad bet — ignore it unless you know that many of the remaining cards in the deck are 10s.

The play of the cards

The players now proceed to play as in the standard social game (see "Social Blackjack" earlier in this chapter). Each player in turn declares a natural if he has one, stands pat, or calls for another card. If any player goes over 21, that player has no option but to concede, because everyone can see her cards. The players suffer no disadvantage from having their cards face-up in this version of the game, because the banker's plays are *forced* — he has to make the plays described in the following list.

After all the players have made their choices, the banker turns over his second card. He then must make one of the following plays:

- ✔ If he has 21, he collects all the bets from those players who haven't gone bust (gone over 21) — but not at the double rate that applies in the social game.

- ✔ If the banker has 17, 18, 19, or 20, he must stick, and he pays all better hands.

    Ties are a stand-off in Casino Blackjack, a difference from the rules of the social game. In the case of a tie, all the bets that are out on the table are returned to the players who made those bets.

- ✔ If the banker has 16 or less, he must take another card until he gets 17 or more or goes bust. This point has a significant impact on players' strategies, as you can read about in "Deciding on a strategy of drawing cards."

One variation, which is by no means universally played, allows players to surrender (by simply saying "Surrender") when faced with a particularly bad hand. When you surrender, you lose only half your stake. If the banker has a 10 up and you have 15 or 16, surrendering is probably your best option, because the banker's chance of beating you is more than two to one. (When the banker is dealt an ace, he looks at his second card to see whether he has a natural, so when play continues, you know that he doesn't have a natural. The fact that the banker doesn't have 21 makes surrendering on an ace less attractive.)

Deciding on a strategy of drawing cards

The banker's plays are compulsory, but the players' strategy isn't. In fact, the sight of one of the banker's cards leads to some fairly complex analysis.

Seeing one of the banker's cards makes a huge difference. Think about it this way: If the banker has a high card — say, a 9, 10, jack, queen, king, or ace — showing, his chance of having a good hand from his first two cards alone is pretty high, because any 8, 9, 10, court card, or ace as his face-down card (and he has more than a 50 percent chance of having one of those cards as his second card) gives him at least 17. Conversely, if the banker turns over a 4, 5, or 6, he can't have all that good a hand off his first two cards.

The sight of that initial card may affect your decision as to what to do on marginal hands — those hands ranging from 12 to 16 — where you aren't sure whether to stay or draw a card. If the banker has a 2 or 3, you're in fair shape as well, because he's unlikely to have a great hand and may well have a poor one.

Of course, most hands aren't marginal at all, but have pretty clear-cut actions. It's never right to take a card on 17 or more (unless you have an ace and a 6), and it's never right to stick on 11 or less, but on hands ranging from 12 to 16, your strategy is affected by what you see in the banker's hand:

- ✔ If the banker has a "good" card (an ace, court card, 10, 9, 8, or 7), take an extra card if your total is more than 11 but less than 17.

- ✔ If the banker has a bad card up (a 4, 5, or 6) stick on any total of 12 or more.

- ✔ If the banker has a 2 or 3, stick on any total of 13 or more.

An example should help you see the logic behind these guidelines. Say that you have a ♦10 and a ♦6 for 16, a lousy hand. If the banker has a 10, court card, or ace up, you're a heavy underdog, but the odds (I won't go into the calculation) say that your best shot is to take another card and to hope to improve your hand. But if the banker has a low card up, your best chance of winning the hand is for the banker to bust. You're definitely better advised to stay where you are and hope that the banker gets a bad second card, and then busts when he's forced to draw a third card.

Unlike Social Blackjack, 2s and 3s don't offer any special possibilities because most casinos don't have five-card trick or special payoff hands, although you may find rare exceptions for five- or six-card tricks (see "Special payoff hands").

Buying a card: when to double down

In Casino Blackjack, the bank is always happy for the player to invest more money, so you can *buy a card* (or *double down*), which means doubling your stake and receiving an extra card face-down, not face-up. You can buy a card regardless of the total of your cards.

Reno casinos don't allow doubling down on any number except 10 or 11.

However, when you buy a card you must double your original stake, and you receive only one card, at which point your turn ends. The fact that you get only the one card may discourage you from buying a card, and in a sense, doubling down does reduce your options, but it can still be very much the right play. Buying a card is another strategy that is heavily influenced by the banker's card; you only do so when the information in front of you persuades you that you are already the heavy favorite to win.

Follow these guidelines about doubling down:

- ✔ Always buy a card when your two cards total 11, no matter what the banker has up.

- ✔ Similarly, double down on a 10 or a court card unless the banker has a 10, court card, or an ace showing.

- ✔ Double down on a 9 when the banker has a low card (anything from a 2 to a 6) up.

- ✔ Double down when you have an ace and a low card (anything from a 2 to a 6) or two cards totaling 8 when the banker has his worst cards showing — that is, either a 5 or a 6. The logic is that because you're the favorite whatever you draw, you want to double the stakes if you can. This move may be less obvious than the relatively straightforward advice of the preceding three guidelines, but doubling down in this case makes sense.

Splitting cards: when to stay together, when to break it up

You can split your first two cards into separate hands and be dealt a separate card for each hand whenever your first two cards are a pair. Again, the casino is always happy to see a player invest more money, and so you may split on any pair if you want.

The one restriction is that if you split aces, you get only one extra card for each hand. In addition, if you make a natural, it pays only single odds. But splitting a pair of aces is still clearly the right play.

At most casinos, if you split a pair and then draw the same card to form another pair, you can split your new pair again to form three hands.

The general approach to splitting up a pair goes along the following lines:

- **Never split a pair of 4s, 5s, or 6s.** Numbers like 8 and 10 are good totals for you because the chances of drawing an ace, king, queen, or jack are quite good. You don't want to break up those hands. And because a 6 is the single least promising card, why voluntarily saddle yourself with two of them as the nucleus of a hand? A total of 12 may not be such a great number either, but it's the best you can do under the circumstances.

- **Split a pair of 8s (because 16 is such a bad total) unless the banker has a 9, 10, court card, or ace.** When the banker has one of those cards, you're favored to lose, and thus you don't want to concede twice your stake. (And following my previous advice, draw a card with your 16 in these circumstances.)

- **Never split 10s or court cards.** By splitting 10s, you give up a sure win in the hope that you win on both hands; not, by any means, the right thing to do unless you're more than 75 percent favored to win both hands.

- **Only split 9s if the banker has an 8 showing.** In this case, you figure to get 19 on one hand and he figures to get 18, so you're improving your position, whereas if you don't split, the hand is likely to be a stand-off.

- **Split 7s if the banker has a 5, 6, or 7 showing.**

- **Split 2s or 3s if the banker has a 7 or lower card showing.**

Going high or low when you have an ace

When you have an ace and another card, your hand has two possible values: a *soft* one, counting the ace as *low* for 1; and a *hard* one, counting it as *high* for 11.

Once again, your policy is affected by what the banker has showing:

- ✔ When the banker has a good card up (an 8, 9, 10, court card, or ace), only stick on 19 or higher. For example, when you have an ace and a 7, draw a card, because you're a favorite to lose if you don't. If you don't get a good card, you can draw another card, or hope that the banker draws a bad card and goes bust.

- ✔ If the banker has a bad card up (anything less than a 7), stick on 18 or higher; never stick on 17 no matter what the banker has showing.

- ✔ When the banker has a 5 or 6 up, you should not only take a card with your ace and low card, but you should also double down and buy a card.

  Doubling down gives you two chances to win. Either you can pick up a good card, or the banker can go bust.

Of course, if you draw a card and go over 21 by using the valuation of the ace as 11, you revert to the other valuing scale, and follow the appropriate strategy defined above.

Blackjack on the Web

You can practice your Blackjack strategy in several places on the Web, and in this section, I name just a few that caught my eye.

At Casino Areneum (www.araneum.dk/casino/ukindex.html), you must go through a quick registration process, and then the site starts you off with 5,000 Cyberbucks (sorry, these bucks have no value outside of Cyberspace). After you finish playing, you can visit the site's chat room to discuss your luck (or lack thereof) with other players.

More online play awaits you at Blackjack Time (test.blackjacktime.com/), where you can compete in tournaments if you feel especially lucky.

Those with Java-enabled browsers (you know who you are) can't miss Virtual Las Vegas (www.virtualvegas.com/newvv/html/strip.html), where you choose your dealer from among three characters. Start out with $2,000 and practice your strategy without losing money!

Chapter 19

Baccarat

· ·

· ·

*B*accarat is the generic name for a game played in casinos all over the world. Punto Banco and Chemin de Fer are currently the most popular forms of Baccarat, so I start with the description of Chemin de Fer (which is played mostly in the United States and the United Kingdom), and then I discuss Punto Banco (the most popular form of Baccarat played in the United States and Europe today). Then I touch on Baccarat a Deux Tables (a form of Baccarat popular in Europe).

You may just want to watch these games when you're at the casino! Most casinos require very large bets at the Baccarat tables. You may prefer to investigate less nerve-wracking games than Baccarat, such as Blackjack.

If you decide to play Baccarat, you'll find the following items at hand when you arrive at the table:

✓ **At least two people:** Playing with more than two people is customary, but the game functions perfectly well with two.

✓ **At least one standard deck of 52 cards, without the jokers**

Discovering the Basics of Baccarat

In all Baccarat games, the players and the banker try to make the total value of their cards add up to 9. You seek to get as close to 9 as possible, but going past the magic number doesn't automatically disqualify your hand.

Bond was a Baccarat man

For a good description of the atmosphere associated with Baccarat at a casino, you can't do better than to read *Casino Royale,* the first of the James Bond books, by Ian Fleming.

When adding up your cards to reach 9, assign the following values to the cards:

- ✔ All the cards between the 2 and 9 retain their face value. A 3 is worth 3 points, for example.

- ✔ All the court cards (the kings, queens, and jacks) count as 0.

- ✔ All aces count as 1.

To see the valuation scale at work, consider the three hands in Figure 19-1.

Figure 19-1:
Three equal
hands in
Baccarat.

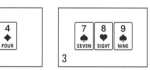

Each of these wildly different hands has the same value — 4.

At the beginning of the game, the player puts down his bet and the banker deals the player and himself two cards face-down. The player's hand is then turned face-up and examined. If the total is an 8 or 9, play comes to a very quick stop; the player wins unless the dealer also has an 8 or 9. If both have an 8 or 9, the hand is declared a tie and the bets go back to their owners.

With any other number besides 8 or 9, the player either takes another card or stays where he is, depending on how close to 9 he is.

The banker then turns over his cards and either draws a card or stays where he is, depending on his total and the draw by the player.

After both the player and the banker are satisfied with their hands, a final comparison is made. The player who ends up closest to 9 wins and collects the bets. In the case of a tie, the bets are returned to the players.

Chemin de Fer

Chemin de Fer (also known as *Shemmy* or *Shimmy*) is the simplest variety of Baccarat. It's also one of the easiest to pronounce — it sounds like *shirr man duh fare*. It's a contest between the banker and as many other players as want to take him on. The only rule that restricts the number of players is that the total bets against the banker can't exceed the banker's bet.

The players sit at a table shaped like a bow tie, and at least two employees of the casino, called *croupiers,* sit in the middle of the bow tie. One croupier has a shoe containing at least three decks of playing cards. (A *shoe* is an automatic dealing device that eliminates any accidents in the dealing.) The other croupier supervises the betting. The casino is not directly involved in the betting — the players are betting among themselves. The casino's only interest in the game is that it collects a commission on the bets.

The first banker (who also deals) is chosen at random, or else the player who offers the largest stake for the first hand becomes the dealer. For example, the largest first bet could be $100. The player who makes this bet puts that amount on the table.

The player to the banker's right then has the option to take on all or part of that $100 by putting his bet on the table (unless someone else beats him to it; see "Cornering the market"). Whatever is left uncovered by that player can be bet by the next player, and so on, until a total bet of $100 is made. For example, if the first player bets $40, then the second player can bid up to $60. If the second player bets $30, then the next player can bid up to $30.

If the players' bets don't cover the banker's bet, the portion of his bid in excess of what is covered is taken off the table and returned to the banker.

Cornering the market

If one player wants to take on the banker for all his bet, she calls out "Banco." (*Banco* sounds like *bank-o.*) This call entitles her to a head-to-head encounter with the banker. If two players make the call, the player closer to the banker's right wins the privilege to compete solo with the banker.

Any player may call out *Banco,* but after a player has done so and lost to the banker once, she gets the chance to recoup her losses on the next round by calling out "Banco Suivi," which sounds like *bank-o swee vee.*

If no one calls Banco or Banco Suivi, then any player may call "Avec la table," which sounds like *ah-vek la table.* Calling Avec la table means that the player, and that player alone, competes directly with the banker for half the banker's bet.

Following the pattern: the play of the cards

The player who made the largest bet plays the cards for the other players, and the banker handles his own cards. I know it sounds strange that one player plays for all the others at the table and can essentially lose someone else's money. It all works out because the player must follow very restricted paths during the play, which you read about shortly.

The dealer deals four cards in total — two to the player who made the largest bet and two to himself.

The player and the banker both look at their cards, and if either or both sides have a hand totaling 8 or 9, they turn their cards face-up immediately. A hand that totals 8 or 9 is called a *natural;* a natural automatically wins the hand. The naturals are known as *Le Grand* (totaling 9) and *Le Petit* (totaling 8), "the big" and "the small" naturals. If one side has an 8 and the other a 9, the 9 wins.

The hands in Figure 19-2 are all naturals. The second hand, which is worth 9, would beat the other two, which are only worth 8 each.

Figure 19-2:
Each of
these hands
is a natural.

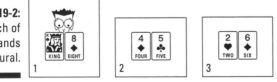

If both sides have a natural or exactly the same number (if both sides have an 8, for example), they have a *standoff,* and the bets are returned to the players. Then the banker makes another bet, which must equal or surpass his previous bet, and the cycle commences again, with players matching all or part of this bet.

If neither side has a natural, the player may take another card — under certain strict and rigidly enforced circumstances, which I outline in Table 19-1.

Table 19-1	The Player's Options
Player's Hand	*Player's Required Action*
1, 2, 3, 4, 0	Draw a card
5	Can take a card if she wants one
6, 7	Stay

If the player can or must take another card, the dealer gives her one face-up.

As you can see, the player has very few options. As a player, you have no real opportunity for free will in Chemin de Fer. The rationale is that the player isn't just playing with her own money, but with that of the other gamblers as well, and she must thus act responsibly.

However, one occasion offers more opportunity for the player to exercise free will. When a player has called *Banco* or *Banco Suivi* and is thus on her own against the banker, some authorities permit the player to do whatever she wants — and the banker can also do whatever he wants. This decision is up to the rules of the individual casino.

The banker then turns his attention to drawing another card or not. The banker has the options shown in Table 19-2. His options are based on the value of his cards and the value of the face-up card he has just given the player, if any.

Table 19-2	The Banker's Options	
Banker's Hand	*Player's Draw*	*Banker's Required Action*
0, 1, 2	Anything	Draw a card
3	1, 2, 3, 4, 5, 6, 7, 0	Draw a card
	8	Stay
	9	Optional
4	2, 3, 4, 5, 6, 7	Draw a card
	1, 8, 9, 0	Stay
5	5, 6, 7	Draw a card
	1, 2, 3, 8, 9, 0	Stay
	4	Optional
6	6, 7	Draw a card
	1, 2, 3, 4, 5, 8, 9, 0	Stay
7	Anything	Stay

Rules work in the player's favor

Chemin de Fer does restrict the player when it comes to taking an additional card, but these restrictions actually work to the player's advantage. If the player has a bad hand (one far removed from a 9), she has the chance to improve it; if she has a good hand (one close to a 9), she can't blow it by drawing another card imprudently. And if a player really craves options, she can always hope for a 5, which offers the potential for four so-so draws (of court cards), four good draws (of the ace, 2, 3, or 4), and five bad draws (of the 5, 6, 7, 8, and 9). In the case of a 5, deciding whether to stay or draw is a close call.

If the player doesn't draw, the banker should stand on 6 or 7 and draw on anything less.

The banker, just like the player, is hamstrung to very restricted playing options. Of course, the required play is the best mathematical option for each side — but it may still seem quite restrictive for the participants.

If the player wins, she collects the winnings (of course, if she's been playing cards for other players, the other players take their winnings). The bank moves around one place to the banker's right, and the whole process starts again.

If the round is a standoff, the bets are returned to the players, and the banker puts up a new stake. If the banker wins, he leaves his winnings on the table to enlarge his stake for the next hand. The banker can't reduce his next bet unless he resigns the bank — it's all or nothing.

Until he resigns the bank, the banker can't take any money off the table from his winnings unless no one wants to match his bet.

Players play until they lose interest or lose all their money, whichever comes first.

Punto Banco

Punto Banco (which sounds like *poont-o bank-o*) is currently the most popular version of Baccarat in casinos in Europe and the United States. Punto Banco resembles Chemin de Fer (see "Chemin de Fer" for the details) with the following differences:

- ✔ The players compete against the bank.

> ✔ The players and the bank can bet on their own cards or on the cards of anyone else at the table. Spectators can bet on both the bank and the players.
>
> ✔ The casino acts as a player, and a player handles the bank.

As in Chemin de Fer, the object of the game is to get your cards to total as close to 9 points as you can.

The players simply bet on whoever they think will win. The casino collects their bets if they lose and pays out the bets (whichever side they backed) if they win.

All the players are seated around the table before the hand starts. Everyone puts down his bet in the space in front of him, backing whichever side that he wants without seeing any cards. The *croupier,* an employee of the casino, deals two cards to herself, as the player, and to the player designated to handle the bank (that player is selected by rotation).

The player and the bank turn over their cards. The croupier then draws a card for the player if the player has 0 through 5, stays (does not draw a card) if the player has 6 or 7, and declares a natural if the player has 8 or 9.

Then the banker decides what she wants to do. She must follow the guidelines outlined in Table 19-3; even if the banker already has a winning hand against the player, if the table requires her to draw a card — she must!

Table 19-3	The Banker's Options	
Banker's Hand	*Player's Draw*	*Banker's Required Action*
0, 1, 2	Anything	Draw a card
3	1, 2, 3, 4, 5, 6, 7, 9, 0	Draw a card
	8	Stay
4	2, 3, 4, 5, 6, 7	Draw a card
	1, 8, 9, 0	Stay
5	4, 5, 6, 7	Draw a card
	1, 2, 3, 8, 9, 0	Stay
6	6, 7	Draw a card
	1, 2, 3, 4, 5, 8, 9, 0	Stay
7	Anything	Stay
8, 9		Declares a natural

The hand that ends up closest to 9 wins.

Baccarat a Deux Tables

Baccarat can also be played with the banker (playing for himself, not for or against the casino) taking on two players simultaneously. This version of the game is known as *Baccarat a Deux Tables* (which sounds like *bah-car-at ah duh tables*), or Baccarat at Two Tables, because the banker sits in the middle and deals out cards to himself and to two players, one to his right and one to his left. The players can bet on either side or both sides. During the play, the banker is trying to beat both opponents, and they are each trying to beat him.

To play Baccarat a Deux Tables, you need

- ✔ **Two players and a banker**
- ✔ **At least one and up to eight standard decks of 52 cards**

In this game, the casino simply acts as an intermediary; the players take on the banker head to head. If the banker beats them, he collects their bets, and if they win, they take his money. The casino gets a percentage of the bets but doesn't pay out winners or collect from losers.

The formalities are similar to Chemin de Fer (see "Chemin de Fer" for the details). The bank puts up its stake, and all the spectators and gamblers around the table can bet on the first or second player or both players, but the cumulative bids can't exceed the banker's bet.

After the bets are made, the banker deals two cards to each side of him and two for himself. The players follow the rules of Chemin de Fer for drawing cards (see "Following the pattern: the play of the cards" for the details), leaving the banker in a quandary on occasion; he can't necessarily follow the optimum strategy with just one hand against both opponents.

At this form of Baccarat, the banker doesn't automatically lose the bank on the loss of a hand. He can remain the banker until his stakes run out.

The casino's profit comes from taking between $2^1/_2$ and 5 percent of the stakes put up by the banker. The casino supplies a *croupier* to assist or advise the banker if he wants one.

Chapter 20

Poker

● ●

In This Chapter

▶ Exploring the general rules of Poker

▶ Picking up the basics of Draw Poker and Stud Poker

▶ Discovering a couple of the other varieties of Poker

● ●

*T*rying to cover the subject of Poker, a game with at least 200 variations, in a few pages may seem like a futile occupation. However, I can give you a brief overview of some of the most popular versions of the game, along with some insight into the strategy of Poker.

To play Poker, you need the following:

- ✔ **At least five players:** Somewhere between six and ten is ideal, but you can cope with fewer or more.

- ✔ **One standard deck of 52 cards:** In some versions of the game, you also need the jokers.

- ✔ **Some chips or counters:** Ideally, use chips of at least two different denominations (different colors or sizes) to make the accounting easier. Money is a perfectly acceptable alternative to chips. In fact, the game is almost always played for money. As a general rule, bring a reserve of at least 80 times the minimum bet.

Getting the Basics Down

Almost every game of Poker shares some common elements. To start with, Poker is a gambling game and a game of money (or chip) management. The aim on each hand is to win money — or, at the very least, to avoid losing too much money. Your object may just be to have fun, but if that's your sole aim, it probably won't come cheap!

To be successful, you must achieve a hand of higher rank than any other player at the table. You win by forcing the other players to drop out of competition or by outranking their cards in a showdown. If you do so, you collect all the bets — commonly known as the *pot* (or *pool* in England*).*

Poker on the Web

The Web offers numerous sites that cater to the Poker player's every whim. At Casino Areneum (www.araneum.dk/casino/ukindex.html) you can sign up for live play and chat. The Intergalactic Casino (intergalactinet.com/casino/videopoker/) is always ready to deal you a hand — choose your favorite game from among several varieties of Poker.

If you have a java-enabled browser, stop in at Virtual Vegas Poker (www.virtualvegas.com/newvv/games/vp/javapoker.html) to enjoy some great graphics and sound effects while you play. After playing, visit the IRC Poker Database (nova.stanford.edu/~maurer/r.g/) to read all about live play and chat over IRC.

Ranking Poker hands

Almost all Poker games, regardless of how many cards the player gets, require you to make the best hand of five cards. The player who can, through the play, construct the highest-ranking hand wins the pot.

In Poker, the suits have no rank — all suits are equivalent. It's the rank of the hand that counts.

The following list details the various hands from highest-ranking (the royal straight flush) to lowest (high card). I also tell you the odds of being dealt such a hand.

- **Royal straight flush:** The top five cards of the same suit; in other words, the AKQJ10 in one of the four suits. This is not an easy hand to achieve; your chances of the dealer dealing you a royal straight flush are 650,000 to 1.

- **Straight flush:** Any five cards from the same suit in consecutive order (such as the 23456 of clubs). In comparison to the royal straight flush, this hand comes up every day, so to speak, clocking in at 75,000 to 1. When two players have straight flushes on the same hand, the higher sequence outranks the lower one (so KQJ109 outranks 87654, whatever suits the cards are in).

✔ **Four of a kind:** Four of any one card — for example, four 7s or four queens. The fifth card in the hand can be anything. If two players have this hand at the same time, the rank of the four cards determines the better hand; four 8s beat four 7s, for example. The odds of being dealt this hand are 4,150 to 1.

✔ **Full house:** Three of a kind and a pair — for example, three 10s and two 9s. If two players each have a full house, the higher three of a kind determines the better hand — so three queens and two 4s outrank three 10s and two 7s. Full houses have odds of 700 to 1.

✔ **Flush:** Five cards of the same suit; the cards don't have to be in a sequence. When two players have flushes, the highest card in each flush determines the better hand; if the top cards are the same, you look at the second card, and so on. Thus ♦A♦8♦6♦4♦3 outranks ♠K♠Q♠9♠8♠3 (aces are always high). Flushes come up with odds of 500 to 1.

✔ **Straight:** Five cards of consecutive rank (in numerical sequence), but the cards can be in any suit. If two players have straights, the top card of the straight determines the winner. So ♠K ♦Q ♠J ♣10 ♣9 outranks ♠J ♦10 ♥9 ♥8 ♦7. The ace can rank high or low to form a straight, but around-the-corner straights (QKA23) aren't permitted. Straights have odds of 250 to 1.

✔ **Three of a kind:** Also knows as *triplets,* this hand consists of three cards of the same numeric value, together with two unmatched cards. As you may expect, ties are split in favor of the higher-ranking three of a kind. The odds are 47 to 1 against being dealt three of a kind.

✔ **Two pairs:** Four cards in two pairs and an unmatched fifth card. Ties are decided by the value of the top pair, then the value of the second pair, and finally by the spare card. Thus KK446 outranks KK443. Two pairs have odds of 20 to 1.

✔ **One pair:** One pair and three unmatched cards is the second-lowest hand. The rank of the pair, followed by the unmatched cards, splits the tie. So KKA64 beats KKQJ7. You pick up a hand with a pair in it twice in every five hands.

✔ **High card:** The weakest hand, *high card* means five unmatched cards. The top card in the hand determines the better collection. If two hands tie, move to the second card, and so on. Your chances of picking up a hand with no combination in it are 50-50.

Spicing up the game with wild cards

Many games of Poker can be played with *wild cards* — certain, predefined cards that can be used as absolutely anything the player wants them to be.

The three most common wild cards are

- **The joker:** Anytime you play with a joker, it's wild. You can use it to represent any card.
- **The 2s, or** *deuces*
- **One-eyed jacks:** If you look at all the jacks in the standard deck of playing cards, you notice that the ♣J and the ♦J are presented to you face-on, while the ♥J and the ♠J are in profile. That means that the ♥J and the ♠J are *one-eyed jacks.* Some people play the one-eyed king, the ♦K, as wild also.
- **The bug:** Some people play Poker with a *bug,* using the joker. You can use the bug to complete a straight or flush or as an ace. You can't use it to make a pair, three of a kind, or four of a kind. So AAABugJ can be a full house but not four aces.

If you play with wild cards, *five of a kind* (four of a kind plus a wild card) takes over as the highest hand possible, above a royal straight flush. If two players both have five of a kind, the hand with the higher value wins — 6s beat 2s and so on.

Getting started

Everyone assembles the chips or money that they need to bet. Players use either money or, more typically, Poker chips. At a casino, where Poker is one of the more popular games, you can buy chips from the casino, replenishing your stock whenever you run out.

When all the players are ready to start, they cut for the deal and the seating rights. The player with the highest card deals the first hand, and the other players seat themselves, in order of the cards cut, around the table. The second-highest player goes on the dealer's left and so on.

In the social game, most groups play *dealer's choice,* which means that the dealer gets to choose what version of the game to play and what cards are wild, if any. The deal rotates after every hand, allowing a new player to choose the game.

In casinos in the United States, you rarely get to choose the game. Even at a table where multiple games are played, the games typically rotate every 20 to 30 minutes rather than letting the players choose. In English casinos, the dealer frequently has quite a bit of choice as to how the game is played. The players remember who is the dealer by passing a little plastic button around the table, and the dealer keeps this button in front of him. Sometimes the button has the permissible choices of games printed on it, and the dealer turns the button so that the relevant game's name is up.

Ante up!

After the dealer has been selected and the chips have been assembled, then the players throw in the *ante*. To explain the ante, you have to understand how the betting works. No one has to bet on her Poker hand if she doesn't want to. To prevent a player from just sitting quietly, being dealt a hand every deal, and then throwing the hand in without cost until she gets the perfect hand, you have the concept of the *ante*. The ante is an advance bet, usually the minimum bet, that you have to pay in order to be dealt a hand. The ante can be a quarter at most in a social game, perhaps a dollar in a casino.

At most games, everyone has to *ante up,* meaning that everyone throws the ante into the center of the table before the deal. The ante serves the double purpose of making everyone contribute something and starting the pot for each hand.

Alternately, the player to the left of the dealer puts in one chip, and the next player puts in two chips. This is known as the *straddle,* the *small blind* and *the big blind.* The next player to bet must put in at least two chips if he wants to stay in. For Draw and Stud Poker, the ante is nearly always used.

The mechanics of betting

After the players put in their ante, the dealer deals the cards, everyone looks at his hand, and the first opportunity to bet goes around the table. The player to the dealer's left gets the first chance to bet.

Everything at Poker takes place in strict rotation, on a clockwise basis. Never do anything until the player on your right has acted.

When it's your turn to bet, if you like your cards, you can stay in the hand by doing any of the following:

- ✔ **You can bet.** To bet, put a stake into the pot. If the other players want to stay in the game, they must bet the same amount.

- ✔ **You can call.** Calling involves putting into the pot an amount equivalent to the previous bet. Calling the bet is also referred to as *seeing* or *matching.* After another player makes a bet, if you want to stay in the game, calling is your least expensive option.

✔ **You can raise.** An even more aggressive approach is to *raise* the previous bet (also called *raising the stakes*), which means betting the amount of the previous bet, plus any extra amount you feel your hand is worth.

For example, say that you're the third player to bet. The first player bets two, and the second player raises the bet by five. After you raise, you can call, which involves putting in seven units (two + five units); or you can call and raise again, say two more, if you really feel like it.

Some play that the players can raise the bet only three times on any round of betting.

✔ **You can check.** Players can also *check,* which means to not make a bet but to stay in the game. You can't check in the middle of a betting sequence — only if you're the first to bet and you don't have a good enough hand to start the betting, or if all the bettors before you have checked.

After you decide what you want to bet, put the stake down on the table, rather than throw it into the pot. This is good etiquette, so that everyone can see what you're betting and they don't have to take your word for it.

If you don't want to stay in the hand (perhaps if the stakes have gotten too high or your cards are hopeless), you can *fold,* in which case you quietly drop out. Put your cards down in front of you and wait for the next hand to be dealt.

One of the interesting things about Poker is that you don't have to bet if you don't want to; you can concede, or fold, whenever you like. Of course, by folding, you lose all your investment thus far — but you don't risk losing more.

The first round of betting comes to a stop only when someone makes a bet (or raises the bet) that everyone else calls or that makes everyone else drop out. A second opportunity for everyone to bet comes later in the hand, which you can find out about in "Continuing after the draw" in this chapter.

If you have a good hand, you can bet as much as you like — to the maximum of the table. Most tables have a limit, described in the sidebar "Making the minimum and maximum bets."

Sandbagging relates to the practice of a player betting nothing, or checking, in the early part of any round (to encourage others to bet) and then raising when someone else makes a bet. Absolutely nothing is wrong with this form of deviousness, although some schools don't allow sandbagging; a player who's first to bet frequently goes for this approach when she's worried that a direct bet may scare the other players out of the hand. Of course, checking and then raising may scare the other players out, too.

Making the minimum and maximum bets

Limit Poker is very popular in the United States. The minimum bet in at-home games can be as low as 5 cents or even a penny. In home games, you frequently play a limit of one unit for the bet or raise in the early stages, with a maximum of two units in the later stages. In casinos, the minimum is generally at least a dollar.

In the United Kingdom, you can play an alternative system in which the maximum bet is limited by how much money is already in the pot. A limit of half the pot restricts the maximum bet still more. For example, say that six people are playing and everybody puts in one unit as an ante. If the first bet is for two, then you can see that bet (making 10 units in the pot at that point) and, if you want, increase the bet

by 10 if you're limited to the amount in the pot or by 5 if you have a half-pot limit. When you're just starting to play poker, I suggest that you stick to the limit of units, not the pot!

If you play *table stakes,* you may not go get new chips or take out more money after a hand starts. If a player has insufficient money to match the last bet, he puts up what he has into a *side pot,* and any further bets from the remaining players get set aside and treated as a separate pot, which all the other players are competing for.

You can also have a financial upper limit (no bet larger than $100, for example), or you can set a range, such as $1 to $50.

If you bet out of turn, you must leave the bet in the pot. If no one increases the stakes, your bet stands, but if someone raises the betting, you can't recover your misplaced wager if you decide to fold; however, you can stay in by contributing the extra needed. As a point of both etiquette and strategy, don't be too eager to contribute your bet, particularly with a good hand. Try to disguise your excitement if you can — or fake it, if you prefer.

Winning ways

The betting and the hand can end in any of the following ways:

- ✔ One player makes a bet or a raise and everybody else folds. The player left after everyone folds becomes the undisputed winner, and she is not required to show her hand. She simply collects all the bets.

- ✔ Everybody can pass on the final round, in which case all players must show their hands immediately in a *showdown.* The highest-ranking hand wins.

- ✔ One player makes a bet, and all the remaining players in the game call the bet. The player making the bet then shows his hand, allowing the other players to put away their hands (fold) if they can't beat it or to show their own hand if they can beat it.

Improving your Poker game

If you follow this advice, I can't guarantee that you will win, but you should limit your losses:

✔ Keep a Poker face (don't show excitement or disappointment, no matter what your hand is like). You avoid costing yourself money when your opponents get a read-out of your hand.

✔ If you do send out signals, deliberately mix up those signals. Your opponents are watching, consciously or unconsciously, for those signals.

✔ Study your competitors. Watch their actions and ask yourself whether they are deliberate or accidental.

✔ Remember that Poker isn't about friendship. Your erstwhile friends are trying to shaft you — do the same to them before they do it to you!

✔ Say anything you like, within reason, even if your comments may be construed as misleading. If anyone listens to you, they only have themselves to blame.

When it comes to the pot, other players' stakes, or their cards, you can look, but you better not touch! Don't touch anything but your own bets and cards. If you're at a casino, let the dealer pass you the pot if you're fortunate enough to win it.

Draw Poker (Five-Card Draw)

In this version of the game, you get to *draw,* or trade in some of your cards for new cards, after the initial round of betting.

The most popular version of Draw Poker is Jackpots (or Jacks or Better), which requires the first bettor to have at least a pair of jacks to make the initial bet. (This game is the origin of the word *Jackpot* in its normal usage.)

In many places, anything goes — a player can make the first bet with anything in his hand, a style of play that increases the potential for *bluffing,* which means pretending that you have a better hand than you do.

Everybody puts in an ante, or a less-common alternative is for the dealer to put in the ante for the whole table (see "Ante Up!" for more information about the ante). The dealer passes out one face-down card at a time, clockwise, to each player, starting on his left, until everyone has five cards. The betting also starts at the dealer's left, and if you play Jackpots, you must have a pair of jacks or better to place a bet. (A player with jacks or better doesn't have to bet if she doesn't want to; she can check if she wants.)

If the first player passes (checks), then the next player to the left has the same options of betting or passing, and so on around the table. If everybody passes, the hand is gathered up, reshuffled, and redealt, with an additional ante.

Some people play that if a hand is redealt, the minimum holding required for the first bet also increases from a pair of jacks to a pair of queens. If everyone passes on the next hand, then the minimum holding required jumps to a pair of kings, and finally to a pair of aces. Sometimes the stakes are also increased when this sort of thing happens. If no one can open with a pair of aces, some play that the requirements for opening start coming down; others play that the requirement for opening goes up to two pairs.

Determining a strategy for the first bet

The first question you need to focus on is when to make the first bet, or *open the betting*. The key issue is how many players haven't yet had the opportunity to open the betting (and who may have much better hands than yours). When thinking about the first bet, keep the following things in mind:

- ✔ As a general rule, if you're one of the last three to make a bet, go ahead and do so on a pair of jacks or better.

- ✔ If four players are left to make a move, only bet if you have at least a pair of queens.

- ✔ With five or six players yet to bet, wait until you have a hand better than a pair of kings.

- ✔ Similarly, wait to make the first bet until you get a pair of aces if seven players are still to bet.

Deciding whether to stay in or to fold is more difficult. First, consider how many other players are already staying in the betting. Obviously, the more players who stay in or, worse, raise the betting, the stronger your hand needs to be to remain in the game:

- ✔ With one other player betting, you should have a pair of kings or better to stay in.

- ✔ With two players, you need any two pairs to stay in.

- ✔ With between three and five players still in, you still need two pairs, but the more players in, the better your top pair should be.

- ✔ With six players in, only remain in the game with three of a kind or better (see "Ranking Poker hands" for more information on the types of hands).

The only other category of hands you need to consider are those that have nothing at the moment but are close to being good hands — hands that are one card removed from a straight or flush. I discuss this type of hand in "The luck of the draw."

The guidelines I give in the preceding lists are just that — guidelines. As you feel more comfortable with the game, you may introduce a little psychology into your decision-making. As you get to know the mannerisms and habits of the people you play against, you can use that information to help you make decisions about how good your hand may be in comparison to the other players' hands.

The luck of the draw

After a player makes a bet, each player in turn has the option of folding, calling, or raising (see "The mechanics of betting" for more on these options). As soon as this initial phase of the betting is over, the players have their one and only opportunity to improve their hands.

The dealer starts with the first player remaining in the game to his left and asks her how many cards she wants. She keeps the good cards of the five that she was dealt and discards the rest face-down. She calls out the number of new cards that she wants or says that she is *standing pat,* meaning that she doesn't want to trade in any cards. The dealer passes the correct number of cards to the player face-down and then moves on to the next player, offering him the draw and receiving an equivalent number of cards in return. At his turn, the dealer also calls out how many cards he is dealing himself.

Looking at the odds

One of the key areas of strategy is knowing what hands are worth staying in the betting with the hope of creating a winning hand. Table 20-1 shows you just how likely — or unlikely — it is that you can improve your collection of cards at the draw.

Before you read this table, keep in mind that if you don't hold at least a pair or four cards to a straight or flush, you should drop out of the bidding immediately, rather than pay for the dubious privilege of attempting to improve an unpromising hand. Damage limitation is one of the most important arts at Poker.

Keep these terms in mind as you read Table 20-1:

- An *inside straight* is four cards of a straight, meaning that you need one specific card. For example, you have 3567, so you need the 4.

- An *open-ended straight* is four consecutive cards, such as 3456. The fifth card to complete the straight can be either the 2 or the 7.

- An *inside straight flush* is having four of the cards needed for a straight flush when the card you need is a specific card. For example, if you have ♦4578, you need the ♦6 to complete your straight flush.

- A *kicker* is a high card, such as an ace.

Table 20-1	Your Chances of Improvement		
If You're Still in the Game with	*And You Draw This Many Cards*	*Your Chances of Getting*	*Are*
An ace	4	A pair	Pretty good
An ace and a king	3	A pair of aces or kings	Good
A pair	3	A better hand	Good
		Two pairs	Pretty good
		Three of a kind	Fair
		Full house	Almost non-existent
A pair and a kicker	2	A better hand	Good
		Two pairs	Pretty good
		Three of a kind	Slim
		Full house	Almost non-existent
Two pairs	1	Full house	Slim
Three of a kind	2	Full house	Slim
		Four of a kind	Poor
An inside straight	1	Straight	Slim
An open-ended straight	1	Straight	Pretty good

(continued)

Table 20-1 *(continued)*

If You're Still in the Game with	And You Draw This Many Cards	Your Chances of Getting	Are
Four cards to a flush	1	Flush	Pretty good
Four cards to an inside straight flush	1	Straight flush	Bad
Four consecutive cards to a straight flush	1	Straight flush	Poor

As you can see, your chances of drawing to a straight aren't all that good, even on an open-ended straight. Drawing to an inside straight isn't recommended unless you need to make a charitable donation. And drawing on three cards to a straight or flush is grounds for confinement in an institution in 35 states in the United States.

Also, the chances of improving a hand when you hold a pair and a kicker are less than the chance of improving your hand when you hold just the pair, because you're trading in only two cards instead of three.

But bluffing issues can enter this equation. When you're known to follow the strategy of drawing two cards when you hold a pair and a kicker, and then you're dealt three of a kind later on and again draw two cards, the other players may assume that you hold a pair and a kicker again, giving you ample opportunity to bluff. (You can find out more about bluffing in "Bluffing Do's and Don'ts" later in this chapter.)

If you call for more cards than you intended, you must make an extra discard before picking up, so that your hand has the right number of cards. If you pick up the wrong number of cards, you're out of the game. If you call for too few, your hand is *fouled,* because you no longer have enough cards for a valid hand.

Most hands aren't won on a pair. Because drawing three cards gives away so much information about your hand, staying in on a pair when more than one other player is betting isn't such great strategy. A pair of aces is the top hand half the time (before the draw) with seven players in. With four players in, jacks are usually the best pair. (All this information argues for betting to the maximum with two pairs, because you want to drive the other players out and not give them the chance to improve their hands.)

Knowing what to get rid of

You may occasionally be faced with the dilemma of what to discard on a hand with more than one reasonable option. This situation arises most often when you have a high pair and four cards to a straight or flush — for example, ♠Q ♦Q ♦8 ♦6 ♦5 or ♦K ♣K ♣Q ♥J ♠10.

Determine whether enough is in the pot and enough players are left in to go for the bet at 5:1 odds. But where you have straight flush possibilities, the odds are with you to keep it and try to complete it.

You don't have to be too worried about other players trying to look at your cards. Nobody wants to run the risk of acquiring the reputation of peeking at another player's cards. But don't voluntarily expose your cards to another player — he may feel less reluctance to look at the cards if you show them to him! Don't show your cards to spectators or to players sitting out.

Continuing after the draw

After everybody still in the game has drawn additional cards, if they want to, a second and final round of betting takes place. This round starts with the player who opened the betting on the previous round or with the last player who raised a bet from the first round. The betting limit, if you are playing with one, is generally doubled at this point.

The betting goes clockwise around the table until everyone left in has called the final bet or until only one player is left in. Whoever has been called shows his hand, and anyone beating that hand must show her hand. You don't need to reveal what you have otherwise. The cards speak for themselves — because all five cards are used, everyone can see what the other players have, and you don't have to claim the hand.

Stud Poker

Stud Poker exists these days in two main varieties, Five-Card Stud and Seven-Card Stud, with different modifications of the same strategies applying to both games. Stud Poker differs from other Poker games in that you get to see part of your opponents' hands during the betting.

Five-Card Stud

In Five-Card Stud, you don't get to draw to replace any cards; what you're dealt is what you get, and that's that. However, instead of picking up all five cards dealt to you face-down, at one turn, you get your cards one at a time, with opportunities to bet after receiving each card.

After paying the ante, each player is dealt one card face-down. This card, which remains down for the course of the game, is known as the *hole card*. Your other four cards are dealt face-up. When everyone has received one face-up card, the person with the highest face-up card has the first opportunity to bet, and then the betting progresses clockwise. If two equal cards are showing, the player nearest the dealer's left (or perhaps the card in the higher suit, the order being spades, hearts, diamonds, and then clubs) makes the first bet.

In some versions of Five-Card Stud, the low card is required to bet first, and that bet has a minimum amount. This rule may also apply to Seven-Card Stud.

When every bet has been called, the third card is dealt out, face-up, to the players remaining in the game. Again, the first bet is made by the highest hand showing after two face-up cards, with a pair outranking any single card, of course. This pattern continues, with four rounds of betting, one after each new face-up card is dealt. At the end of the final bet, all the players left in the game show their hole cards, and the best hand takes the pot. (See "Ranking Poker hands" for more information on the types of hands.)

If you're going to throw in your hand at Five-Card Stud, turn your upcards down and hand in your cards, rather than turning your concealed cards up. No one should know the true identity of your hole card.

Five-Card Stud offers few uncertainties; with only one piece of concealed information, you have little room for a deep bluff. Most of the picture is on display. It quickly — and perhaps expensively — becomes clear to you that you shouldn't stay in the betting when you can see that a player has a better hand, no matter what your hole card is.

Similarly, don't pay out good money to stay in a hand when you have three cards to a flush; the chances of completing it are really very slim. On the other hand, bet the limit whenever you have a pair showing that outranks any other pair visible at the table. And when you have a concealed pair, bet on it immediately, if you're not beaten by a visible pair in someone else's hand.

Damage limitation is critical at this game. With a low hole card, if you don't form a pair immediately, you should probably fold. If your hole card is an ace or court card, stay in for the minimum bet. After a couple of cards, if your hand, when combined with the hole card, is lower than any other player's upcards, you should seriously consider dropping out, unless you feel like bluffing. The point is that if you need a good draw to beat that player, he is equally capable of improving his hand in the same way. And never play on with another player who has a pair up, unless you can beat it with your hole card.

Some people reduce the deck to 40 (by taking out the 12 lowest cards) cards to make the hands more interesting; the fewer cards in the deck, the better everyone's hands are likely to be. When you do so, you should also change a flush to beat a full house, because the flush becomes more rare.

Seven-Card Stud — "Down the River"

Nobody can level the charge of predictability against Seven-Card Stud. This game is conceptually parallel to Five-Card Stud, but it has a great deal more uncertainty in it because the pattern of cards creates so many more unknowns.

After putting in the ante, the order of dealing is two cards down, four up, and one down. (See "Ante up!" if you need more information on the ante.) The pattern of betting generally follows that of Five-Card Stud, starting after the first face-up card, but you have a fifth round of betting after the final card is dealt face-down.

The interesting thing about this game is the fact that virtually nothing can be predicted about anyone else's hand, except by the pattern of their betting. For example, if all you can see up in another player's hand is ♦7 ♣9 ♥K♦4, that player can literally have almost any hand at all, from a king-high set of odd cards through one or two pairs or three or four of a kind. And that hand has room for a flush or straight flush in diamonds, or a straight just about anywhere. What's more, even if that player has a great hand, he's had no reason to have been betting strongly so far. If his first two hole cards are the ♣4 and the ♠4 and the final hole card is a 7, the hand was bad enough to have been thrown in earlier in the face of strong betting.

One of the critical things in Seven-Card Stud is to remember the upcards of the other players, especially those who have folded, so that you can eliminate the most unfavorable possibilities from your opponents' hands. In the preceding example, if you're holding a full house with three aces and competing against this player, you may be cheered to note the ♦6 and a 4, 7, and king among the other players' cards. You know, then, that you're exposed only to the risk of four 9s; you can beat any other hand automatically. (See "Ranking Poker hands" for more information on which hands beat other hands.)

Of course, the sight of the cards that you may want in someone else's hand is frequently enough to depress you into folding rather than staying in. Watching the *dead cards* (cards that have already appeared) is critical to appreciating the mathematical odds correctly. If you want a 3, and you see two of them appear in other people's hands, then only two 3s are left for you, not four, and your chances of getting one are cut in half.

When the showdown takes place at Seven-Card Stud, you should announce what your hand is; unlike, say, Five-Card Stud, the selection of the cards means that you have an element of choice, so make everyone's life easy by announcing your hand.

At Seven-Card Stud, you may be tempted to stay in with bad hands (just in case something good happens). Please don't do it! On average, over the course of the evening, you lose more money by staying in on nothing for a couple of rounds and then going out than in any other way. You can lose your money on moderate hands so easily; why voluntarily surrender it on bad hands? Drop out after the first three cards unless you have the makings of a straight or flush, have a pair, or have three (or perhaps two) high cards.

And the same advice applies in midhand when one of the other players has you beaten on the open cards. If you can't beat him even with the inclusion of your hole cards, why should you get lucky later on? Anyway, what is to stop that player from having something in reserve?

The typical winning hand at Seven-Card Stud, if play continues to the very end of the hand, is a flush — that should be good enough to win most hands. A straight is much more problematic; it's better than an even chance to win, though. However, most games don't go that far; most hands are won with just two pair or better, because all the other hands drop out when one player is betting strongly in midgame.

Low-Ball

In Low-Ball, low hands win over high hands. Low-Ball is played along the same lines as Five-Card Draw, except that the value of all hands is turned upside down. The best hand is one where no cards match. Worse than that is a pair, and so on. (See "Ranking poker hands" for the standard ranking of the hands.)

This form of hand valuation produces two issues:

✔ Does a straight or flush count, giving you a disastrous hand, or can you ignore that element of the hand? The general view here is that you can ignore the fact that you have a straight or flush and treat your hand as five unmatched cards.

> ✔ Should the ace be high or low? The common sense answer here is that if you can count an ace as high or low at regular Poker (as you do in 5432A), you can do the same at Low-Ball.

Depending on your view of straights and aces, three hands are possible as the lowest (and therefore best) hand:

> ✔ 5432A, commonly referred to as a *wheel*, is best.

> ✔ 6432A, if you don't ignore straights, is second best.

> ✔ 75432, if you insist on aces being high, is third best.

If you're playing Draw Poker Low-Ball, do not under any circumstances draw two cards to keep three low cards. Your chance of getting what you want is equivalent to that of drawing two cards to a straight — and I have told you what a losing prospect that is!

Hold 'Em

Hold 'Em is one of the most complicated and most popular games around. The object of the game is to combine the face-down cards that the player is dealt with some face-up cards that are available to everyone. These face-up cards in the center of the table are called the *flop*.

Each player gets two cards face-down, and then a round of betting takes place. After that, three cards, which will be common to everyone, are put face-up on the table and then another round of betting takes place. Then another card is dealt face-up with another round of betting, and finally a fifth and final face-up card is dealt, with the last round of betting following that.

The player must use both his face-down cards and any three of the five face-up cards to make the best possible five-card hand that he can. (See "Ranking Poker hands" for more information on the types of hands.)

Generally, you play Hold 'Em without any wild cards.

Your best strategy is not to bet money to call other players' bets if you have a moderate or poor hand. Don't hope to improve your hand with a favorable draw. If your two cards are both low and not a pair, drop out unless the two cards are in sequence (such as a 67) or in the same suit. Even if your cards look reasonably favorable for a straight or flush, be prepared to drop out if the first three face-up cards don't leave you well placed to complete your hand into the straight or flush you're looking for.

Bluffing Do's and Don'ts

Bluffing entails betting on bad or moderate hands or changing fewer cards than you need to do at the draw in the attempt to look like you have a good hand.

Keep the following points in mind as you develop your bluffing strategy:

- **Don't be too stolid.** Keep in mind that you have to speculate to accumulate, and if you aren't caught bluffing occasionally, you're not doing it enough.

- **Do study your opponents' actions at the table.** Try to work out how often they bluff, and try to see whether you could have read their body language when they were bluffing if you had been paying attention. In fact, try to watch a group of players before joining them. Your chances of reading their behavior are much higher when you're not tied to one position at the table and you don't have to worry about your own hand at the same time.

- **Do try to work out the temperaments of your fellow players before you start to play.** If you can see that someone is unprepared to surrender any pot to a potential bluff, make sure that you exploit that weakness in him, but don't try to bluff him out. You know in advance that bluffing won't work.

- **Don't try to bluff when you're outgunned by the number of players still in the hand.** If more than three players are still in the pot, the odds are that one of them thinks that he can beat whatever is the bluff hand you're pretending to hold. Keep your bluffs for the smaller number of players.

- **Don't bluff against the evening's big winner.** Such players have more money to burn than usual and are likely to invest it in seeing the hand through to its conclusion.

- **Don't show your bluff.** Try to avoid showing your hand after a successful coup, unless you don't intend to bluff much more that evening.

- **Don't get caught bluffing too often.** If you get caught bluffing more than 50 percent of the times that you try it, change your strategies and possibly your opponents. You may be moving in too tough a crowd.

Part VIII
Specialty Games

The 5th Wave   By Rich Tennant

"Why do I say you're too competitive? For starters, you're playing Solitaire with marked cards."

In this part . . .

When reading the title of this part, you may logically ask "What makes these games so special?" My first answer is that you play these games with special people — namely yourself and children. The more truthful answer is that these games don't really fit in anywhere else in the book, but they're such great games, I couldn't leave them out. To that end, I've grouped some pretty diverse games into this part — everything from Solitaire to War to Go Fish! Enjoy.

Chapter 21

Solitaire

● ●

In This Chapter

▶ Discovering Solitaire basics

▶ Exploring some common versions of Solitaire

● ●

1 show you many different versions of Solitaire in this chapter. The games don't have all that much in common except that you can play them with a single deck of cards (and they happen to be *my* favorite Solitaires). These games range from "automatic" Solitaires, where you can make every move immediately without thought or forethought, to Solitaires where you can plan the game for at least ten minutes, if you want to. None of these games is easy, so if you win any of them, you'll feel a sense of achievement. In fact, I have never managed to win some of the Solitaires that I discuss in this chapter.

To play Solitaire, you need the following:

 ✔ **One player**

 ✔ **One standard 52-card deck of cards:** You usually don't need jokers in games of Solitaire.

 ✔ **Space to spread out the cards**

Acquainting Yourself with Solitaire Terms

Before you start exploring the various games of Solitaire, you need to know a little technical vocabulary:

 ✔ When you initially deal the cards in Solitaire, the pattern of the cards is known as a *layout* or *tableau*. The layout can consist of *rows* (horizontal lines of cards), *columns* (vertical lines), and *piles* of cards (a compact heap, frequently of face-down cards, sometimes with the top card face-up). You can move tableaus under the correct circumstances, which are dictated by the rules of the particular Solitaire you're playing.

✐ *Building* involves placing one card on top of another in a legal move. The definition of a *legal move* varies according to the individual rules of the Solitaire.

✐ In games where the objective is to build up cards on some of the original cards, the base cards are known as the *foundation*. As a general rule, after you place cards on a foundation, you can't move them. You may build on a tableau as well, in some cases.

The tableau and the foundation may sound like very similar items, but they differ in a few important ways. The object of a Solitaire is to build up the foundation; the tableau is just an intermediary home for the cards as they make their way to the final destination — the foundation. You use the tableau to get the cards in the right order to put them on the foundation.

✐ When you move a complete row or column, you create a *space* or *gap* into which you can often move whatever card(s) you like.

✐ Frequently, you don't use all the cards in the initial layout; the remaining cards are called the *stock*. You go through the stock to advance the Solitaire.

✐ When working through the stock, you frequently have cards that you can't legally put into the layout. In such cases, the unused cards go to the *waste-pile*.

✐ *Redeals* take place in the middle of a Solitaire when you've exhausted all legal moves. The rules of the Solitaire may allow you to redeal by shuffling and redistributing the unused cards in an attempt to advance the game.

✐ Many Solitaires permit one "cheat" — you can move an obstructing card or otherwise advance the game. This process is also known as a *merci*.

Accordion

The game Accordion is also known as Methuselah, Tower of Babel, or Idle Year (presumably because of the amount of time you need to keep playing the game to win at it).

Accordion is a charmingly straightforward game that can easily seduce you into assuming that it must be easy to solve. Be warned — I've never completed a game of Accordion, and I don't know anyone who has! This challenge makes success at the game doubly pleasurable.

Accordion also takes up very little space — a major benefit because you tend to play Solitaire in a cramped space, such as a bus station or an airport lounge.

The objective of Accordion is to finish up with a single pile of 52 cards — if you can. Relative success is reducing the number of piles to four or fewer. Your chances of complete victory are certainly less than one in 1,000, based on the lack of success that I and others have had!

Looking at the layout

The layout for Accordion is simple. Shuffle the deck well and then turn over the top card in your deck and put it to your left to start your layout. Then turn over the next card. If the card is either the same suit (both clubs, for example) or the same rank (both jacks, say) as the first card, put the second card on top of the first. If you don't have a match, use the card to start a second pile. Then turn over a third card and compare it to the second card; again, if the suits or ranks of the cards match, put the third card on top of the second card; if not, start a third pile with the third card. You can't match the third card with the first card, though. Continue by going through every card in the deck in this way. I told you it was easy! The game ends after you turn over the last card.

Shuffling the deck well is important because you're going to work your way through the deck one card at a time, so you don't want to have all the diamonds coming together, for example.

One additional rule: When matching cards (of suit or rank) are three cards apart, you can combine them in the same way as if the cards were adjacent. In other words, you can build the fourth card on the first one. A couple of examples can help you see what I mean.

At the start of the game, your initial cards may look like one of the examples in Figure 21-1 after you have laid out three cards.

Figure 21-1:
Cards near
the start of
a game.

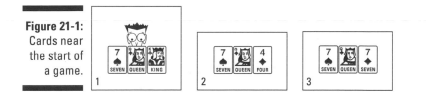

In the first set of cards, you must create three different piles because the cards are unrelated in rank or suit. In the middle example, you can put the ♦4 on top of the ♦Q (because they're in the same suit), leaving you with only two piles. In the bottom example, you can put the ♦7 on top of the ♦Q, which then allows you to combine the two 7s, resulting in a single pile.

To see how you can combine cards that are three places away from each other, look at Figure 21-2.

Figure 21-2:
Matching cards that are three places away from each other.

After you turn up the ♣Q, you can place the ♣Q on the ♦Q (because they are three apart and match in rank) and then put the ♣K on the ♣Q (same suit). The ♥J then moves to the first row.

Laying the cards out in lines of three helps ensure that you identify the cards that are three apart properly.

Choosing between moves

When moving the cards, you frequently have to be careful to make the plays in the correct order to set up more plays. You may have a choice of moves, but you may not be sure which to do first. Look at a possible scenario in Figure 21-3.

After you turn up the ♥4, you can place the ♥4 on the ♥9, which opens up a series of moves that you can play. The best option is to move the ♥4 onto the ♠4 and then move the rest of the cards into their new spaces.

Because the ♠K is three cards away from the ♣K, you can combine the two cards and then move the ♥4 onto the ♥J. Now the ♦9 is three cards away from the ♦Q, so combine those two cards. Note that if you move the ♥4 before you move the ♠K, you miss out on two possible moves.

Making an available play isn't always mandatory. When you have a choice of possible moves, play a couple more cards to help you decide which move is superior.

Figure 21-4 shows you how waiting can help you make up your mind when you have a choice of moves.

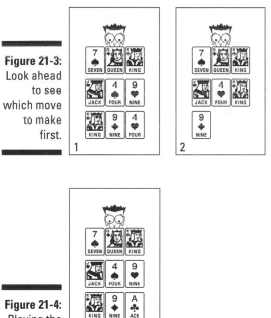

Figure 21-3:
Look ahead
to see
which move
to make
first.

Figure 21-4:
Playing the
waiting
game.

At this point, it's unclear whether to put the ♠A on the ♣A or on the ♠K, because your piles don't indicate whether you want to keep aces or kings on top of your piles. If several piles have kings on the top, you might want to avoid hiding the ♠K. Instead of jumping the gun, you turn over another card to see what happens, which turns out to be the ♠J.

Now you can see daylight: Put the ♠J on the ♠A, then on the ♠K, and then put the ♠J on the ♥J. Now you can put the 9s together. Next, put the ♠4 on the ♠J, allowing the ♣A to go on the ♣K and the ♦9 to go on the ♦Q. Then put the ♠4 on the ♠7, and you're down to three piles. Wasn't that fun? Getting a series of moves to come together like that makes up for the hundreds of unexciting ones.

Play continues until you end up with one pile of cards — good luck!

Calculation

Different people have their own criteria for what makes a good game of Solitaire. Calculation should satisfy most tests because you can solve it in a fair amount of the time (so long as you work at it), it takes up little space, and you can either devote your full attention to it or play without thinking — depending on your mood. However, unless you plan your plays carefully, you're likely to become completely stymied fairly early on.

In this game, only the card rankings matter; the suits of the cards are irrelevant. The object of the game is to build up four piles of cards on the foundation, from the ace on up to the king.

You begin the game by taking out an ace, 2, 3, and 4 from the deck and putting the four cards in a row from left to right, horizontally. These cards are the foundation on which you build — you hope — using all the rest of the cards in the deck. You build on each of the foundation piles one card at a time; however, you build up each pile in different sequences:

- ✔ On the ace pile, you can only put the next higher card — that is, the play sequence must go A23 and so on.
- ✔ On the 2 pile, you go up in pairs: 468 and so on.
- ✔ On the 3 pile, you go up in intervals of three: 69Q25 and so on.
- ✔ And you won't be surprised to know that on the 4 pile, you go up in fours: 8Q37J2 and so on.

For each of the four piles, you have 13 moves available, at which point you reach the king, and the pile is complete.

You turn up cards from the stock one at a time. If the card you turn over has no legal place, put it directly on top of one of the four waste-piles that you create below the foundation. As soon as the card becomes a legal play on a foundation, you may take the card from the top of the waste-pile (but not from the middle of the waste-pile) and move it up.

In Calculation, when you have a legal move (you can put a card on one of the foundation piles), go ahead and make it. Don't wait to see what other cards you may turn up, because you may end up burying a card you could have played.

You can't move cards from one waste-pile to another; after a card is on one pile, you can only move it to the foundation. And just because a waste-pile is empty doesn't entitle you to move cards from another waste-pile into the gap.

The waste-piles are arranged so that you can see all the lower cards in them to maximize your strategic planning.

Kings are exceptionally bad news at this game. They're always the last card to go on each of the foundation piles, and when you put them on the waste-pile, they may block everything beneath them. In a strange way, it's good to turn up kings at the beginning of the game — you can put them on the bottom of each of the waste-piles or put them all together in one pile. As a general rule, try to keep one waste-pile for the kings. However, when two or three kings appear early, it's a reasonable gamble to use all four piles and not keep one for the kings.

Figure 21-5 shows an example of the start of a game. Having selected your ace, 2, 3, and 4 from the deck, you start turning over the cards one at a time.

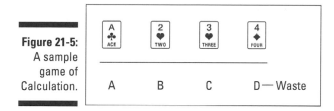

Figure 21-5:
A sample game of Calculation.

Now you go through the cards one by one. These are the moves that you make:

You Turn Over a . . .	And Put It . . .
8	on the 4
6	on the 3
4	on the 2
7	on pile A
King	on pile B (Good)
King	on pile B (Better)
9	on the 6
6	on the 4
2	on the ace
5	on pile A
Ace	on pile C

(continued)

(continued)

You Turn Over a . . .	And Put It . . .
Queen	on the 9
King	on pile B
10	on pile D
9	on pile B
3	on the 2
Ace	on pile C (duplicating cards is generally a bad idea, but sometimes it can't be helped)
Jack	on pile C
8	on the 6; now move the 10 from pile D to the 8 (queens are now going to be good news)
3	on pile D (you might place it on pile A, hoping to develop pile A on the 2 sequence)
2	on the queen (good decision last move!); now the 5 from pile A goes onto the 2
3	on pile D
Ace	on pile B
5	on pile A
7	on pile C
10	on pile C
Queen	on the 10; ahh! now move the ace from pile B, the 3 from pile D, the 5 and 7 from pile A, and the 9 from pile B
9	to pile A (you know that you won't need a 9 for some time, because neither of the outside foundation piles use 9 at the start and both inside piles have their 9s already)

At this point, the game is taking shape very healthily, and you're likely to complete the Solitaire successfully. You're in a particularly good position because with three kings out of the way, you're unlikely to block yourself too badly.

Try to construct lines in the waste-piles in reverse. For example, if your 4-pile is lagging, waiting for a queen, and you put a 7 on a jack on a waste-pile, then put a 3 on top of the 7 if it comes up. You hope that when the queen emerges, you can put the 3, 7, and jack on at one time and advance matters efficiently.

Care to take a bet?

The story of why there is a Solitaire called Canfield is a good one. At the turn of the century, Mr. Canfield ran a gambling salon where he made a bet with his customers. By paying $50, the customer received a well-shuffled deck of cards to play an abbreviated form of the game that now bears Mr. Canfield's name. For every card in the foundation piles at the moment when "time" was called (after three turns through the stock), the customer received a return of $5. The odds of winning the bet were heavily weighted in favor of the proprietor, but customers still flocked to take up the bet. The problem from the casino owner's perspective was that the game required that a casino employee watch over every single gambler who wanted to take up the bet, thereby reducing the profitability of the game.

Canfield

Canfield is one of the most commonly played Solitaires in the Western world. People often erroneously refer to this game as Klondike, which also appears in this chapter (see "Klondike"). To further complicate matters, Canfield is also known as Demon Thirteen in the United Kingdom.

To play Canfield, place 13 cards in a pile with only the top card face-up; this pile is called the *reserve* or the *heel*. To the right of the reserve, spread out four cards, called a *tableau,* on which you can build by using the cards from the reserve or the *stock* (the remaining 34 cards in the deck). Above the tableau, place a single face-up card, which acts as the base-card of a foundation from which each suit will be built up.

The object of Canfield is to get rid of all 13 cards in the reserve pile. You get rid of cards from the reserve pile by placing them in legal positions in the tableau.

You build in the tableau by placing a card that is one rank lower and of the opposite color on a top card in the tableau. For example, you can legally put the ♣2 on a either the ♠3 or ♦3. After the ♣2 is on the top of the pile, you can place either the ♠A or ♦A on it. If you place the ♦A on the ♣2, you can then place either the ♣K or the ♥K on the ♦A, and so on.

Take the remaining 34 cards, the stock, and work your way through them in threes, taking the top three cards at a time and putting them into a waste-pile while preserving the order of the three cards. You have access to only the top card in the three, but if you use the top card — that is, you put it on the tableau or foundation — you gain access to the second card and so on.

After going through the stock in threes, you turn up the last card out of the 34, and this card is accessible. When the stock comes out in threes, you treat the last three cards as a regular group of three. If you have two cards left over at the end of the stock, you get to look at and use them both separately.

After you work your way through the stock, pick it up and start again; continue until you either finish the game or get stuck and can't move any further.

As soon as another card equivalent in rank to the foundation base-card emerges from either the reserve pile or the stock, pick the card up and put it in a separate pile in the foundation, above the tableau. You can play only the next highest card of the relevant suit on the foundation.

The cards (even a whole pile of cards) in the tableau can be moved onto other cards in the tableau, so long as you observe the opposite-color rule.

You always have the option of placing the top card in the reserve pile on the foundation or on the tableau.

Take a look at the layout at the start of the game in Figure 21-6.

Figure 21-6:
Starting a
game of
Canfield.

This layout is a very promising start to a game of Canfield. The ♣Q joins the ♦Q at the top of the foundation, in a separate pile. This move creates a gap in the tableau where you can place a card from the reserve pile.

You can move a pile of cards from one space in the tableau to another; you're not limited to moving single cards.

The ♥3 goes on the black 4, and the black 2 goes on the red 3. Another card from the reserve pile fills the gap in the tableau that was left by the black 2.

One variation that makes Canfield more difficult is to build up the foundation from the ace, meaning that you don't give yourself a foundation card to start with. To compensate for no foundation card, some players use a reserve pile of only 11 cards.

Klondike

Klondike, frequently misnamed Canfield, is by far the most frequently played Solitaire that I know. You need only a little time to play, and you don't need much space to set it up. In addition, you have a good chance of winning at Klondike — you may find yourself winning half the games you play

Klondike requires little tactics or strategy to play. It's an ideal game for children, perhaps for that very reason, and I think that Klondike was the first Solitaire that I ever played. Klondike is also an ideal Solitaire for a spectator, who can lean over the player's shoulder and say things like "Put the red 7 on the black 8," until the player loses patience and punches him in the nose. This happens often when I play Solitaire.

The object of Klondike is to build up piles of the four suits from the ace (the lowest card) to the king on the foundation. You don't start with any cards in the foundation; you collect cards for the foundation during the course of the play.

To build the initial layout, or *tableau,* deal seven piles, with one card in the first pile, two in the second pile, three in the third, and so on. Turn over the top card of each pile as you deal out the cards.

When dealing out the piles, deal seven cards face-down to form the seven piles; deal the next six cards to form the second layer of each row (except the row on the far left), then the next five cards to form the third layer, and so on. If you lay out the cards in this way, you avoid any problems from imperfect shuffling.

You can then build on the top cards of each pile by putting lower-numbered cards of the opposite color on the top cards. Your building-up cards come from the stock.

You can move the turned-up cards around (leaving the face-down cards in place), and whenever you move a group, you turn over the new top card.

When you've used all the cards in a pile, you create a space. You can move any pile headed by a king — and only one headed by a king — into the space, and then you turn another card over on the pile from which you moved the king pile.

Whenever you turn up an ace in the tableau (or in the stock), move that card to the foundation and start a new foundation pile. You may then take any top card from the tableau and move it onto the foundation, where appropriate. For example, after you have the ♦A in the foundation, you can take the ♦2 when it becomes available and start building up the diamonds.

To start the game, play the cards in the stock, which should have 24 cards in it. Go through the stock three cards at a time, putting the cards into a waste-pile. You have access to only the top card of each set of three cards. If you use that top card, you gain access to the card below it, and so on. When you finish going through the stock, gather up the stock and go through it again.

You may go through the stock only three times. If you haven't persuaded the Solitaire to work out, you lose the game. However, most people that I know ignore the three-times rule and just continue with the Solitaire until it works out, which it does a fair percentage of the time.

As an alternative, you can go through the stock one card at a time and only one time. I haven't concluded whether you're more likely to get the Solitaire to work out with this rule or not, but instinctively, I feel that it must do so. Some people play that you can go through the deck one card at a time on three separate occasions before calling the whole thing off.

La Belle Lucie

As far as I'm concerned, La Belle Lucie (which is also known as Midnight Oil, Clover Leaf, the Fan, or Alexander the Great) is the best Solitaire that I've played. Every move is critical. The game requires great planning and fore-thought while rewarding the player with a healthy chance of success.

I've been known to take more than ten minutes to make a move while planning the intricacies of competing strategies, and it's certainly not unusual for players to take a few minutes at a time to plan a move.

The objective of La Belle Lucie is to build up all four of the suits from a foundation of the ace through to the king.

Getting started

In La Belle Lucie, you start by dealing all the cards face-up in piles of threes; make sure that each card in every trio is visible. You fan each trio so that you can see a top, middle, and bottom card. The last four cards go in two piles of twos. Your aim is to move cards around the tableau, freeing up cards that build up the foundation.

Whenever an ace is exposed on the top of a pile, you can start building a foundation on that pile. The next card to go on the ace is the 2 of that suit, and so on, up to the king of the suit. If no ace is exposed, then you just have to uncover one by moving the cards around.

You get three tries (or *cycles*) to move all the cards into suits. At the end of each cycle, you pick up all the cards that are not on the foundations, shuffle them well, and distribute them in trios again.

Making your moves

You can move cards in the tableau onto the card one lower than themselves in rank, but beware! Each card can be moved only once, and you can only move one card at a time, which is critical. For example, as soon as the ♦7 goes on the ♦8, the ♦8 can never be moved again unless both cards go onto the foundation in the diamond suit. You can't move the ♦7 and ♦8 onto the ♦9 because only one card at a time can be moved. The ♦8 has thus been "buried." Until the next redeal, you can't move this card, unless the ♦A through the ♦6 goes into the foundation, whereupon the ♦7 and ♦8 also go onto the foundation.

However, this rule doesn't matter if the ♦8 is at the bottom of a pile; no cards are trapped by the move. The rule does matter if the ♦8 covers something else. Note that kings never move — therefore, you want them at the bottom of piles.

Bear in mind that the purpose of the game is to build up all the suits in order, starting with the ace. So you try to get the aces out from their piles. If they're at the top of their piles already, so much the better. If not, you have to try to excavate them, but at the same time, you have to plan the sequence of moves that brings the card to the top. It isn't a good idea to play five moves to get out the ♦A and then discover that in the process the ♦2 gets permanently buried. Of course, sometimes burying a card may prove inevitable. The skill of the game is to bury as few cards as possible by making your moves in the right order, and to bury only those cards that seem less relevant at the moment, such as jacks and queens. Kings automatically trap everything below them; so if you're worried about burying the ♦J by putting the ♦10 on it, and the ♦Q is below the ♥K, relax! You've cost yourself nothing — you were never going to get to move the ♦J anyway.

Another example of a potentially bad holding is something along the lines of ♦Q ? ♦10. Even if you ever get to put the ♦10 on the jack, doing so freezes the ♦J. The ♦J can't be moved again, because you can't move the ♦10 and ♦J onto the ♦Q.

Sometimes you get mutually impossible moves, as shown in Figure 21-7. With the base shown in Figure 21-7, you can't move the ♦6 until you clear the ♥2; and you can't move the ♥2 until you free the ♦6 to get at the ♥3. So neither card moves until the ♥A is free, when the ♥2 can go to the foundation.

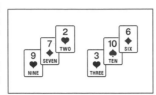

Figure 21-7:
Only one
series of
moves can
get you out
of this
mess.

Certain moves are risk-free at the start of the game; you can always move any queen onto the king of the same suit (because kings are stuck anyway). After you move the top two cards of a pile of three and the card at the bottom of a pile is exposed, you can put the relevant card on top of it without worrying about the consequences. (When a card is at the bottom of a pile, you can't trap anything underneath it if you render it unable to move because nothing is underneath it to trap.) Moreover, whenever a card is *stuck* (as, for example, if you put the ♦7 on the ♦8; you make both cards immobile), you may as well build more cards such as the ♦6 and ♦5 on top of it. In fact, doing so can only help your chances of getting more cards out.

The initial layout for a sample hand appears in Figure 21-8 (the top card in each trio appears on the right).

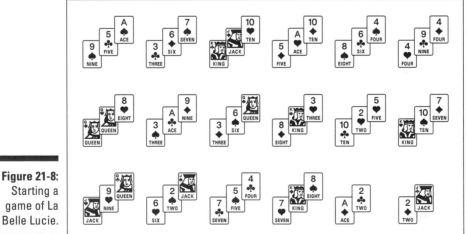

Figure 21-8:
Starting a
game of La
Belle Lucie.

This layout has some encouraging features: All the kings are reasonably placed (they're either at the bottoms of their piles or at least don't trap too many cards), and three of the aces are immediately accessible — a very fortunate combination of events. The bad news is that the ♥J and ♥9 are on top of one another, ensuring that the ♥10 (which traps the fourth ace) won't move this cycle.

Make the automatic moves: Take off the ♠A and start a foundation pile for spades; put the ♦9 on the ♦10 (because the ♥10 can't move, the ♦J can't come free, so you may as well build on the ♦10); and then take off the ♣A, the ♣2, and the ♦A.

The next card to go for is the ♠2. You can get it easily by putting the ♠J on the ♠Q; but before you do that, can you put the ♠Q on the ♠K? To make that move, you need to put the ♥3 on the ♥4, and to do that, you need to move the ♦4 on the ♦5. That last move is impossible because the ♦5 is trapped below the ♥A. So put the ♠J on the ♠Q and take up the ♠2, ♠3, and ♠4.

Figure 21-9 shows an interesting combination of piles.

Figure 21-9:
Your game a few moves later.

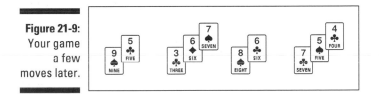

You want to clear the ♠4 away to get the ♠5 out, and you want to clear the ♠7 away to get the ♣3 out. Should you put the ♣4 on the ♠5, or the ♠5 on the ♣6 and then put the ♣4 on the ♠5? The answer is that you need to keep the ♠8 (below the ♣6) free. Put the ♣4 on the ♠5 and free the ♠5 for the foundation. Now put the ♣6 on the ♣7, the ♠7 on the ♠8, and ♦6 on the ♦7. (Because the ♦8 is under a king, it's stuck for the duration, so you can't move the ♦7.) The ♦3 is now free, which allows you to move ♣3 through ♣8 onto the foundation.

The preceding example shows a relatively simple problem. The degree of interaction can get considerably more convoluted. This element of trading off one move against another is what makes La Belle Lucie such good fun.

The ♣9 is stuck (you can't move the ♦4), the ♠6 is stuck, and the ♥A is stuck, which just leaves diamonds. The ♦2 comes out easily enough, by putting the ♣J on the queen. However, the ♦3 is under the ♠Q and the ♠J, so you take the ♦2 out, which ends the first cycle.

Starting the next cycle

Keep your foundations but pick up the cards left in the tableau, shuffle them well (they've been in sequence, so an imperfect shuffle can restrict your mobility), and deal them out in threes again. If you have two cards left over, make one pair; if one card is left over after putting the cards out in threes, as at the start, make two pairs out of the last four cards.

Wrapping things up

You have three cycles to get out, and if you fail at the last turn, you're allowed one cheat or *merci* by moving a single card in the tableau; whether you want to pull one card up or push one card down is up to you.

Poker Patience

Poker Patience is, in theory, an undemanding Solitaire. It takes only a minute or two to play, and you can approach the game frivolously or seriously. I do both in this section.

To start with, you need to know the ranks of Poker hands. In ascending order, they are as follows:

- **One pair:** Two of a kind
- **Two pairs**
- **Three of a kind**
- **Straight:** Five cards in consecutive order; for example, from ace through a 5, or from 7 to jack
- **Flush:** Five cards in the same suit
- **Full house:** A three of a kind and a pair
- **Four of a kind**
- **Straight flush:** A straight with all cards in the same suit

Aces can be either high or low — your choice.

The objective of the game is to lay out 25 cards to form a square, five cards by five cards. In the process you want to make ten poker hands (five across and five down) and score as many points as possible.

Scoring 200 points counts as a win. Various scoring systems are shown in Table 19-1.

Table 19-1	Scoring Systems for Poker Patience		
Poker Hand	*U.S. Scoring*	*U.K. Scoring*	*Barry's Scoring*
A pair	2	1	2
Two pairs	5	3	5
Three of a kind	10	6	10
Straight	15	12	25
Flush	20	5	15
Full house	50	10	50
Four of a kind	70	16	70
Straight flush	100	30	100

The U.S. scoring system has a major flaw in it (which has been corrected in the U.K. method of scoring). The flaw is based on the fact that although flushes are rarer at Poker, they are considerably easier to play for at Poker Patience than straights. To fix this problem, reverse the scoring table, as in the version that I recommend.

To start, turn over one card and put it face-up, then you go on to the next, building your grid in any direction you like — up and down or right and left. But although you can put any card anywhere you like in the grid and you can expand the cards out in any direction you like, each card must be at least touching another card, whether it is adjacent to another one or linked diagonally by touching the corner of another card.

After many years of playing Poker Solitaire, I've decided that the right way to play (particularly when using my scoring table) is for straights to be set out in one direction (vertically or horizontally) and full houses or four of a kinds to go in the other direction. If you use that layout and decide for straights to go in the horizontal rows, you have excellent reasons for putting the cards in columns either with themselves or with numbers five less than or five more than themselves. By making this separation by fives, you help the formation of straights.

When playing Poker Patience, sooner or later, you run into a useless or unplayable card. When this happens, don't panic; instead, start a junk row or junk column. Inevitably, at least one row won't score as much as you want it to score.

Look at the layout in Figure 21-10 to see the theory at work. The matrix is updated after every two cards, although each card is turned over individually. After ten cards, the basic structure is going well. The nucleus of the straights is fine on the horizontal lines and all the pairs are matched up.

In Figure 21-11, you can put the ♠9 on the bottom row, but completing the straight and collecting points always produces a warm, fuzzy feeling.

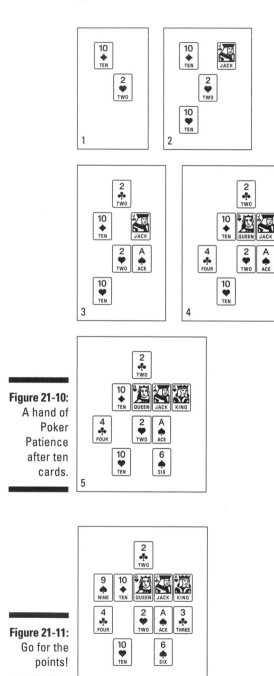

Figure 21-10:
A hand of
Poker
Patience
after ten
cards.

Figure 21-11:
Go for the
points!

Play continues in Figure 21-12. The ♥8 may have gone under the ♣3, but it seems premature to abandon the right-hand column. The ♠Q scores the full house, so abandon the straight in the fourth row.

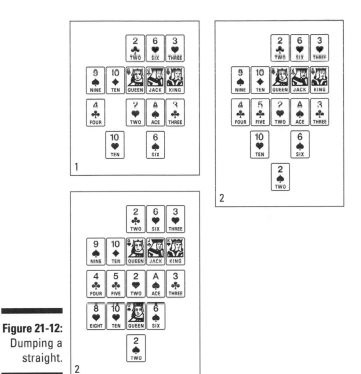

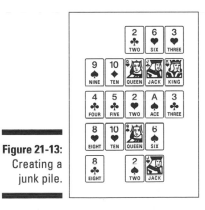

Figure 21-12:
Dumping a
straight.

In Figure 21-13, the bottom row has become a junk pile. One row and column normally does.

In Figure 21-14, a lucky last card sees you scramble to respectability; two straights and two full houses plus three of a kind is 160, and three pairs take you to 166.

Figure 21-13:
Creating a
junk pile.

Figure 21-14:
Making
something
out of this
big mess.

After you finish playing, you can carry out a further exercise in mental agility by trying to rearrange the cards to score as many points as possible. This rearrangement is really only worth doing if you have a straight flush, when you can rack up big numbers. Using all the cards in high-scoring combinations (flushes or higher) is a real coup. I've managed this feat about five times, and on one memorable occasion, I discovered that my initial arrangement was the highest possible with the cards I'd been dealt. Unfortunately, a game that successful will probably never happen again.

Some people also count the long diagonals (from top right to bottom left and vice versa) in the scoring. Planning the scores on the diagonals too carefully is pretty difficult, but it can be done — or you can just regard any score on them as a bonus.

You can also play Poker Patience as a competitive game for two players or more, if you like. One player calls out the cards he's drawn at random, and then both players try to arrange their own grids to maximize the scores. The highest score wins.

Solitaire on the Web

The Web offers a wide variety of sites for the Solitaire enthusiast. You can find tons of Solitaire games to play online; for example, discover a fun Solitaire called Marble Solitaire at www.cosmix.com/playground/java/solitaire/, where the object of the game is to remove all the pebbles from a cross by "jumping" one pebble over the other. For a Solitaire with a different flavor, download software for a fun game based on the rules of Cribbage at members.aol.com/dartcypro/crib.htm. At Pretty Good Solitaire 97 (www.goodsol.com/) you can download a collection of 160 Solitaire games for Windows 95 and Windows NT— nearly every popular and classic Solitaire game is included in the package.

Chapter 22

Children's Games

In This Chapter

▶ Picking up on the best children's games

▶ Discovering new games to play with your friends

*T*hese days, most children seem to be born with a remote control in their hands. However, some children are lucky enough to be given decks of cards when they're young (as was the case with me).

The games in this chapter are suitable for the very young and also for the slightly older child. No matter what your age (or the age of your children) you'll find a game in this chapter that you'll all enjoy playing together.

Beggar My Neighbor

Beggar My Neighbor, also known as Beat Your Neighbor Out of Doors and Strip Jack Naked, is a very simple game, requiring no strategy or planning at all. The objective of the game is to win all the cards from the other players.

To play Beggar My Neighbor, you need the following:

▶ **Two to six players:** You can play with more than six players in a pinch.

▶ **A standard deck of 52 cards:** With four or more players, add a second deck of cards. This game has the great advantage that you don't really need a complete deck of cards — the fact that a card or two is missing is almost irrelevant. Don't forget to remove the jokers!

To begin, one player deals out the whole deck in a clockwise rotation, dealing the cards face-down and one card at a time so that each player gets about the same number of cards. The players don't look at their cards; they just form them into a neat pile, face-down in front of them.

The player to the left of the dealer turns over the top card from his pile and places it in the center of the table (or floor, if you happen to be playing there).

Different things can happen now, depending on what card has been turned over:

- If the value of the card is between 2 and 10, the card has no special significance, and the play goes on to the next player.

- If the card is a *court card* (an ace, king, queen, or jack), the game becomes a little more exciting. The next player then has to pay a *forfeit*, meaning that she has to turn over some of her cards onto the central pile. If the turned-over card is an ace, the second player must turn over four cards one by one onto the pile; if the card is a king, he has to pay three cards; if a queen, two cards; and if a jack, one card.

If all the forfeit cards the player turns over are between 2 and 10, then the player who turned over the court card takes up the whole pile and puts it under his own cards. But if the player turns over another court card during the course of the forfeit, then the debt is deemed paid off, and that player doesn't have to turn over any more cards. Instead, the next player must pay the forfeit dictated by the second court card and hope to turn over a court card in the process or concede the whole central pile to that player.

When a player has no more cards left, she is out, and the game continues without her. The last player in the game, who accumulates the whole deck, wins.

Your success at Beggar My Neighbor depends on the luck of the draw; if you get a good smattering of court cards, you will probably win. If someone feels bad because he lost, you may want to remind him of that. But that doesn't mean you can't congratulate him if he wins!

Because the game theoretically can go on for a long time — and is ideal for long car journeys, waiting for planes, or similar situations — you can also agree that the player with the most cards at a certain predefined time is the winner.

Snap, Slapjack, and Animals

Snap, Slapjack, and Animals are close cousins to the school of games that target acquiring other people's cards, such as Beggar My Neighbor. For Snap, Slapjack, and Animals, speed is the key to winning the game. In all these games, the player with the quickest reactions wins. These games are among the very few card games that depend *entirely* on physical dexterity.

Snap

Get ready for a fast and furious game!

To play Snap, you need the following:

- **Two or more players**

- **A standard deck of 52 cards:** Play Snap with a single deck of cards if you have fewer than four players; add a second deck if more players compete. Playing this game with a less-than-brand-new deck is a good idea — the cards can take a beating (literally) during the play.

   You don't need a full deck of cards to play Snap — a card or two may be missing from the deck. You can also play Snap with special cards designed for another game (such as an Old Maid deck), as long as most of the cards have backs identical to other cards in the deck.

The dealer deals out the whole deck of cards face-down, one card at a time to each player, going in a clockwise rotation. It doesn't matter that some players get more cards than others. What does matter, however, is that the players don't look at the cards they get.

Each player, starting with the player to the left of the dealer, takes a turn flipping over the top card of his pile and putting the card face-up in front of him. After a few turns, each player has a little pile of face-up cards in front of him.

This process continues until one player turns over a card onto her pile that is the same rank as the top card on some other player's pile. As soon as that happens, the first person to call out "Snap!" takes the two piles that have matching cards on them. When you win a person's pile, you just put it off to the side.

Frequently, two players make their call simultaneously. In this case, the two piles with the same card on them are put together, face-up, in middle of the table. Then each player continues to turn over a top card onto their pile until someone turns over a card that matches the card on top of the pile in the middle of the table. The first person to shout "Snap pool!" wins the pile in the middle of the table.

When a player mistakenly calls out "Snap!" her own pile goes into the center of the table; the first player to call "Snap pool!" at the relevant moment gets her pile.

When a player turns over all her cards into the pile in front of her, she just picks up the pile and uses it again.

The player who ends up with everyone else's cards wins the game.

Establishing several informal rules can avoid bloodshed at this game. For some reason, Snap brings out the worst competitive instincts in people, myself included:

- ✔ **Set rules about the proper way to turn over your card.** The player can't turn over the card so that she sees it first, which means that she must flip over the card in a single motion onto her pile.

- ✔ **Get an impartial witness to decide on all close calls.** Obviously, choose someone who isn't actually playing the game.

A devious player remembers the order of her pile (or of another player's pile) when the pile gets small, so as to gain a big edge in the calling. Keep an eye on the cards as the game draws to a close; if you don't, you put yourself at a disadvantage. If you want to avoid this situation, you can agree to shuffle your pile when you have worked your way through it.

You can play a couple of variations to the basic game which may make Snap more appropriate for the age range of the players:

- ✔ In Simplified Snap, which is suitable for three or more players, all the players put their turned-over cards on a single pile of turned-up cards in the middle of the table. Players call "Snap!" whenever the top card on the pile coincides with the last card played. This method allows you to focus on only one place, rather than looking around at all the piles at the same time. Because all the action is in one place, this variation may be good for younger players.

- ✔ By contrast, the target of the game in Speed Snap is more challenging, and thus may be better for older players. All players turn over their cards at the same moment so that the reaction process speeds up. To make sure that all the players turn over their cards simultaneously, the umpire (or one of the players) must say "One, two, three!" and all players turn over the cards on three. Whenever any two of the cards just turned over match, whoever calls out "Snap!" fastest wins the two piles.

Animals

Animals is a much louder version of Snap. To understand how to play Animals, you need to read "Snap" in this chapter. The major difference between Snap and Animals is the way you call out for the cards.

Make sure that you have the following items to play Animals:

- ✔ **Two or more players**

- ✔ **A standard deck of 52 cards:** It doesn't matter if a few of the cards are missing.

- ✔ **Pencils and scraps of paper**

At the start of the game, each player selects an animal, preferably one with a long and complicated name, such as *duck-billed platypus* or *tyrannosaurus rex*. Each player then writes the name on a piece of paper and puts the paper in the middle of the table.

Everyone shuffles the papers around, takes one, and then announces the name of the animal. Then play begins, and it goes just like Snap.

When two players turn up matching cards, those players are the only ones who can win the cards. They must each try to call out the other person's animal name first, and whoever succeeds wins both piles.

A variation on this game (sometimes called Animal Noises) calls for everyone to select a common animal, such as a cat or dog. To win the cards, the two players who turn up matching cards must finish making the noise of her opponent's animal before he does the same to her. Whoever finishes the noise first wins her opponent's pile of cards. If you play this variation, select an animal with a long call, such as a rooster; saying "cock-a-doodle-doo" takes longer than "meow" — if your call is really long, then it takes your opponent longer to say it.

If a player calls out a name at the wrong moment, he concedes all his cards to the animal (or animal noise) he called out. Making the wrong call or naming the wrong animal at the appropriate moment costs you nothing by itself, but you're likely to lose your pile because the other player may beat you to the punch.

Slapjack

Slapjack involves physical agility rather than verbal dexterity and memory. Young children can play this game; they just need to be able to tell the difference between a jack and a king or queen.

Assemble the following items to play Slapjack:

- ✔ **Two or more players**
- ✔ **A standard deck of 52 cards:** Although you don't need a complete deck, make sure that you have all the jacks in the deck.

Slapjack can totally wreck a deck of cards.

The dealer deals out the entire deck, face-down, to all the players, one card at a time to each player in a clockwise rotation. At the end of the deal, each player should have a neat stack of cards in front of him. No one looks at his cards.

Beginning at the dealer's left, each player takes a turn playing a card face-up onto a single stack in the center of the table.

Play continues relatively peacefully until someone plays a jack. Whoever slaps the jack first wins all the cards in the middle of the table. That player takes the cards from the middle of the table and adds them to the bottom of the pile in front of her. The player to the slapper's left starts the next pile by placing a card face-up in the center of the table.

If you slap the wrong card, you must give a card from your face-down pile to whoever it was whose card you slapped.

After all a player's cards are gone, he isn't automatically out of the game; he stays in for one more chance, waiting to slap the next jack that gets turned over. If he fails to do that, he's out.

The first player to get everyone else's cards wins.

Spirits run high in Slapjack, so you may need to define some rules before the game starts:

- Whoever turns over a card does so by turning the card *away* from him, so that he can't peek at it in advance.
- The players should rest their slapping hand on the table and make the player who puts out the card slap with her other hand, which must also rest on the table.
- When you aren't sure who slapped first, the hand closest to the jack always wins the day.

War

War is a great game for relatively young children. The object is to acquire all the cards, which you can do in a few ways.

To play War, you need the following:

- **Two players**
- **A standard deck of 52 cards**

Start by dealing out the deck one card at a time, face-down, so that each player gets 26 cards, which he keeps in a pile, without looking at them. Then each player turns over a card simultaneously; whoever turns over the highest card picks up the two cards and puts them face-down at the bottom of his pile.

The cards have the following ranks, from highest to lowest: ace, king, queen, jack, and then 10 through 2.

The game continues in this manner until both players turn over a card of the same rank, at which point you have a *war*. A war can progress in one of three ways:

- ✔ Each player puts a card face-down on top of the tied card and then one face-up. Whoever has the higher second face-up card takes all six cards.

- ✔ In a slightly more aggressive version of War, each player puts *three* face-down cards on the table, not one, and thus the competition is for ten cards, not six. This option has the advantage of speeding up the game, which can drag a little — even for children!

- ✔ The third version is potentially even more bloodthirsty. When a war takes place, the number of cards at stake depends on the value of the equal cards. If the equal cards are 7s, you each count off seven face-down cards before turning a card over. If the equal cards are court cards, you turn down ten cards before squaring off. For an ace, count out 11 cards.

Make sure to choose which way you want to wage your wars before the start of the game.

Whoever wins the cards gathers them up and puts them at the bottom of her pile. The first person to get all the other player's cards wins.

You can also play War with three players. The dealer deals out 17 cards to each player, face-down. The remaining card goes to the winner of the first war. The players take turns flipping over one card. The highest card of the three takes all three cards. If two players tie for the high card, they each turn down three cards and then turn over one, and the highest card of the turned-over cards collects all the cards in the pile; if there is a draw at this point, you fight another war. If all three of the players turn over the same numbered card, a double war takes place; each player turns down six (not three) cards, and again, the winner takes all, or you carry on fighting wars with a further three cards until a winner emerges.

Fish

The Fish family features three commonly played games: Go Fish, Authors, and Happy Families. All three games attempt to achieve the same aim: Namely, each player tries to make as many complete sets of four of a kind (*sets*) as he can.

Go Fish

Get out yer pole — you're about to go fishin' fer sets (four cards of the same kind).

To play Go Fish, you need the following:

- ✔ **At least three players**
- ✔ **A standard deck of 52 cards**

Each player gets ten cards. You pretend as you deal out the deck that you have one more player than you really do. With four players, for example, deal out ten cards (one by one, face-down, in a clockwise rotation) in five piles. Add the two leftover cards to the fifth pile and leave that pile of 12 cards as the *stock* in the middle of the table.

Starting with the player to the left of the dealer, each player takes a turn asking any other player at the table a question in the form of "Do you have any Xes?" (*X* is the rank of card asked for; 4s or queens, for example.) The player asking the question must have at least one X to pose the question.

If the person asked has an X or two, she hands them over, and the questioner's turn continues. The questioner can then ask the same player, or any other player, if they have a card in a particular set. As soon as the questioner completes a set of four cards, she puts the cards down on the table in front of her and continues her turn.

The game becomes more difficult if the responder only has to provide one card from the relevant set, even if she has more than one card in that set. Then the questioner has to ask again and risks wasting a turn.

If the person asked has no cards of the rank specified in the question, he replies "Go Fish," and the player who asked the question takes a card from the stock. If the card that she draws from her stock completes a set, she must wait until her next turn to put the set down on the table. The turn passes to the player who sent his rival fishing.

Some play that if the card you draw from the stock completes any set in your hand, your turn continues.

The player who collects the most sets wins. However, if one player puts all her cards into sets before the stock gets used up, then she wins.

Authors

Authors resembles Go Fish in many ways, with a few interesting exceptions that make it a far more subtle game in many ways.

To play Authors, you need the following:

- ✔ **At least four players**
- ✔ **A standard deck of 52 cards**

The dealer deals out all the cards at the start of the hand, giving each player one card at a time, face-down, in a clockwise rotation.

You play Authors and Go Fish along similar lines (see "Go Fish" for the details). The big difference between the games is that questions must relate to specific cards rather than to a type of card. So a player asks "Do you have the seven of spades?" rather than asking for 7s in general.

The additional rules on asking questions are quite specific:

- ✔ **You can't ask for a card if you already have that card in your hand.**
- ✔ **You can't ask for a card unless you have at least one card of that set already in your hand.**

Of course, if you have two cards of a set in your hand, hearing someone else ask for a third card in the set may pinpoint who has the other cards in that set. If A successfully asks B for the ♦Q, he clearly now has two queens, so you can collect them from him at your next turn if you get the chance. In a four-player game, for example, if you, as D, hear A unsuccessfully ask B for the ♦Q, then you know that A has one queen and that C has the ♦Q — unless you have it.

In this game, an unsuccessful question means that the turn passes to the left, rather than to the player unsuccessfully asked for a card. Just as in Go Fish, when a player completes a set, she places it on the table.

Decked out with Authors

At one time, people played Authors with special decks of cards bearing the pictures of famous authors on them. These decks are not readily available now, though they're coming back into fashion; in any event, the regular deck works very well in its stead.

When you run out of cards, either because your hand has been picked clean or because you've made your hand into sets, you're out, and the game continues without you until all the sets have been completed and no one has any cards left. Whoever has the most sets at the end wins.

If you ask for a card when you have nothing in that set, fail to provide a card when you're asked for it, or even fail to put down a set as soon as you can, the fine is giving one set to the player to your left — a pretty severe charge!

Happy Families

Happy Families is most common in the United Kingdom — Happy Families is essentially the U.K. equivalent of Authors.

You need the following items to play Happy Families:

- ✔ **Four players**
- ✔ **A special deck of cards:** Instead of the regular suits, each of the four "families" consists of a husband, wife, and two children, such as Mister Bun the Baker, Mrs. Bun the Baker's Wife, Master Bun the Baker's Son, and Miss Bun the Baker's Daughter. As an alternative, the deck can consist of four animals; again, a father, mother, and two young ones is typical.

The same rules about asking questions apply to Happy Families as do to Authors:

- ✔ **You must have a card in the set for which you are asking.**
- ✔ **You can't have the card for which you ask.**
- ✔ **You must specify a particular member of the family rather than asking for the set in general.**

Your goal is to make sets. If a player has the specific card you ask for, that player must give it up. If not, the turn passes to the player who doesn't have the card you asked for. The player who makes the most sets wins.

Concentration

Concentration is also known as *Memory*. The object of the game is to make as many pairs of cards as possible.

To play Concentration, you need the following:

- **At least two players:** Concentration is an ideal game for developing the memory of children over the age of six. Children younger than that tend to step on the cards as they're playing and to lose focus while waiting for a turn.

- **A standard deck of 52 cards:** Typically, you play Concentration with a single deck of cards; for six or more players, add a second deck.

- **Some space:** You spread all the cards out face-down on the floor or on another flat surface, so you actually need quite a bit of room for the game.

The dealer shuffles the cards well and then spreads all the cards face-down on the floor. The dealer chooses whether to line up the cards in rows and columns or whether to spread them out at random.

The more orderly the rows, the easier to remember where the cards are, and the less advantage a player with a good memory has.

Each player takes turns flipping over two cards from anywhere in the layout. If the cards are the same rank, two 7s, for example, she has a pair, and she takes the cards off the floor, puts them in her pile, and tries again. Conversely, if the cards have different ranks, she turns them back over. Then the next player tries his luck, and so on. You can turn over any card on any turn, whether someone else has already turned it over or not.

When you start to play this game, you may well find yourself getting completely confused, because you try to remember everything and end up forgetting it all. Realize your own limitations and stick with a base of four to six cards that you can definitely recall, and let the rest pass by until you match up a few cards.

Play continues until all the cards have been matched. The player with the most pairs wins the game.

Cheat

Children love Cheat (which is also called I Doubt It) because it gives them the opportunity to develop their deceptive powers in a way that their parents approve of. Most children master the art of lying convincingly and looking guilty when telling the truth very quickly.

You need the following to play Cheat:

- **Three or more players:** You can play with up to 12 players.

- **A standard deck of 52 cards:** You normally play Cheat with a single deck of cards with up to five players. With six to 12 players, use two decks.

The object of Cheat is to get rid of all your cards as quickly as possible. To do that, you play your cards face-down, announcing what you have put down — but you don't have to tell the truth.

The dealer deals out all the cards one at a time, face-down, and the player to the left of the dealer is first to play. The players then pick up and look at their cards.

The first player puts down a number of cards into a central pile on the table, squaring the cards up so that it is impossible to see precisely how many cards he has put down. He then makes an announcement about his play, along the line of "three 6s" or whatever he considers appropriate. This statement can be false in more than one way. He may put down more or fewer cards than he claims, and he may put down completely unrelated cards to what he claims. The other players put their cards on top of his.

Some people require that the play must consist of the correct *number* of cards, whether or not they are what you claim them to be.

If no one challenges the claim (and anyone can do so), the turn moves clockwise to the next player. The next player also makes his play face-down, and he has three choices:

- **He can claim to be playing the same rank as the previous player:** Staying with the example that the first play was claimed to be three 6s, the player can take this choice by putting down a number of 6s.

- **He can claim to be playing cards of one rank higher:** If the player put down 6s, "cards of one rank higher" means as many 7s as he wants.

- **He can claim to be playing cards of one rank lower than the previous move:** In this case, a number of 5s.

The player isn't allowed to pass. He puts his cards face-down on the table, on top of the previous play. Of course, he can lie, too!

The next player has exactly the same set of options (play the same rank as the previous player, or one higher or one lower), and so on, until someone makes a challenge.

To make a challenge, someone calls out "Cheat," and the player accused has two options:

- ✔ He can concede (gracefully or otherwise) by picking up the entire pile.
- ✔ He can turn over the cards he just put down to demonstrate that he was telling the truth, in which case the challenger must pick up the whole pile.

The player who picks up the pile from the center gets to start the next round, with whatever number he wants.

In the case of a dispute as to who called out "Cheat" first, the player nearest to the left of the accused has priority.

The winner of the game is the person who succeeds in playing all his cards and getting out. A player can accomplish this task either by withstanding a challenge on his final turn or by no one challenging the player who goes out before the next player has made a play. In practice, someone always challenges a player going out, but if a player can conceal that he has no cards left on his last play (not easy to do!), he may avoid a challenge.

Some people play that the second player's turn is far less flexible; if the first player plays 6s, the next player must play 7s, and the one after that must play 8s. This variation takes away some of the flexibility in the play, but makes it much easier for younger children to determine what they should do. Because only one play is possible, everyone knows what comes next.

Old Maid

Old Maid allows you to use a fair amount of simple psychology in the game, making it an ideal game for younger children.

All you need to play Old Maid is the following:

- ✔ **At least three players**
- ✔ **One or more standard decks of 52 cards with a single queen removed:** Use a single deck of cards for up to six players. For seven or more players, use two decks, but take care that the decks have the same backs. You can play the game with special commercial decks, too, with animal faces on the cards and just one Donkey in the deck. Or you can play with a special Old Maid deck, with an ugly Old Maid card in it.

The object of the game is to get rid of all the cards in your hand and not be left with the one unmatched card, the solitary queen, or *Old Maid*.

The dealer deals out all the cards, one by one, face-down, in a clockwise rotation. Each player starts by removing every pair of cards that she has (a pair can be two 5s or two kings, for example). These cards are simply set aside face-up on the table, so that everyone can see how many pairs each player has.

Take care not to remove any three of a kind — just pairs.

After that, the player to the left of the dealer fans out her cards face-down and offers them to the player to her left to take one card. The player who is offered the cards must take one of them and then looks at it to see whether it forms a pair with another card in his hand. If it does, he discards the pair onto the tabletop.

Whether the card he draws forms a pair or not, that player spreads his cards face-down and offers his hand to the player to his left, who must then choose a card, and so on.

The game continues, with players dropping out as they get rid of all their cards. Eventually, one player is left with the lone queen and gets tormented by the other players with taunts of "Old Maid!" until the new hand starts.

Both France and Germany have special versions of Old Maid. In France, they take out three jacks from the deck, leaving only the jack of spades, the *vieux garçon* or "Old Boy." The Germans have special decks with a Black Peter card, often showing a cat in military attire. In each game, the loser is the player left with the odd card.

You can use a certain element of psychology or reverse psychology to persuade people to take the queen away from you. If you arrange your cards with some of the cards more prominently positioned than others, other players think that you are trying to pass off the prominent cards. Make sure that the prominent cards are "safe" ones, and you increase the chance that the player takes one of the other cards — perhaps the queen. Conversely, try to read the mind of the player offering you cards; would he hide the queen away or try to pass it off on you? Or has he not gotten into these mind games and has arranged his cards at random? Only the Old Maid knows for sure.

Part IX
The Part of Tens

The 5th Wave   By Rich Tennant

"It's jacks or better to open, and the low card in your hand is wild...until my Mom walks in, and then we're playing Go Fish, got it?"

In this part . . .

Do you want to know how to improve your temper, or your temperament, or simply to become a better player by sharpening your memory? Well, nothing is impossible, if you focus on this part of the book. We can't promise you the earth, but if you read up on the tips in this part, you may discover ways to improve your technique. I also provide you with a short list of places to go after you've finished reading this book and have caught the Card Playing Fever.

Chapter 23

Ten Ways to Improve Your Game and Have More Fun

- -

In This Chapter

▶ Building up your memory for cards

▶ Keeping your cool

▶ Remembering to have fun

- -

*P*laying cards is supposed to be fun, so I don't want to catch you studying this chapter as if it's a homework assignment. Just keep these tips and hints in mind as you play — you'll find yourself playing better and having a better time, too.

Befriending Your Partner

When playing a game with a partner, you may experience times when it seems like your partner is actually playing for the opponents. Your partner may totally misinterpret what cards you want played, or he may blindly lead a card that the opponents have been hoping for the whole game.

No matter what happens, never criticize your partner at the table; he's trying to do as well as he can, too! If you upset him, you end up with a partner who may not be pulling his weight for your team, and you may relax your opponents. Why do that?

If your partner does something stupid but gets a good result, that's a good moment to let him know (courteously) that he may have committed a technical inaccuracy. If his action gets a bad result, don't comment on it unless asked to.

If you have a misunderstanding, don't correct it at the table unless the same problem is likely to come up again in the very near future. Make note of the incident and discuss it later with your partner, if at all possible. Don't discuss the problem too soon after the accident; everyone has an ego and automatically defends himself, so wait for the competitive fires to die down before revisiting the scene of the crime.

Giving Yourself a Reality Check

Almost all card games incorporate some element of chance, so bear in mind that you're not going to be perfect at a game; try your best but don't get angry with yourself if you make a mistake.

Write down your own mistakes and review them after the game. You can allow yourself to make mistakes, but if it bothers you, and you really want to improve your game, writing down your mistakes can help you avoid making the same mistake twice.

Keeping Your Opponents at the Gate

At some point, you will experience the thrill of victory — whether it's winning the game or just making a smart play. When one of these glorious moments is upon you, you must resist the urge to proclaim your victory from the highest mountaintop.

Never gloat when you get a good result, no matter how aggravating your opponents are (yes, even if they have won every single game that night, and you finally manage to score a game). When you advertise a victory, you're showing that you lack control — which can be good information for your opponents.

Besides, gloating openly about a win doesn't give you nearly the same thrill as resting secure in the knowledge that you just pulled off something great. Irritating your opponents by your results proves infinitely more satisfying than irritating them by your mannerisms or comments.

Record your opponents' disasters, too, if they seem relevant to you, so that you can be sure that those mistakes don't happen to you.

Acting Brave in the Face of Disaster

You can't win every hand. Many times in the course of whatever game you play, you will make a wrong move, or the dealer may give you the absolute worst cards in history.

When the Fates put some obstacle in your way, just move on to the next hand without comment, if you can. Your ability to absorb bad results without comment may throw off your opponents. Besides, your behavior will show a lot of class, too.

Knowing When the Time is Ripe

You can't be in top form all the time. Sometimes, you may not have enough time or energy to really devote yourself fully to the game. Or maybe you just don't feel like playing.

Whatever the reason, if you can't give yourself fully to the game, don't play, particularly if you're playing for money. If your heart and mind really aren't in the game, you won't play well, and the people you're playing with won't have any fun.

Bearing this tip in mind can mean the difference between keeping and losing friends. For example, a friend related the following story to me. He was invited to go play cards one Friday night at a friend's house. It sounded like a great idea at the time, so he accepted. By the time Friday night rolled around, he had been through a really tough week at work, and he was really exhausted. But he thought, "I told my friends that I'd be there, and so I should go." When he arrived at the friends' house, he noticed that they, too, looked a little tired. They all sat down at the table and the first hand was dealt. When the play started, the friends both played so poorly that they almost cried. At the end of the first hand, one of the friends explained that they had been up all night tending to their sick dog. That was all my friend needed to hear. He explained that he was likewise too exhausted to play well. They all just looked at each other, laughed, threw in their cards, and called it an evening. My friend said that they all still laugh about that night to this day.

If you're in the middle of a game and things aren't going well, take a break in mid-session, even if it's only to wash your face. Do anything that you can think of to break a sequence of bad luck.

To be courteous to the other players, try to keep your break down to around five minutes. You don't have to make excuses to take your break, as long as you aren't running away from the table after every hand. Everyone needs a break from time to time.

Counting on Lady Luck

Be superstitious! If you enter a session of cards expecting to do well, your positive approach frequently translates into good results. So if you do well when scoring with your lucky pen, make sure to continue using it.

Cutting Yourself Off

If you're playing for money, don't try to recover your losses by desperate gambling; doing so only makes your situation worse.

If you have a set limit and you lose that amount, then stop playing. Don't even think about going out to get more money and trying to recoup your losses.

And don't play for stakes larger than you can afford to lose. If you do, you become sufficiently uncomfortable by the idea of losing that you don't play your best.

Even if you aren't playing for money, remember that the secret to a long life is knowing when it's time to go. If you're not having a good night with the cards, then just call it quits.

Painting a Picture of the Cards

When you first start playing a game, you may have your hands full just remembering the basics of the game. As you become more comfortable with the play, however, you should start thinking about what cards your opponents may hold. You can slowly assemble a picture of the other players' cards by observing the clues that they give off:

   ✔ **Watch their body language.** Many less-tricky players show their disappointment about bad cards and don't hide their joy over good cards. If you know that a player reacts this way, watch him closely.

However, don't forget that a truly savvy player may try to throw you off the track by conning you with a false reaction (smiling when she has bad cards, for example).

- ✔ **Listen to the bidding.** If a game has a bidding phase, this is your best opportunity to get information about your opponents' cards. Your opponents normally base their bids on the cards they actually hold; however, watch out for the players who cry wolf — if the rules of the game allow it, your opponents may deliberately overbid a bad hand in order to cut their losses or put you off the scent.

- ✔ **Watch for negative inferences.** Observing the cards that your opponent doesn't want can help you discern which cards he may be after.

If you can, don't focus on the problems in your own hand to the exclusion of other players' cards. One of the biggest challenges that I have when playing cards is that if I have a problem, I can be oblivious to the other, irrelevant small cards being played around me — until I suddenly realize that those cards weren't so irrelevant.

Marching to the Beat of Your Own Drum

You may have played with this guy before. You know the one — he practically makes you punch a time clock when it's your turn to play, and he starts tapping his fingers on the table if he thinks you're taking too much time making up your mind on what to do. What a drag this guy is, not just to you, but to everyone at the table.

Play the game at your own tempo, not that of the dominant player at the table. Many players get an edge from playing fast and encouraging other players to match their tempo. Don't fall into their trap; keep your own time.

Talking Through the Cards

Mentally speak the cards to yourself as they're played. By verbalizing the cards (internally), you get a separate part of the brain working on the cards in addition to the eyes. The more ways you can set the cards in your mind, the better chance you have of recalling them.

However, don't move your lips as you do your mental inventory of the cards. Just as your first-grade teacher scolded you for moving your lips as you read, your fellow players will never let you forget it if they see you mouthing out all the cards. In addition, you don't want to give away how you developed such a good memory for the cards — the other players may catch on to your trick and start to do it, too, thus eliminating your advantage.

Counting Down to Victory

Knowing how many cards the opponents have in a suit can help in some games. Count back from 13 if you're missing only a few cards in a particular suit. For example, if you're playing Bridge and you hold eight cards in a suit between your hand and your partner's hand, the opponents have only five cards. So as their cards in the suit appear, count back from five.

An alternative approach for a particular suit is just to count the cards as they are played, rather than adding in the cards in your own hand. This works well in most games where you can't see your partner's hand.

Keeping a count on all the suits can be exhausting. Try to work out at the start of the hand which are the key suits and focus on those, not on all the suits. In some games, such as Barbu and Hearts, focus on low cards only.

Having Fun

Whoever came up with the phrase "Winning is the most important thing" probably didn't get invited to too many parties. There is absolutely nothing more boring than playing cards with someone who acts like she's constructing a nuclear missile every time she plays a card.

Keep in mind that it's only a game, and don't take things too seriously. Doing so not only cuts into the other players' enjoyment, but it may also hurt your game. The more pressure you put on yourself, the more tired and frustrated you get, and the worse you play.

Chapter 24

Ten Places to Find More Information on Your Game

. . . .

In This Chapter

▶ Finding the answers to your questions

▶ Getting more advanced with your game

. . . .

*E*ven if you're just starting out with a game, don't be afraid to ask more-experienced players for advice; most people are only too flattered to be asked for help. You may find the following sources of information particularly helpful when you have a question about your game:

The Internet

Almost all games have a Web page or discussion group, and you can even play some games live on the Internet. Cyberspace gives you the chance to ask a question or debate a move with players all around the world, day or night. (I list Web sites for you to visit in many chapters in the book.)

Gaming bodies

Contact the official governing body for your game and ask for details of local clubs where you can play. You can often find these organizations listed in the phone book and on the Internet.

Books

The bookstore is full of books devoted to particular games. Reading about a game gives you a chance to work through potential problems in your game away from the table, where it doesn't cost you anything.

Newspapers and magazines

Read newspaper columns that feature the game you're interested in — you'll discover the latest techniques and hear about upcoming tournaments. More and more magazines are also appearing on the Net, sometimes with a delayed publication date, sometimes requiring payment of a negligible annual fee before viewing.

Running with the big dogs

Playing with people who are better than you at a particular game gives you first-hand instruction on improving your game.

Tournaments

Actually playing with the experts would be ideal, but sometimes world-class players only play with each other — but you can still watch their moves.

Going to the mountain

Some vacation spots, such as Las Vegas and Reno, offer ample opportunity for you to practice and discover advanced techniques in many different games.

Clubs

Some clubs are devoted specifically to one game, such as Bridge clubs. However, most clubs offer more than just a game; clubs also commonly offer some kind of instruction in the game that's played there. Don't be shy about looking up clubs in the telephone book or finding out details from sponsoring authorities. Most clubs actively recruit new members, and they will be only too happy to accommodate beginners.

Index

(continued)

• G •

• *O* •

Score Cards

Score card for Rummy, Gin Rummy, Piquet, Clobyosh, and Cribbage
(Feel free to photocopy this score card as many times as you'd like.)

Player 1 _____	Player 2 _____

Player 1 _____	Player 2 _____

Score Cards

Score card for Rummy, Gin Rummy, Piquet, Clobyosh, and Cribbage
(Feel free to photocopy this score card as many times as you'd like.)

Player 1 _____   Player 2 _____

Player 1 _____   Player 2 _____

Score Cards

Score card for Oh Hell!, Hearts, Pinochle, Setback, Eights, Fan Tan, and President
(Feel free to photocopy this score card as many times as you'd like.)

Player 1	Player 2	Player 3	Player 4

Player 5	Player 6	Player 7	Player 8

Score Cards

Score card for Oh Hell!, Hearts, Pinochle, Setback, Eights, Fan Tan, and President
(Feel free to photocopy this score card as many times as you'd like.)

Player 1	Player 2	Player 3	Player 4

Player 5	Player 6	Player 7	Player 8

Score Cards

Score card for Canasta, Whist, Euchre, and Spades
(Feel free to photocopy this score card as many times as you'd like.)

Team 1 _____   Team 2 _____   Team 1 _____   Team 2 _____

Score Cards

Score card for Canasta, Whist, Euchre, and Spades
(Feel free to photocopy this score card as many times as you'd like.)

Team 1 _____	Team 2 _____

Team 1 _____	Team 2 _____

Score Cards

Score card for Barbu (Feel free to photocopy this score card as much as you'd like.)

Game	(Dbls) West	(Dbls) North	(Dbls) East	(Dbls) South	Total
West					
Trumps					
Fan Tan					
Hearts					
Last Two Tricks					
No Queens					
Barbu					
Nullo					
North					
Trumps					
Fan Tan					
Hearts					
Last Two Tricks					
No Queens					
Barbu					
Nullo					
East					
Trumps					
Fan Tan					
Hearts					
Last Two Tricks					
No Queens					
Barbu					
Nullo					
South					
Trumps					
Fan Tan					
Hearts					
Last Two Tricks					
No Queens					
Barbu					
Nullo					

Score Cards

Score card for Barbu (Feel free to photocopy this score card as much as you'd like.)

Game	(Dbls) West	(Dbls) North	(Dbls) East	(Dbls) South	Total
West Trumps					
Fan Tan					
Hearts					
Last Two Tricks					
No Queens					
Barbu					
Nullo					
North Trumps					
Fan Tan					
Hearts					
Last Two Tricks					
No Queens					
Barbu					
Nullo					
East Trumps					
Fan Tan					
Hearts					
Last Two Tricks					
No Queens					
Barbu					
Nullo					
South Trumps					
Fan Tan					
Hearts					
Last Two Tricks					
No Queens					
Barbu					
Nullo					

IDG BOOKS WORLDWIDE BOOK REGISTRATION

Register This Book and Win!

We want to hear from you!

Visit **http://my2cents.dummies.com** to register this book and tell us how you liked it!

- ✔ Get entered in our monthly prize giveaway.

- ✔ Give us feedback about this book – tell us what you like best, what you like least, or maybe what you'd like to ask the author and us to change!

- ✔ Let us know any other *...For Dummies* topics that interest you.

Your feedback helps us determine what books to publish, tells us what coverage to add as we revise our books, and lets us know whether we're meeting your needs as a *...For Dummies* reader. You're our most valuable resource, and what you have to say is important to us!

Not on the Web yet? It's easy to get started with *Dummies 101®: The Internet For Windows® 95* or *The Internet For Dummies®,* 4th Edition, at local retailers everywhere.

Or let us know what you think by sending us a letter at the following address:

...For Dummies Book Registration
Dummies Press
7260 Shadeland Station, Suite 100
Indianapolis, IN 46256
Fax 317-596-5498

BUSINESS AND
**GENERAL
REFERENCE
BOOK SERIES
FROM IDG**

**COMPUTER
BOOK SERIES
FROM IDG**